# CROSS BORDER COMMERCE
*With Biblical Worldview Application*

# CROSS BORDER COMMERCE
## *With Biblical Worldview Application*

### Second Edition

## Brian C. Satterlee

Raleigh, North Carolina

CROSS BORDER COMMERCE: WITH BIBLICAL WORLDVIEW APPLICATION. 2ND EDITION

ISBN 13: 978-1-934748-12-1

The Author thanks Megan Miller and Matthew Pedersen for their help in editorial review of the textbook.

Published by Synergistics International Inc.
Raleigh, NC 27615
info@si-corp.net

*Dedicated to my beautiful Grandchildren, with the greatest expression of love!*

*Cricket DeLainey Bell Satterlee*
*Finn William Satterlee*
*Samuel Brian Satterlee*
*Luke Elijah Satterlee*

# ABOUT THE AUTHOR

Brian Satterlee holds earned doctorates in both Business Administration and in Higher Education. He has been teaching college-level courses since 1980 and currently serves as Professor of Business Administration at Liberty University, where he teaches the MBA courses International Business, Global Financial Markets, and Developing Global Markets. In 2004 he was recognized with the Liberty University Chancellor's Award for Teaching Excellence.

In addition to his academic career, he is experienced in business and industry. During the 1970s and early 1980s, Dr. Satterlee worked in the construction industry, experiencing increasing levels of responsibility and authority in both technical and managerial positions. He has been a successful entrepreneur and engaged in various small business enterprises over the years. During the mid-1990s, he was invited to the Caribbean islands of Grenada and Dominica and to the Central American nation of Belize, where he was instrumental in assisting non-governmental organizations create and sustain economic development activity.

Dr. Satterlee has served as consultant to numerous organizations and government agencies in areas such as productivity improvement, leadership, technology, and innovation. Other executive-level positions include serving as business school dean, graduate school dean, and dean of continuing education.

A member of the Oxford Round Table, he has authored books in the areas of Strategic Management, Knowledge Management, E-Commerce, and International Business. He has published 24 scholarly papers nationally within his disciplines and has been invited to speak at 25 professional conferences, both national and international.

# TABLE OF CONTENTS

# PREFACE

The Small Business Administration (SBA) reports that over 99 percent of all independent enterprises in the United States have fewer than 500 employees, The SBA 2012 report data indicates that there were 27.9 million small businesses, and 18,500 firms with 500 employees or more. Specifically, small businesses produce:

- 99.7 percent of U.S. employer firms
- 64 percent of net new private-sector jobs
- 49.2 percent of private-sector employment
- 42.9 percent of private-sector payroll
- 46 percent of private-sector output
- 43 percent of high-tech employment
- 98 percent of firms exporting goods
- 33 percent of exporting value

Cross border commerce, also known as international business or global business, offers exciting possibilities for small businesses. Yet, less than half of American businesses may pursue the opportunities of cross border commerce. Why is this so? Some say doing business overseas is too risky, or that impenetrable regulations make it seem impossible to conduct cross border commerce, or that they do not see an appropriate return on the investment of their time and money. Others point to the fact that they do not have the resources of larger firms that can employ international specialists, or that they would like to engage in cross border commerce, but do not know where to begin. The underlying motivation for each of these reasons for not engaging in cross border commerce is clear: fear of the unknown associated with doing business overseas. The source of this fear is lack of knowledge regarding globalization and global business. The solution, then, is to become educated in the essentials of cross border commerce in an efficient and effective manner.

*Cross Border Commerce* was written to provide the essential skills and knowledge needed to succeed in the global business arena. While most books on the subject focus almost entirely on the business needs of large corporate operations, *Cross Border Commerce* recognizes that the vast majority of readers are not employed by large corporations; thus, the focus is primarily geared toward medium-to-small organizations providing the essentials needed in a conducive and thorough manner of presentation. In addition to serving the needs of most business readers, this book is different from others in the field in three related and major aspects. First, the business content is written in an easily readable, concise, and no-nonsense manner: without the many nice-to-know but non-essential aspects added to other books in the field. The second aspect is price: the typical textbook in this field retails for almost twice the cost of this book. The much greater price is needed to offset the many nice-to-know but non-essential aspects, as well as the enormous costs associated with supporting large publishing corporate operations. The third aspect is the biblical worldview integration: taking what is learned academically and engaging the student with how to apply this from a Christian worldview and perspective.

## ORGANIZATION OF BOOK

The contents of this book are presented in a logical manner wherein specific knowledge is built sequentially: each chapter builds upon the preceding chapter's topics. The chapters are subdivided into smaller subsections, providing the essential business concepts needed to prepare for doing business overseas. Chapters One through Six provide the foundational essentials for understanding cross border commerce. Chapters Seven and Eight provide specifics regarding global market entry and global operations management issues and Supplemental Material regarding working overseas is provided at the end of Chapter Eight.

Chapter One provides the foundational knowledge regarding globalization and global business. Building upon the foundation established in Chapter One, Chapters Two and Chapter Three guide the reader through the major environmental aspects impacting cross border commerce: cultural, political, legal, and economical (including the elements of risk). The reader is now ready to discover the more advanced concepts in Chapter Four and Chapter Five, which provide essentials regarding international trade theory, the roles of government in cross border commerce, global financial markets and monetary systems, and foreign direct investment (FDI). Chapter Six is devoted entirely to the topic of international trade agreements and regional economic integration.

Now that the readers are knowledgeable in terms of globalization and the essential concepts of international business, they are ready to apply this foundation to the practical side of cross border commerce: making business decisions regarding where to expand and how to operate overseas. Chapter Seven covers the decision processes used in determining the conditions needed for expansion into global markets, key factors for success, and the modes of market entry. Chapter Eight provides the essential decision-making process needed to effectively and efficiently manage overseas operations, whether service or production.

## FEATURES FOR LEARNERS AND PROFESSORS

*Cross Border Commerce* provides learners from diverse academic backgrounds an overview of the theoretical knowledge and practical experiences needed to be literate and competent in the field of cross border commerce. While the book assumes that learners will have limited knowledge in the topic prior to enrolling in their course, the content provides exit learning and competencies comparable to those experienced in courses which require prerequisite knowledge or prior coursework in the field. Thus, this book is suitable for undergraduate and graduate courses in International Business, Global Business, and Global Management in which no prerequisite knowledge or prior coursework are required for enrollment.

*Cross Border Commerce* is especially suitable for those professors who desire to maximize learning in online courses. Many online professors lament the fact that their learners do not properly know how to study. Further, the busy demands in their learners' lives diminish the amount of time they have available to devote to their studies. The understandable end result of these two factors is that learners may choose to focus only on completing and submitting the online assignments at the expense of substantive long-term learning.

A unique learning feature of Cross Border Commerce is the inclusion of an organic learning system that helps the reader develop excellent study habits. The organic learning system requires readers to engage in a series of educational exercises located at the end of each Chapter. The Exercises, based on proven educational principles, are intended to be completed in the following sequential order:

- *Observational Analysis:* The observational analysis is to prepare and detail a broad overview of the Chapter. The learner is encourages to first read the Chapter to establish the main themes and principles being discussed. At this point the learner should take advantage of the space for notes provided on each page of the Chapter, jotting down thoughts or questions immediately as they arise from the reading.
- *Key Terms Analysis:* The Key Terms Analysis establishes the foundational vocabulary used within the Chapter. This section is set up in a matching format enabling the learner to easily compare and contrast the specifics between key terms. Building upon the results of completing the Observational Analysis, the Key Term Analysis allows the learner to go back through the notes they have taken to fill-in the textbook blanks, in preparation for any assignments due for the Chapter.
- *Theoretical Analysis:* After establishing the foundations of the textbook by gaining a general overview and flow of the chapter as well as determining and gaining an understanding of specific key terms that are vital to understanding the chapter, the learner is ready to engage the theoretical nature of the text. Learners are encouraged to do a second reading of the text trying to gain a higher understanding of the text by looking at the more nuanced aspects of the reading. The theoretical sections encourages the learner to think, with greater focus, on the inner workings of the broader concepts and strategies, as well a more applicable understanding of the key terms. Study at this level completes a holistic and inductive examination of the text, equipping the learner with the educational foundation necessary for scholarly research and writing in the field.
- *Practical Analysis:* This helps bridge the gap between the theoretical and educational aspects of the chapter as well. Learners are encouraged to complete some or all of these questions in order to establish how the educational theories play out in a real-world setting.

- *Biblical Worldview Application:* This section takes what is learned academically and engages the student with how to apply international business topics from a Christian worldview and perspective.

Supplemental material regarding working overseas is provided at the end of Chapter Eight. This material includes various topics dealing with working overseas as an expatriate including (1) motivations to accept an expatriate assignment, (2) expatriate selection procedures and success indicators, (3) adjusting to cultural change, (4) compensation and taxation issues for expatriates, (5) tips for doing business in select nations, and 6) personal security issues that may arise while working overseas.

Finally, a complete set of ancillary instructional materials is available to professors who adopt this book for their courses.  The ancillary instructional materials include sample course syllabi, test-banks for each Chapter (objective-type items/questions with key, and short essay questions), power-point lecture slides for each Chapter, sample threaded discussion questions, and sample course projects (graduate and undergraduate). Please contact info@si-corp.net for details. In an effort to ensure only qualified professors receive the ancillary materials, the publisher will contact the educational institution to verify the validity of the request.

# CROSS BORDER COMMERCE
*With Biblical Worldview Application*

Second Edition

Brian C. Satterlee

# Global Commerce
# and Trade

## CHAPTER OVERVIEW

Globalization, the growing integration of economies and societies worldwide, is recognized as one of the most important topics in international business. The pendulum of opinion swings from approval on one side to disapproval on the other. On the positive side, rapid economic growth and poverty reduction in some developing nations have been perceived as a positive aspect of globalization. From the negative end, significant international opposition exists over concerns that it has increased inequality and environmental degradation.[1]

No precise, widely agreed-upon definition exists for such an extensively used term as globalization. The array of definitions seems to be increasing rather than narrowing over time, taking on cultural, political, and other connotations—in addition to the economic. However, the most prevalent thinking on globalization refers to the observation that in recent years a quickly rising share of economic activity in the world is taking place between people who live in different nations, rather than in the same country.[2]

Globalization is not a new phenomenon but has been an aspect of humanity from earliest times, as widely scattered populations gradually became involved in more extensive and complicated economic relations. The growth of modern globalization began towards the end of the nineteenth century, mainly among the nations that are today developed or prosperous. The growth of globalization slowed considerably during the first half of the twentieth century. This slowdown was caused by many factors, including a worldwide sense of growing protectionism in a context of bitter national and great power strife, world wars, revolutions, rising authoritarian ideologies, and massive economic and political instability.

Since World War II (WWII), the pace of globalization has been steadily increasing. International relations have continually improved since the end of WWII. The improved post-war relations were brought about in part by the creation of institutions such as the General Agreement on Tariffs and Trade (GATT) known today as the World Trade Organization (WTO), which provides the enforceable agreement for signatory member nations to conduct global business. Additionally, developing nations were invited to become engaged on a wide range of multilateral international trade issues for the first time in history.

The pace of globalization continued to accelerate during the last decade of the twentieth century. Nations in their desire to capitalize on the new economic realities of the twenty-first century eliminated or reduced barriers to international trade and investment. Opening to the outside world has been part of a more general shift towards greater reliance on markets and private enterprise. This is especially the case as many developing and communist countries realized that high levels of government planning and intervention were failing to deliver the desired development outcomes.[3]

Chapter One provides an overview of Globalization. The overview begins with a section that provides the functional definitions to be used throughout the text, describes the importance of global trade, and discusses the concept of global business. Next a historical overview of international trade is provided. Driving forces and the rise of the multinational corporation are described as well as a discussion of the political, social, economic, and cultural impacts of business globalization. The chapter concludes with an exploration of the mindset and characteristics of a successful global business manager.

# THE GLOBALIZATION MOVEMENT

Some believe that globalization amounts to the selling of America to the world. While the U.S. is the largest worldwide exporter of culture, realistically these exports are "bringing a kind of market masala* to everyone in the world. Despite the embrace of polyethnic imagery, market-driven globalization doesn't want diversity. Its enemies are national habits, local brands and distinctive regional tastes."[4] Thus, the term "glocalization" has been coined to explain the phenomenon that the globalization of a product or service is more likely to succeed when that product or service is adapted specifically to each locality or culture to which it is marketed. More specifically, the term describes the tempering effects of local conditions on global pressures.

## *Prime Characteristics and Outcomes of Globalization*

The prime characteristics and outcomes of globalization can be described as follows:

- Globalization creates interdependencies among nations. As nations rely increasingly on global trade, they become more dependent upon the functioning of a global economy. A nation with a strong international trade presence has a much higher dependency profile than that of a nation with limited (or little to no) participation in the global marketplace. Consequently, critics argue that interdependency reduces a nation's strength and dilutes its ability to be self-sufficient. Proponents on the other hand argue that self-sufficiency is not the best measure of a nation's strengths and weaknesses and that interdependency can actually foster a more contributive and harmonious society.

- Globalization requires transparency. In the well-integrated global economy, a consumer might be oblivious to the origin of the product he or she is consuming. This oblivion is especially true when the origin is immaterial to the purchasing decision, as in the case of commodities. Transparency is less effective for products with brand recognition or differentiation. For example, consider the U.S. consumer who prefers to purchase a Japanese-manufactured automobile for its perceived superiority in reliability or a German-engineered automobile for its distinctive design. Whether transparent or not, the impact of globalization affords this consumer the option of deciding between locally produced goods or foreign imports. In another example, a consumer product such as a digital camera might contain components manufactured in Taiwan, assembled in Thailand, marketed by a French firm, and ultimately distributed in Canada. Globalization is demarcated by the way it transparently integrates all of these separate activities to form a single, seemingly inconsequential purchasing decision for the local consumer.

- Globalization requires that business people understand the ideal goal of having a seamless international marketplace. Financial professionals must be aware of the monetary impact of globalization, including its effect on macroeconomic and microeconomic models, accounting regulations and differences in legislation, and foreign exchange considerations. The economic environment is worldwide. Marketing professionals must be aware of the broad competitive landscape,

---

* Masala - a mixture of many spices in Indian cooking.

including the negotiation protocols peculiar to each nation in which business is conducted. They must favorably negotiate pricing models to capture each local market because the product territory is worldwide. As a result, the consumer should benefit from the increased number of product alternatives made available in this global marketplace. Overall, the competitive environment is more cutthroat (a term used here to describe those situations in which firms tend to compete with each other in unpleasant and unfair ways), but becomes more integrated than ever.

- Globalization involves the blending and merging of various cultures; however, it is not the same as assimilation. Assimilation historically resulted from situations where immigrants were isolated from their home cultures.[5] Globalization is an integrative model that is contrary to the results of isolation produced by arcane immigration models. Integration of cultures is more desirable than assimilation, as the integration allows the better elements of that culture to remain intact. Assimilation requires the rejection of the old culture with total acceptance of the new.

Globalization and its impact on international commerce is one of the most discussed topics in the world of business today. Likewise, the decisions and actions made by business professionals impact the future directions and perspectives of globalization. At the same time, no one doubts that globalization has led to the growth of world trade and output. The following sections of this chapter cover these growth patterns, both worldwide and in the USA.

### Characteristics of Globalization
- Interdependencies among nations
- Transparency
- Desire for seamless international marketplace
- Blending and merging of cultures

### Growth of World Trade and Output (1992—Present)

The World Trade Organization (WTO) was established in the early 1990s to help foster international trade and resolve disputes.[6] Many question the necessity of the WTO, but it was originally created in order to provide uniform standards and rules of engagement to a growing international trade market. International trade growth was also fueled in the 1990s by government legislation that created a more favorable trading environment. The North American Free Trade Agreement (NAFTA) was enacted in order to facilitate the importation and exportation of goods and services among the signatory nations (United States, Canada, and Mexico) by reducing trade tariffs and restrictions. NAFTA was originally projected to create two hundred thousand jobs per year in the U.S. alone. The results show that in actuality the job mix has simply changed.[7] Mexico emerged as a viable location for manufacturing facilities due to its low wage costs and close proximity. Canada is also a viable location for production facilities and service industries, due to its highly skilled labor force and close cultural similarities. Today this manufacturing emergence is increasingly shifting to Asia—especially China, Taiwan, Thailand, and Malaysia.

Gross Domestic Product (GDP) is the official measure of total output of goods and services in a nation's economy. The rank of the top 5 countries by GDP as of 2012 in trillions of dollars are:

1. United States ($16.2)

2. China ($8.2)

3. Japan ($5.9)

4. Germany ($3.4)

5. France ($2.6)

The annual growth rate for gross domestic product (GDP) in the United States from 2000 to 2009 has been 2.70 percent. There has been positive annual growth above 2 percent every year from 1992 to 2007 with the exception of 2001 at 0.9 percent and 2002 at 1.8 percent; GDP then suffered a decrease of -.3 percent in 2008 and -2.8 percent in 2009. The highest growth rates occurred in 1997 (4.5 percent) and 1999 (4.8 percent).[8] It has increased an average of 2.37% from 2010 through 2012. A major driver for this growth was the demand for technology-based products and services. The U.S. is home to some of the world's leading hardware and software manufacturers. For example, Apple®— the world's largest software company—is headquartered in the state of California.[9] The increase in demand for technology-based products and services has created a job market for highly-skilled workers who demand higher salaries, which results in increased consumer purchasing power. These increases have all attributed to the growth rates witnessed in the United States over the past decade.

The GDP of nations outside of the U.S. has also risen steadily. China, the most populous country in the world, has emerged as a cost-leading manufacturer of products ranging from consumer goods to industrial equipment. China's GDP annual growth rate for 2012 was 7.70 percent and is currently projected at 7.60 percent for 2013. Elsewhere, Vietnam—a country fraught with devastation and crippling sanctions after the Vietnam War—has emerged as a major exporter of furniture. Thailand has emerged as a leading manufacturer of semiconductors. According to the International Monetary Fund, Vietnam had GDP growth of 6.24 percent for 2011 and 5.247 and 5.30 percent projected for 2012 and 2013 respectively. Thailand had GDP growth of .077 percent for 2011, 6.49 percent for 2012, and 3.107 projected for 2013.

Middle Eastern nations have also experienced GDP growth. In oil-producing nations such as Saudi Arabia (GDP 8.57 percent 2011, 5.126 percent 2012, and 3.57 percent projected 2013) and Kuwait (GDP 6.30 percent 2011, and 6.186 and .821 percent projected for 2012 and 2013 respectively), an increase in global energy demand has been a financial windfall. India's growth has also topped expectations. India (GDP 6.33 percent 2011, 3.24 percent 2012, and 3.79 percent projected 2013) is particularly attractive as a U.S. trade partner because of its highly educated, English-speaking workforce. Services that can be easily contracted to third parties, known as outsourcing, make up a large portion of foreign direct investment in India. [10]

*Brief Summary of Current U.S. International Trade Competitive Situation*

The United States is a major consumer and producer in the international marketplace. As reported by the U.S. government CIA World Factbook in 2014, the 2012 estimated

GDP purchasing power parity of the United States ($16.24 trillion) ranked first in comparison to other economies, with the European Union ($15.54 trillion) coming in at a close second.[11] The top five export partners of the United States consist of:

1. Canada

2. Mexico

3. China

4. Japan

5. United Kingdom

United States' imports primarily come from the following countries:

1. China

2. Canada

3. Mexico

4. Japan

5. Germany

Canada and Mexico consistently rank as two of the leading suppliers to the United States making up over 25 percent of total trade to the U.S. NAFTA was a major contributor to continental trade growth between the United States, Mexico, and Canada because it eased quotas, tariffs, and customs procedures. [12]

### *Why Global Business and International Trade is Important to the U.S.*

First, the international market allows for domestic vendors to optimize production through the use of foreign vendors under potentially more favorable economic conditions. Production is efficient when any increase or decrease in output would cause a disproportionate increase in the cost of production and when there is no alternative that would lead to a more profitable production of a given product. In international trade, these alternatives include outsourcing production to foreign firms. Nations with lower wage costs can often produce more efficiently. Therefore United States firms rely heavily on operations in lower wage cost nations for tasks such as manufacturing, which can be easily reassigned. Through outsourcing, the domestic firm is able to focus its resources on areas in which it maintains a distinct competitive advantage, such as service offerings or research and development. In a recent survey of financial executives, 73 percent of the respondents consider outsourcing to be an important component of their long-term growth strategies.[13] Overall, outsourcing usually results in lower consumer prices, which would rise considerably if domestic firms were forced to procure similar items locally.

Second, the international market removes the boundaries of local market territories, thereby increasing the potential market audience. In other words, territorial boundaries that define potential markets are removed. This redefines a global business market as representing the entire world. When a domestic firm considers to expandh its market globally, there is potential to develop a much larger revenue base. Additionally, firms that are losing domestic business can recapture and often expand sales by strategically pursuing customers overseas. This global view can be particularly useful to a firm that competes through product differentiation. For example, the U.S. international trade involvement can be seen in its export of coal.[14] The U.S. holds one of the largest coal reserves in the world. Many nations rely on U.S. exports of coal to service their own national infrastructure needs. U.S. firms could not recognize most of this revenue in the absence of an international trade market.

Third, foreign direct investment allows domestic firms to receive capital financing from foreign entities. It also provides financing to international markets as part of a diversified investment vehicle. The funds from foreign direct investment make up a sizable amount of capital expenditure in the U.S. Japanese-based Honda Motor Company and Toyota Motors have built automobile manufacturing facilities in the Midwest and Southern United States, which have infused billions of dollars of capital into the U.S. economy.

> ### Reasons International Trade is Important to the United States
>
> 1. Maximizing production and efficiency.
> 2. Increasing market audience.
> 3. Receiving foreign direct investment.

Other examples include foreign firms that maintain corporate operations in different global locations. For example, Schlumberger—a company with 2013 earnings revenue of 45.27 billion USD—is incorporated in the Netherlands Antilles, traded on the New York Stock Exchange, and maintains its headquarters in Houston, TX.[15] A portion of its income is still subject to taxation within the United States. The healthy international business environment enables the U.S. to attract foreign firms, add jobs, tax revenue, and technology to its economy. Just as the U.S. receives foreign capital it also invests heavily in other nations. Without a positive international trade environment foreign investment of any type would not be possible.

Globalization has created a thriving market for international trade and can be classified as a narrower focus on this trade activity. In addition, global business can be examined in an individual or collective context and can be compared and contrasted with domestic business.

### Global Business

In a broad context, global business can be considered as business without boundaries. As a collective term global business includes all domestic businesses with transactions in the international market. Additionally, global business includes all transnational or multinational businesses. These are enterprises that manage production establishments or deliver services in at least two nations. Multinational corporations (MNCs) are often divided into three broad groups based on production, operations management, and functionality:

1. Vertical integration extends a firm's competitive scope within the same industry by performing production activities normally provided by a supplier or distributor. The integration can be backward into sources of its inputs or supplies or forward into distribution of its outputs toward the end-users.

2. Horizontal integration occurs when a firm expands its business by creating or acquiring activities dealing with similar products, that are substitutes for the business' products and/or acquiring other competitors that offer similar products.

3. Diversified integration occurs when a firm expands its business into different products that are not similar to current lines.

NOTES

Global business can also be examined as it relates to individual business entities. When a firm in one nation exchanges products, services, resources, or capital with a firm located in another nation, this exchange constitutes an international transaction. The frequency of international transactions can help determine whether an individual business also qualifies as a global business.

A business with frequent international transactions is a global business. In congruence with globalization principles, the entire world is one large market. The astute global business professional discerns between domestic and international customers. Firms pursuing international commerce consider differences between domestic and international standards, languages, cultural preferences, and government regulations. A well-known saying in global business circles is, "think globally; act locally." What then are some of the major differences and similarities between domestic and international business?

### Differences and Similarities with Domestic Business

A global business has considerable operational differences from that of a strictly domestic business. First, a global business must consider the broader geographical scope in which it operates. Second, it must understand that each market contains different cultural influences that will affect the product marketing mix. Third, it must take into account market factors, such as foreign exchange rates, which can materially alter operating conditions. Finally, the management of a global business requires carefully selected and trained leadership, salesmanship, and support staff.

The scope of a domestic business is specific. A domestic business' scope is generally confined to a local marketing territory. The territory can be made up of a single city, county, state, or multi-state area. In a global business, this scope is expanded to include other countries over a far greater geographical area. A global business must

> **Global Business Differences**
> - Scope
> - Cultural influences
> - Market factors
> - Management practices

carefully consider the nations in which it can compete, giving special attention to each nation's unique blend of challenges, competitive landscape, and environmental factors. To illustrate, a winter clothing manufacturer concludes that consumers located in tropical regions have little interest in their winter clothing line. To be profitable the firm either has to exclude this region from its target audience or find another product that will be suitable to the tropical region.

The second difference between global and domestic business management is observed in a nation's culture. Culture is defined as the set of shared attitudes, values, goals, and practices that characterize a particular category. In this business context the category is the particular region or nation that is foreign to the domestic firm that is closely correlated to consumer spending patterns. A domestic business operates in the "comfort of its own backyard," whereas a global enterprise operates within foreign cultures that may be entirely different from the well-known domestic market. Even the most subtle differences require thorough evaluation before an appropriate product marketing mix can be determined. A study of the correlation between advertising effectiveness and ritual behavior concludes that "the notion of advertising as simply transferring ritual meaning to a product through straightforward association . . . does not adequately describe the complex interaction between the two institutions."[16] For example, an alcoholic beverage manufacturer could face great difficulty in trying to market its product in a country where a strongly influential religious community discourages the consumption of alcohol.

The third difference between global and domestic business is that management takes into consideration market factors. Market factors are the demographic, sociologic, and economic forces that vary from one region to another. One area of particular concern is the exchange of foreign currencies. Countries have their own unique currency systems complete with different denominations. In order to translate the domestic country's currency into the foreign country's currency, an intermediary—typically a foreign exchange market—is often required. This foreign exchange market adds overhead to the cost of buying and selling in almost all foreign markets. To make matters worse, some governments impose artificially inflated or fixed currency exchange rates. For European nations, the introduction of the Euro has significantly reduced the burdens previously associated with foreign currency exchange in this region.

The fourth difference between global and domestic business management is the need for global business leaders to be equipped with special management skills. The global business manager must have a wide perspective of foreign affairs. General world market knowledge in addition to knowledge specific to each target country, is necessary in order to make decisions about which markets would best complement the firm's competitive strategy. Another difficulty often faced by the global business manager is with customs, which can vary greatly from one country to another. For example, the use of government bribery is a routine part of business operations in a number of nations, but the U.S. considers this practice illegal. The global business manager must be equipped to respond to such challenges in ways that best perpetuates the firm's interests and maintains the integrity of the individual. One of the greatest challenges of working in this environment is doing so without sacrificing corporate or personal integrity.

The old adage says that, "those who fail to learn from history are doomed to repeat it." This saying is especially true for those engaged in global business. Armed with a good understanding of the impact of globalization on business, as well as knowledge of similarities and differences between global and domestic business, we now turn our attention to a brief discussion of the historical developments in global business.

## HISTORICAL DEVELOPMENTS

International exchange is often thought of as a recent concept; however, there is evidence to suggest that the first international trade took place as early as 2500 BC. Starting in Phoenicia, historical records indicate a steady progression of trade throughout the Middle East, Africa, Europe, and Asia. Global trade was greatly enhanced during the second millennium AD with the widespread use of vessels, rail, and air transportation options. Improvement in transportation, advances in communications technology, and trade-friendly legislation have all contributed to the desire to produce a seamless global economy.

### To the Time of Christ

Phoenicia was one of the oldest examples of an international trading community, dating back to 1100 BC.[17] The Phoenicians made up for their lack of arable land by trading precious metals and textiles with surrounding communities. Another early trading civilization was found in Africa, where the Berbers would cross the Saharan desert to trade salt. International trade was involved in the building of Solomon's Temple which was completed in the tenth century BC. Solomon, king of Israel, entered into a trade agreement with Hiram I, king of Tyre, for the supply of timber from the forests of Lebanon. The timber was brought in great rafts by the sea to Joppa and dragged to Jerusalem to be used in the construction of the temple. Hiram also provided labor for the task. In return Solomon provided food for Hiram's royal household. The entire pact was recorded in the Old Testament book of I Kings: 5:

> When Hiram king of Tyre heard that Solomon had been anointed king to succeed his father, David, he sent his envoys to Solomon, because he had always been on friendly terms with David. Solomon sent back this message to Hiram: "You know that because of the wars waged against my father David from all sides, he could not build a temple for the Name of the LORD his God until the LORD put his enemies under his feet. But now the LORD my God has given me rest on every side, and there is no adversary or disaster. I intend, therefore, to build a temple for the Name of the LORD my God, as the LORD told my father David, when he said, 'Your son whom I will put on the throne in your place will build the temple for my Name.' So give orders that cedars of Lebanon be cut for me. My men will work with yours, and I will pay you for your men whatever wages you set. You know that we have no one so skilled in felling timber as the Sidonians." When Hiram heard Solomon's message, he was greatly pleased and said, "Praise be to the LORD today, for he has given David a wise son to rule over this great nation."

> So Hiram sent word to Solomon: "I have received the message you sent me and will do all you want in providing the cedar and pine logs. My men will haul them down from Lebanon to the sea, and I will float them in rafts by sea to the place you specify. There I will separate them and you can take them away. And you are to grant my wish by providing food for my royal household." In this way Hiram kept Solomon supplied with all the cedar and pine logs he wanted, and Solomon gave Hiram twenty thousand cors of wheat as food for his household, in addition to twenty thousand baths of pressed olive oil.† Solomon continued to do this for Hiram year after year. The LORD gave Solomon wisdom, just as he had promised him. There were peaceful relations between Hiram and Solomon, and the two of them made a treaty.

> King Solomon conscripted laborers from all Israel—thirty thousand men. He sent them off to Lebanon in shifts of ten thousand a month, so that they spent one month in Lebanon and two months at home. Adoniram was in charge of the forced labor. Solomon had seventy thousand carriers and eighty thousand stonecutters in the hills, as well as thirty-three hundred foremen who supervised the project and directed the workmen. At the king's command they removed from the quarry large blocks of quality stone to provide a foundation of dressed stone for the temple. The craftsmen of Solomon and Hiram and the men of Gebal cut and prepared the timber and stone for the building of the temple.[18]

Perhaps the most well-known example of international trade in this era was the Pax Romana or Roman Peace. This Latin term refers to the Empire in its glorified prime. From

---

† One hundred twenty thousand "cors" of wheat amounts to approximately 125,000 bushels. Twenty thousand "baths" of pressed olive oil amounts to approximately 115,000 gallons (about 440 kiloliters).

the end of the Republican civil wars and beginning with the accession of Augustus in 27 BC, this era in Roman history lasted until 180 AD with the death of Marcus Aurelius. Though the use of the word "peace" may be misleading as this period refers mainly to the great Romanization of the western world. The Roman legal system, which forms the basis of many western court systems today, brought law and order to the provinces. The Legions patrolled the borders with success; though many foreign wars still existed, the internal empire was free from major invasion, piracy, or social disorder on any grand scale.[19]

## Through the Middle Ages to the Renaissance

International trade continued to develop through the Middle Ages. Stone roads started to appear throughout Europe, and regular trade networks extended all the way to Africa and Asia. Travel was a time consuming and hazardous activity. The upper class who were an elite concentration of wealthy individuals often of noble heritage, only traveled by horse-drawn carriages and enjoyed lavishing lifestyles. Peasants and slaves were not so fortunate having to travel without the benefit of even horses or camels and often left to perform manual labor.

In 1215 the Magna Carta Libertatum was chartered as a way to formally recognize the legal limitations of a king's power. This charter is sometimes credited with stimulating the growth of free trade during this time period. Even today modern democratic societies refer to the Magna Carta as a key legal baseline. Elsewhere the Ming Dynasty in China built a powerful naval fleet with high hopes of exploration and expansion. Some scholars assert that these Chinese expeditions were the first successful voyages to America.

Modern trade history began with the exploration of the Western Hemisphere by Christopher Columbus in 1492. Once discovered the Americas were quickly colonized by European nations to become critical provincial trading resources. Transatlantic trade flourished, but not without peril. The sea vessels of this time were slow and dangerous, relying exclusively on wind power for propulsion. Most manufacturing methods were still manual-labor intensive.

Western history records numerous periods of trade growth, from the discovery of America by Spanish traders to the establishment of the Dutch East India Trading Company. One interesting example of global trade from that period of time involves the processing of cocoa into chocolate. Chocolate is processed from the seeds (or beans) of the Cacao tree, which grows in South America and other equatorial and tropical climate regions.

The Mayans, an indigenous people of Central America, introduced Spanish explorers of the early sixteenth century to xocolatl by making chocolate-type drink based on the cocoa bean. The Mayans enjoyed xocolatl for at least two-thousand years before their encounter with Spanish explorers. Soon after the first taste of this delicious beverage Spanish traders imported cocoa to various European ports where sugar was eventually added to process hot chocolate. Originally the Spanish processed the imported cocoa beans into various powder, butter, and liquor modalities. Later, with the rise and development of the West India Trading Company, the Netherlands became the prime processors of cocoa. Demand for the product grew in dramatic fashion, and investors expanded cocoa tree plantations into other tropical climate regions, such as Africa, the Caribbean, Hawaii, South America, and Southeast Asia.

## NOTES

### To the Industrial Revolution

The Industrial Revolution heralded the introduction of mass production, improved transportation, technological progress, and the industrial factory system. Social and economic changes during this period enabled the transition from a stable agricultural and commercial society to a modern industrial society that relied on complex machinery rather than hand tools. Exploration and trade from Western European nations during the Renaissance led to an increased supply of precious metals from the New World. This resulted in rising prices, which stimulated the growth of industry and fostered an international economy based on money rather than barter. Expansion of trade and the money economy stimulated the development of new institutions of finance and credit. During the eighteenth century an expanding and wealthier population demanded more and better goods.

In the productive process coal came to replace wood. The Industrial Revolution was characterized by a marked surge in manufacturing techniques that included mass assembly, electricity, and new forms of propulsion. One such innovation was the steam engine—an economical form of self-propulsion. The steam engine brought about the first efficient forms of mass transportation using machine power. As a result transatlantic and transpacific transit times were greatly reduced.[20] The steam engine was also used to create manufacturing systems capable of mass production. Developed nations, such as the United States and Britain, used mass production as a competitive advantage to increase their dominance in the world's marketplace.

Consequently the focus of trade shifted from Mediterranean to Atlantic ports chartered companies were organized and continued improvements in navigation and ship construction sped long voyages. As a worldwide trade evolved, local trade barriers were reduced, stimulating global trade. Modern credit facilities also appeared, such as the state bank, the bourse (the European term for stock exchange), and the futures market. Additionally, the promissory note and other new media of exchange were created.

### To the Information Age

The Information Age is the era where information is considered to be a valuable resource, and its capture and distribution generates competitive advantage to organizations. While the era technically could be traced to the invention of the telephone and the telegraph in the late 1800s, it rose to the forefront in the early 1970s with the advent of the microprocessor. Modern increases in trade activity can be attributed to the improvements in communications networks.

In 1866 the telegraph opened the first transatlantic communications channel to facilitate real-time communication over long distances. By the early 1900s radio and telephone networks were widespread in developed nations followed by televisions several decades later. Pax Americana, Latin for "American peace," is the period of relative peace in the Western world since the end of World War II in 1945, which coincided with the dominant military and economic position of the U.S. Pax Americana places the U.S. in the military and diplomatic role of a modern-day Roman Empire. During this period no armed conflict has emerged among major Western nations themselves, and no nuclear weapons have been used, although the U.S. and its allies have been involved in various regional wars.

In 1957 the launch of the Sputnik 1 satellite paved the way for orbital electronic devices. Toward the end of the 1980s the personal desktop computer became a commonplace household fixture. These technologies converged towards the close of the twentieth century to form the basis of the Internet, a distributed communications network that connects computers and electronic devices around the world in real time. In a trade context the Internet is used for E-commerce, which enables millions of consumers each day to buy and sell products. Common ways that businesses use the Internet include managing field-based operations, employing workers in remote locations, monitoring inventories, and knowledge management. The Information Age has connected the world and greatly expanded the opportunities for true global businesses.

The preceding section presented a concise description of advances in global trade throughout select periods of recorded history. Early globalization efforts clearly were driven by the desire to increase wealth of the ruling class, and later to increase standards of living for the general populace. The modern globalization movement is driven by a complex array of issues and interventions. The following section discusses these driving forces of contemporary globalization.

## DRIVING FORCES

A number of forces are driving the trend towards globalization. First, reductions in barriers to trade have allowed goods to more easily pass between international borders. Second, reductions in barriers to foreign investment have allowed foreign investors to benefit from growing markets outside of their own. Third, advances in communication and transportation technologies have greatly improved the speed at which international parties can communicate and move goods across borders. Finally, the rise in prominence of multinational corporations has greatly impacted the pace of globalization.

### *Reduction in Barriers to Trade*

Barriers to trade can affect the ease with which a country can import and export goods. Barriers to trade include the following:

- Tariffs or taxes on imported goods

- Quotas or the restriction of the import of something to a specific quantity

- Embargoes or the prohibition of commerce and trade with a certain nation

- Sanctions or economic actions of one nation, or group of nations, against another group as part of a trade dispute

Cooperative trading agreements have significantly reduced these barriers. In North America, the most notable example is NAFTA which is a cooperative agreement between the United States, Canada, and Mexico that ensures the smooth passage of goods between these countries. An example of similar reduction in certain European countries can be observed in the European Free Trade Association (EFTA).

NOTES

### Reduction in Barriers to Foreign Investment

Foreign investment includes the direct financial investments of foreign entities into the host economy. This is a type of inbound foreign investment. Foreign investment also includes the outbound investment of host country capital into foreign economies. Example of inbound foreign direct investment includes the 2002 acquisition of Equilon Enterprises by Royal Dutch/Shell of the Netherlands and Saudi Aramco of Saudi Arabia. The Energy Information Administration reported the following:

> U.S. petroleum refining and marketing saw two major foreign direct acquisitions in 2002. The largest was a three-way transaction that resulted from an agreement that allowed Chevron and Texaco to merge in 2000. At that time, the U.S. Federal Trade Commission and several State commissions would only consent to the merger if Texaco divested all of its U.S. refining and marketing assets, which it held through Equilon Enterprises and Motiva Enterprises. These two companies were joint ventures of Texaco, Royal Dutch/Shell (Netherlands and United Kingdom), and, for Motiva only, Saudi Aramco (Saudi Arabia). In a three-way deal, the other joint owners purchased Texaco's shares of Equilon and Motiva in a transaction valued at $4.1 billion. After the acquisition, Royal Dutch/Shell owned 100 percent of Equilon, and Royal Dutch/Shell and Saudi Aramco each owned 50 percent of Motiva. The two joint ventures marketed petroleum products through 23 thousand branded service stations in the United States and owned 8 refineries, 30 thousand miles of pipeline, and a trading enterprise.[21]

Foreign direct investment is an attractive option for firms looking to diversify their investment portfolios and creating opportunities for firms looking to enter emerging markets.

Risks to foreign investment vary. One risk can occur when a foreign government limits the ability of foreign investors to expatriate funds in order to mitigate economic uncertainties. Emerging market economies can also be highly volatile. The recognition of the impact of such barriers led countries to form the independent Organization for Economic Co-operation and Development (OECD).

**Driving Forces**
- Reductions in barriers to trade
- Reductions in barriers to foreign investments
- Advances in communications and transportation technologies

OECD provides a cooperative venue for establishing guidelines and cooperation in free-trade markets.[22] Participation in such organizations instills confidence in investors looking to make foreign investments and reduces an important barrier to foreign investment. Additionally, legislative bodies are now highly sensitive to the criticality of international trade and have enacted legislation designed to expedite and stimulate foreign investment.

### Communication Technology

Communication technologies are used by the global business professional in the processing and transfer of messages and information. The technologies are used in various applications:

- Television and radio broadcasting
- Multimedia applications
- Internet
- Graphic design
- Digital and analogue audiovisual communication
- Networked communication
- Advertising
- Journalism
- Mass media
- Instructional design

Innovation in networking technologies has significantly reduced the barriers of communication between distant operating locations. Local area networks are now used within most retail operations to network point-of-sale registers to inventory systems.[23] Wide area networks are commonly implemented across operating locations so that each location can access real-time inventory information from other locations. Finally, the Internet has allowed companies to commercialize access to their product offerings in the form of electronic commerce systems. E-commerce has exploded into a multi-billion dollar industry since its widespread adoption in the late 1990s.

### *Advances in Transportation Technology*

Transportation technologies now include a full range of ocean, rail, automotive, and aerial options. Ocean vessels evolved from slow, labor-intensive ships into modern diesel-driven vessels that can survive even the harshest climates with minimal crews. Most countries also use extensive rail networks to move heavier items within a continent. Diesel-powered trucks traveling through elaborate highway systems are used to deliver freight to even more specific destinations. Each of these transportation options have benefited heavily with the introduction of the ISO standard cargo container.[24] The International Standards Organization (ISO) is the world's leading developer of International Standards. ISO standards specify the requirements for state-of-the-art products, services, processes, materials and systems, and for good conformity assessment, managerial and organizational practice. ISO standards are designed to be implemented worldwide.[25] Standard ISO cargo containers, also known as isotainers, can be loaded and sealed intact onto container ships, railroad cars, planes, and trucks.

Alternatively, commercial aircraft can be used to move more sensitive freight quickly over long distances. Finally, integrated communications networks are used to link ocean, rail, automotive, and air transportation together and allow real-time freight movement optimization. Despite record high energy costs, the options for moving freight are more efficient than ever.

### *Multinational Corporations*

The final driving force for globalization is the multinational corporation (MNC). Any corporation or enterprise that manages production establishments or delivers services in at least two countries may be considered a MNC. Very large MNCs have budgets

**NOTES**

that exceed those of many nations. Thus, the largest MNCs operate with a considerable amount of purchasing power. Forbes Inc. has compiled a list of the top 2000 multinational firms, as determined by their sales, profits, assets, and market value. The table on the next page lists the top twenty-five companies of Forbes' 2000 Rank for 2013.[26]

A study examining the largest economic entities reveals that as of 2012, 40 percent of the 100 largest economic entities and 58 percent of the 150 largest economic entities are corporations. It is interesting to note, since 2000 the proportion of the largest economic entities that are corporations has fallen 20 percent. The shift is due to "the clear movement of economic power from West to East as the economies of rapidly developing economies (RDEs)" and fast growing companies headquartered within these regions move up in the ranking of global economic power.[27] This finding is significant because there can be a notable difference in the way a nation conducts business versus the way a large corporation conducts business. A nation typically is most interested in serving its citizens without bias or qualification. A corporation, on the other hand, has the primary goal of maximizing the wealth of its shareholders. As multinational corporations continue to grow at a rate that outpaces many countries' entire economies, careful consideration must be given to the role of each in the global economic environment.

Having discussed the driving forces of globalization, we now turn our attention to the impact of globalization in terms of political, economic, social, and cultural aspects of doing business across borders.

| Rank | Company | Country | Sales | Profits | Assets | Market Value |
|------|---------|---------|-------|---------|--------|--------------|
| 1 | **ICBC** | China | $134.8B | $37.8B | $2,813.5B | $237.3B |
| 2 | **China Construction Bank** | China | $113.1B | $30.6B | $2,241B | $202B |
| 3 | **JPMorgan Chase** | U.S. | $108.2B | $21.3B | $2,359.1B | $191.4B |
| 4 | **General Electric** | U.S. | $147.4B | $13.6B | $685.3B | $243.7B |
| 5 | **Exxon Mobil** | U.S. | $420.7B | $44/9B | $333/8B | $400.4B |
| 6 | **HSBC Holdings** | U.K. | $104.9B | $14.3B | $2,684.1B | $201.3B |
| 7 | **Royal Dutch Shell** | Netherlands | $467.2B | $26.6B | $360.3B | $213.1B |
| 8 | **Agricultural Bank of China** | China | $103B | $23B | $2,124.2B | $150.8B |
| 9 | **Berkshire Hathaway** | U.S. | $162.5B | $14.8B | $427.5B | $252.8B |
| 10 | **PetroChina** | China | $308.9B | $18.3B | $347.8B | $261.2B |
| 11 | **Bank of China** | China | $98.1B | $22.1B | $2,033.8B | $131.7B |
| 12 | **Wells Fargo** | U.S. | $91.2B | $18.9B | $1,423B | $201.3B |
| 13 | **Chevron** | U.S. | $222.6B | $26.2B | $233B | $232.5B |
| 14 | **Volkswagen Group** | Germany | $254B | $28.6B | $408.2B | $94.4B |
| 15 | **Apple** | U.S. | $164.7B | $41.7B | $196.1B | $416.6B |
| 16 | **Wal-Mart Stores** | U.S. | $469.2B | $17B | $203.1B | $242.5B |
| 17 | **Gazprom** | Russia | $144B | $40.6B | $339.3B | $111.4B |
| 18 | **BP** | U.K. | $370.9B | $11.6B | $301B | $130.4B |
| 19 | **CitiGroup** | U.S. | $90.7B | $7.5B | $1,864.7B | $143.6B |
| 20 | **Petrobras** | Brazil | $144.1B | $11B | $331.6B | 4120.7B |
| 21 | **Samsung Electronics** | South Korea | $187.8B | $21.7B | $196.3B | $174.4B |
| 22 | **BNP Paribas** | France | $126.2B | $8.6B | $2,504.2B | $71.3B |
| 23 | **Total** | France | $240.5B | $14.1B | $224.1B | $115.5B |
| 24 | **AT&T** | U.S. | $127.4B | $7.3B | $272.3B | $200.1B |
| 25 | **Allianz** | Germany | $140.3B | $6.8B | $915.8B | $66.4B |

NOTES

NOTES

# MACRO IMPACTS

Globalization has impacted the political, economic, social, and cultural aspects of international community members. Political and cultural environments of some nations have become more polarized. While most become more subdued, a few become more extreme. Economic health varies in moderate correlation with the amount of international trade activity in each host country. Social systems have been forced to adapt to a new composition of workers and ethnicities—some without success. Finally, cultural impact has emerged as a focal point in international debate concerning the toll of globalization.

## *Political Impacts of Globalization*

Much debate continues over the political effects of globalization. Opponents of globalization claim that globalization has led to widespread government corruption as indicated through the extensive use of bribery. However, one could argue that globalization is not to blame for this political corruption; but, that these practices were likely preexisting and have only recently gained exposure in the arena of public debate. The results of the 2013 Transparency International's Annual Corruption Index ranks countries' on their countries perceived corruptibility.

|   | *Least Corrupt Country* | *Most Corrupt Country* |
|---|---|---|
| 1 | Denmark | Somalia |
| 2 | New Zealand | North Korea |
| 3 | Finland | Afghanistan |
| 4 | Sweden | Sudan |
| 5 | Norway | South Sudan |
| 6 | Singapore | Libya |
| 7 | Switzerland | I raq |
| 8 | The Netherlands | Uzbekistan |
| 9 | Australia | Turkmenistan Venezuela |
| 10 | Canada | Syria |

The results reveal that nations such as Denmark (1), Australia (9), and the United States (19) are far less accommodating to corrupt practices, whereas Vietnam (116), Russia (127), and Syria (168) are far more tolerant. U.S. managers routinely rank bribery as being an unethical practice. Respondents in some nations find the use of bribes as a critical leveraging tool that facilitates necessary compromise in business exchange.

Proponents of globalization point out the positive influences upon the political environment. An increasing importance of international trade has led nations to establish specific policy departments that deal exclusively with maintaining favorable foreign relations. Overall, this has brought about a much higher increase in global awareness, as well as legislation to ensure minimum standards in a given level of economic participation. U.S. labor laws have been constructed to prevent domestic companies from employing underage workers—even in foreign countries—which have been estimated to be in excess of 150 million child workers between the ages of five and fourteen or 16 percent of all children in this age group.[29]

The multinational company typically views the political landscape in terms of political risks. Political risks can be classified three ways: transfer, operational, and ownership control.

- Transfer risk includes the risk of debt consolidation—the debt of a country in a critical financial situation will be rescheduled for repayment over an extended period as a result of an agreement between the countries concerned. This can impair the ability to exchange capital and other real products between countries.
- Operational risk can be defined as the risk of monetary losses resulting from inadequate or failed internal processes, people, and systems—or from external events. Losses from external events, such as a natural disaster, which damages a firm's physical assets, or electrical or telecommunications failures, which disrupt business, are relatively easier to define than losses from internal problems, such as employee fraud and product flaws. These internal and external events can disrupt the day-to-day operations and production of the business.
- Ownership control risk includes government policies or actions that inhibit ownership or control of foreign operations. This governmental interference can disrupt the actual ownership of an entity.

Each of these variables requires constant monitoring on the part of the firm to ensure that governmental disruptions are kept to a minimum.

### Economic Impacts of Globalization

The health of a given economy can be measured in part by the number of exports it has relative to the number and economic value of its imports. Economic health is considered negative when a country imports considerably more than it exports. Imported and exported goods must also take into account services provided such as consulting, which are provided along with the physical product. Generally globalization has increased the market opportunity for countries to undertake both importing and exporting activities, allowing for an infusion of capital from foreign investors. New foreign sources of capital help to create new businesses and increase spending in research and development activities. However, foreign capital can be unsettling in a market with great volatility—either from political or socioeconomic forces. Significant fluctuations in currency exchange rates can reduce the actual value of each dollar that a foreign investor has vested in his or her foreign portfolio, potentially prompting the investor to withdraw from a market entirely. Withdrawals bring negative consequences such as closures and layoffs, leading some to question the appropriate amount of foreign investment leverage required to maintain a healthy economy, while mitigating disruption to domestic ownership.

### Social Impacts of Globalization

Social implications of globalization are generally integrative. New jobs created by international demand have led to growing populations in urban areas known as urban sprawl. Each new wave of economic activity brings about the inclusion of communities further and further from the city's center. In many modern economies businesses focus on greater social responsibility that lead to more investments in benevolent or humanitarian efforts. The world economy's purchasing power and its benefits can be seen in the international relief provided to victims of the 2010 Earthquake in Japan. The 8.9 magnitude earthquake that struck off of Japan's coast on March 11 and the tsunami it triggered that caused severe damage in the Asia Pacific regions. The surge

NOTES

of water reached 30 feet high and traveled more than three miles inland. More than an estimated 15,000 people were killed by the earthquake and subsequent tsunami. It is the nuclear meltdown that the tsunami caused that everyone is talking about and will likely be talking about for years to come. This almost automatic reaction of benevolence has caused some critics to question the excessiveness of such benevolence.[30] A nation would most likely suffer severe backlash if it were to shun commonly accepted social expectations, whether or not they harmonize with local expectations.

### Cultural Impacts of Globalization

A nation's culture consists of the behaviors and characteristics that are unique to its citizens. Globalization has created what critics refer to as a melting pot or clash of various cultural identities. Sometimes this clash becomes violent especially as a result of religious tensions and riots in some nations. For the most part globalization is a unifying act that requires people to work together. The heightened exposure that ensues usually fosters greater appreciation for diversity. As globalization becomes more embedded in daily life, tolerance must continue to increase in order to avoid unnecessary polarization—again reinforcing the notion that globalization is not assimilation.

The astute global business professional understands the driving forces and impacts of globalization on trade. Additionally, he or she has the ability to translate this knowledge into practice. As many have said, "knowledge is power." In reality knowledge is potential power; only applied knowledge is power. The following section discusses the application of this knowledge by the global business manager.

## THE GLOBAL BUSINESS MANAGER

The global business manager is responsible for many different types of management and leadership activities: operations, procurement, accounting, marketing, industry-specific technologies, staffing—just to name a few. In addition to standard management qualifications, the complexities of the international operating environment require additional qualities that few candidates fully possess. The global business manager must possess a strong international awareness and must understand the unique factors that contribute to the success of a global business, including formal education. The global business manager also must have an appropriate mix of relevant experience in global business ventures.

### Global Mindset vs. the Provincial Mindset

Global businesses transcend physical borders; therefore, the global business manager must possess proficiency in managing a business in any location in which a firm is operating, since the manager is the key coordinator of activities between disconnected operating locations. In addition, the global business manager must be able to juggle the issues that affect each country individually without accentuating the issues of any one country. Managers sometimes use the input of their subordinates concerning decisions about a firm's direction. However, a global business manager in an international setting must consider that line managers probably lack the contextual awareness to suggest the most optimal change. Therefore the global business manager must resist any urge to instinctively trust line managers and instead apply his or her discipline and critical thinking capacity to formulate decisions that are most conducive to the international operating environment. Maintaining a global perspective is critical because each provincial market will contain issues that are unique to its region.

### *Knowledge, Skills, and Attributes Needed for Success*

A common set of knowledge, skills, and attributes—a human resources concept known as KSA—has been identified as that which best expresses the ideal global business manager's qualifications. KSA are usually outlined in a job requisition. No one formula exists for the perfect global business manager so KSAs will not by themselves ensure success. Each KSA that a candidate holds will improve his or her chances for contributing effectively to an international venture's success. The most successful venture is likely to be the one where all of its participants are contributing most effectively.

The first component of KSA is knowledge. Knowledge is the information that a candidate possesses in the area of given disciplines. In business, such disciplines will include accounting, controlling, operations, and staffing. In international business, these disciplines are expanded to contain a contextual facet for each country under consideration. The ideal candidate possesses knowledge in areas pertinent to each country in which the firm operates. For example, staffing practices in socialist France vary from the unregulated labor market in China: a manager of a French multinational corporation with a manufacturing facility in China would require first-hand knowledge of which practices are most effective in each of these two countries in order to prevent failure. Other disciplines that are beneficial, regardless of countries, include knowledge in areas of outsourcing, international law, and global economic principles.

The second component of KSA is skill. Skills are much more narrowly defined than knowledge areas in that they represent quantifiable measures. One example is computer literacy. A minimum standard of proficiency in Microsoft Office® might be required, as the candidate will be responsible for preparing contracts in Microsoft Word or making presentations using Microsoft Power Point. Another skill is proficiency in foreign language. Fluency in a foreign language can be especially beneficial in multinational firms in which several different languages are spoken. For example, the surge in demand for Arabic speaking U.S. citizens after 9/11 and the resulting War on Terror.[31]

The final component of KSA is attributes. Attributes are the characteristics that are unique to an individual's learning experiences or character. Unlike formal knowledge or skills, these characteristics and personality traits are less likely to be taught. However, these can be acquired through understanding and experience. A desirable attribute in a global manager is the ability to manage cross-cultural relationships. An individual who possesses diplomatic traits will naturally be more likely to be successful when dealing with conflicting personalities—often present in cross-cultural relations. Another desirable attribute is the ability to multitask and work efficiently and effectively under pressure. The international business involves a far greater number of variables than that of domestic business, so the ability to adapt to change while managing stress is of critical importance. General management attributes such as friendliness, written and oral communication style, and soft-skills involving leadership qualities are as relevant and desirable in international management as they are in general domestic management.

*How These May be Obtained*

Knowledge, skills, and attributes are obtained principally through education and experience. Education includes formal learning that often results in a certificate or degree. A highly desirable degree in the current marketplace is the Master of Business Administration (MBA). MBA program offerings have grown substantially over the past decade as a result of this high demand. Professional training is used to complement formal classroom learning. Professional training, such as Six Sigma certification, are especially effective at keeping managers abreast of the latest technologies and business practices.

Managers gain experience by the actual hands-on encounters with KSAs in a real, working environment. While education is typically the starting point of a manager's career, past performance (experience) is arguably the most important predictor of a manager's ability to handle a given situation. Education and experience are both necessary components in handling the complex tasks of managing a global business. Staffing is similar for a domestic business manager and a global business manager. The major difference between the two is that in global business, failure is compounded.

## KEY CONCEPTS

- Characteristics of the successful global business professional
- Driving forces: advances in communications technologies
- Driving forces: advances in transportation technology
- Driving forces: reduction in barriers to trade
- Global business
- Globalization cons
- Globalization pros
- Glocalization

- Gross domestic product
- Historical examples of international trade
- Impacts of globalization: political, economic, social, cultural
- Importance of global trade
- Interdependencies among nations
- Top U.S.A. global trading partners
- Transparency among nations
- World Trade Organization

# Chapter 1 Exercises: Observational Analysis

*Ponder on the following key concepts and ideas as you read the chapter*

1.  How globalization has changed and accelerated within the last decade. The major factors and driving forces that are responsible for this exponential transformation.

2.  The historical events that have laid the foundation for global business as it is today. The impacts of globalization in the 21$^{st}$ century and how it has affected the political, economical, social, and cultural landscape of countries and their dealings with one another.

3.  The differences and similarities between a domestic and global business. The knowledge, skills, and attributes a manager must possess in order to be effective managing a global business.

4.  Start a list of books, journals, and scholarly websites that would aid in the understanding of the chapters main concepts and ideas. Start a journal for your own thoughts and ideas. What outside sources support your conclusions?

# Chapter 1 Exercises: Key Terms Analysis

*Match the answers by writing the correct letter in the space provided*

| | |
|---|---|
| _____ 1. Global business manager | A. Provides a venue for guidelines in a free trade market |
| _____ 2. Integrated communications networks | B. Growing integration of economies/societies worldwide |
| _____ 3. Global business | C. Immigrants isolated from their home country |
| _____ 4. OECD | D. Conveys the ideal global business manager's qualification |
| _____ 5. Operational risk | E. Responsible for different types of management activities |
| _____ 6. Magna Carta Libertatum | F. The prohibition of commerce/trade with a certain nation |
| _____ 7. Embargoes | G. One nation trades with a firm located in another nation |
| _____ 8. Ownership-control risk | H. Includes the risk of debt consolidation |
| _____ 9. Horizontally Integrated MNCs | I. Tempering effects of local conditions on global pressures |
| _____ 10. Globalization | J. Failed internal process/people = risk of monetary losses |
| _____ 11. Driving forces for globalization | K. Government actions inhibit control of foreign operations |
| _____ 12. Glocalization | L. Link ocean, rail, automotive, air transportation to allow real-time freight movement |
| _____ 13. Transfer risk | M. Expands competitive scope within same industry |
| _____ 14. Assimilation | N. Different products similar to current lines |
| _____ 15. Diversified integrated MNCs | O. American Peace |
| _____ 16. International market | P. Reductions in barriers to trade |
| _____ 17. World Trade Organization (WTO) | Q. Different products not similar to current lines |
| _____ 18. Pax Americana | R. Help foster international trade and resolve disputes |
| _____ 19. Vertically Integrated MNCs | S. Removes boundaries of local market territory to increase potential market audience |
| _____ 20. Knowledge, skills, and attributes | T. Formal recognition of legal limitations on a king's power |

# Chapter 1 Exercises: Theoretical Analysis

*Analyze the questions and select the best answer based on the reading of the chapter material*

1. Foreign direct investment is an attractive option for firms looking to diversify their investment portfolios, creating opportunities for firms looking to enter emerging markets.

    a. True

    b. False

2. As globalization becomes more embedded in daily life, tolerance must continue to increase in order to avoid unnecessary polarization—again reinforcing the notion that globalization is not assimilation.

    a. True

    b. False

3. The global business manager must possess a strong domestic awareness and must understand the unique factors that contribute to the success of a global business, including vast working experience.

    a. True

    b. False

4. Advocates for globalization believe that globalization promotes:

    a. Rapid economic growth

    b. Environmental degradation

    c. Economic inequality

    d. Protectionism

5. The global business manager must resist any urge to instinctively trust line managers and instead apply his or her discipline and critical thinking capacity to formulate decisions that are most conducive to the international operating environment.

    a. True

    b. False

6. Which of the following is NOT true about globalization?

    a. Began towards the end of the nineteenth century

    b. Is a new phenomenon

    c. Creates interdependencies among nations

    d. Requires transparency

7. International exchange is a recent concept.

    a. True

    b. False

8. United States' imports primarily came from which of the following countries?

    a. United Kingdom

    b. Russia

    c. Germany

    d. France

9. Standardization requires that business people understand the seamless international marketplace.

   a. True

   b. False

10. The Pax Romana heralded the introduction of mass production, improved transportation, technological progress, and the industrial factory system.

    a. True

    b. False

11. The Industrial Revolution heralded the introduction of which of the following.

    a. Mass production

    b. Improved transportation

    c. Technological progress

    d. All of the above

12. NAFTA facilitated the importation and exportation of goods and services between the United States, Mexico, and Canada.

    a. True

    b. False

13. Barriers to trade include all of the following except:

    a. Tariffs

    b. Quotas

    c. Embargoes

    d. FDI

14. All of the following occurred during the Information Age except

    a. Information was considered to be a scarce resource

    b. Radio and telephone networks were widespread in developed nations

    c. The launch of the Sputnik 1 satellite

    d. The personal desktop computer became a commonplace household fixture

15. Economic health is considered positive when a country imports considerably more than it exports.

    a. True

    b. False

16. Which of the following is NOT a driving force of Globalization?

    a. Reductions in barriers to trade

    b. Increased restriction on foreign investments

    c. Advances in communications and transportation technologies

    d. Rise of the multinational corporation

17. Pax Americana, Latin for "American peace," is the period of relative peace in the Western world since the end of World War II in 1945, coinciding with the dominant military and economic position of the U.S.

    a. True

    b. False

18. Which of the following is a barrier to trade?

    a. Mergers and acquisitions

    b. Subsidies

    c. Sanctions

    d. None of the above

19. Globalization has created what critics refer to as a melting pot or peaceful cooperation of various cultural identities.

    a. True

    b. False

20. ISO standards specify the requirements for state-of-the-art products, services, processes, materials and systems, and for good conformity assessment, managerial and organizational practice.

    a. True

    b. False

21. Which of the following is true regarding ISOs?

    a. Standard ISO cargo containers, known as isotopes, can be loaded and sealed intact onto container ships

    b. ISO standards are designed to be implemented domestically

    c. ISO stands for The International Standards Organization

    d. ISO standards specify the restrictions for state-of-the-art products, services, processes, materials and labor

22. Globalization has impacted the aspects of the international community

    a. Political

    b. Economic

    c. Social

    d. All of the above

23. Which of the following is a type of political risk for global managers?

    a. Cultural

    b. Financial

    c. Transfer

    d. Organizational

24. The World Trade Organization (WTO) was established in the early 1970s to help foster international trade and resolve disputes.

    a. True

    b. False

25. KSA stands for _____, _____, and _____.

    a.   Knowledge, skills, abilities

    b.   Knowledge, standards, attributes

    c.   Knowledge, skills, attitudes

    d.   Knowledge, skills, attributes

# Chapter 1 Exercises: Practical Analysis

*Write a short essay in the space provided to each of the following questions.*
*Please use outside references for each answer to support your ideas and thoughts.*

1. Conducting international business (Global Business) involves more variables than that of domestic business. However, a firm must understand the aspects of domestic business before ever considering going "global."

   a. Give some aspects that are crucial for a firm or business to understand on a domestic level before considering going global.

   b. What structures need to be in place and/or changes might a business need to make to their domestic structure in order to be able to sustain a global vision and mindset?

2.  Many factors are driving the trend toward globalization, and there are many outcomes that have resulted from a more integrated world.

    a.  Conduct an Internet search on Thomas L. Friedman's (2006) book The World is Flat, based on your research, what are some driving forces that have shifted the world into a new era of globalization?

    b.  Outsourcing is one of the major outcomes of globalization; what are some pros and cons of outsourcing? Does it have a positive or negative effect on the economy, society, labor, or trade? Explain your answer.

3. The activities and responsibilities that a business manager is responsible for within a domestic firm are vast (operations, procurement, accounting, staffing, etc.) making the qualifications high.

    a. What additional requirements/qualifications would a business manager need in order to be able to be qualified within an international operating environment? Why are these additional qualifications so important?

    b. Can all domestic managers be global managers? Why or Why not?

4. Knowledge and Skills are crucial for any manager to be effective and successful, whether managing a domestic or global business. Design a plan of action that a domestic manager can take to obtain knowledge and skills required for success in the global business environment.

# Chapter 1 Exercises: Biblical Worldview Application

*Write a short essay in the space provided to each of the following questions.*
*Please use biblical references and research, where applicable, to support your ideas and thoughts.*

1. In this chapter, we examined the characteristics of the successful global business professional. How does this apply to Christians?

   a. Access and Read the Internet article *How to be a Christian business owner: Doing business with integrity.* http://www.sharefaith.com/guide/church-business/business-integrity.html

   b. List (from top to lowest priority) what you believe to be the 10 most important characteristics of the Christian Business Professional.

   c. Provide a brief explanation for each why you think they are the most important aspects for the global business manager.

2. In this chapter, we discussed the driving forces of globalization, and their impacts on global business. In what ways do you think these same driving forces are impacting Christian global outreach organizations, such as overseas missions operations?

    a. Conduct an Internet search of a Christian overseas missions' organization of your choice and provide a brief description of how they operate overseas.

    b. Describe, briefly, how the driving forces of globalization discussed in the chapter are impacting the overseas missions' organization chosen above.

3. In this chapter, we discussed Multinational Corporations as a driving force for globalization and the impact they have economically, socially, politically, and culturally.

    a. Conduct an Internet search and list 5 top ranking global companies that promote a spiritual and biblical proponent within their business operations.

    b. Provide a brief overview of the main business activities of each company.

    c. Explain and give examples how each business integrates a biblical worldview and mindset within the company and its products and services.

# Aspects of
# Culture

## CHAPTER OVERVIEW

Culture is the set of shared attitudes, values, goals, and practices that characterize a society, or in the business sense, an organization.[1] Culture provides answers to questions pertaining to who, what, why, and when and how for a specific group of people. Business culture provides answers to questions pertaining to who, what, why, when, and how of any particular organization or type of business. The concept of business culture becomes increasingly complex when applied to a multinational corporation (MNC). Since the MNC culture evolved from the employees of more than one nation, the variables that comprise that specific culture are potentially limitless. One can commonly find that numerous different subcultures exist within the confines of the culture in any particular nation. The global manager must understand the complexities of the relationships between the different subcultures within any particular culture or nation and organizational operations in several different nations.

The purpose of this chapter is to discuss the relational complexities that potentially exist between a culture and a foreign organization seeking to do business in that culture. Major topics of this chapter include the following:

- Cultural paradigms

- The dimensions of culture

- An examination of the major aspects of cultures (major world religion, ethics across cultures, values and attitudes across cultures, business manners and customs across cultures, social structures and organizations, and education)

- The major theories of analyzing and understanding cultures from a business and managerial perspective

## MANAGERIAL PARADIGMS AND CULTURE

When the topic of culture is discussed within the context of international business management, one should consider the influence of three major cultural paradigms: ethnocentric, polycentric, and geocentric. Ethnocentrism is the belief that one's own culture is superior to all others and the standard by which all other cultures should be measured. Ethnocentric cultures hold a general contempt for members of other cultures. Ethnocentrism may manifest itself in attitudes of superiority or sometimes hostility. Violence, discrimination, proselytizing, and verbal aggressiveness are other means whereby ethnocentrism expresses itself.[2] Ethnocentric corporations are home-country oriented with key management positions located at the domestic headquarters. Ethnocentric managers believe that home-country nationals are more intelligent, reliable, and trustworthy than foreign nationals. Home-country nationals are recruited and trained for all international positions. Many international companies exhibit an ethnocentric philosophy. The standard international company finds great difficulty communicating in different languages and accepting cultural differences. International strategic alternatives are limited to entry modes, such as exporting, licensing, and turnkey operations—because "it works at home it must work overseas."[3]

Polycentrism, as the opposite of ethnocentrism, promotes openness towards other cultures, opinions, and ways of life. Intercultural actions and correlations are interpreted not only with the background of own cultural experiences, but when the independence of other cultures is recognized. Polycentric cultures relativize values and see them in the whole context.[4] Polycentric organizations are host-country-oriented corporations. The polycentric firm establishes multinational operations on condition that host-country managers "do it their way."

> Headquarters is staffed by home-country nationals, while local nationals occupy the key positions in their respective local subsidiaries. Host-country nationals have high or absolute sovereignty over the subsidiary's operations. There is no direction from headquarters and the only controls are financially oriented. No foreign national can seriously aspire to a senior position at headquarters. Strategically, the MNC competes on a market-by-market basis because it believes that "local people know what is best for them.[5]

The geocentric organization's primary objective is to develop an integrated system with a worldwide approach where subsidiaries operate in a highly interdependent manner. The entire organization focuses on both worldwide and local objectives. Every part of the organization makes a unique contribution using its unique competencies. Geocentrism requires collaboration between headquarters and subsidiaries to establish universal standards with permissible local variations. Diverse regions are integrated through a global systems approach to decision making: good ideas come from and flow to any country, resources are allocated on a global basis, geographical lines are erased and functional, and product lines are globalized. The best people are sought to solve problems within legal and political limits. Competence is what counts not national origin. The reward system motivates managers to surrender national biases and work for worldwide objectives.[6]

The astute global-business professional is aware of the impact of the managerial-cultural paradigm in use for each overseas situation. Regardless of the managerial-cultural paradigm in use, the business professional recognizes that an understanding of the major dimensions of culture are essential for success in doing business overseas.

## DIMENSIONS OF CULTURE

The dimensions of culture may be categorized as Communication, Religion, Ethics, Values and Attitudes, Manners, Customs, Social Structures and Organizations, and Education. The savvy global manager seeks to understand each of these dimensions as they impact decision making, negotiations, and ongoing operations critical to long-term success. The astute global manager knows how to effectively integrate the new culture with the existing culture.

### *Communication*

Global business professionals encounter various cultures throughout the world. Individuals and organizations within each culture communicate in manners unique to their culture. The necessity for the global business professional to understand the dimensions of culture has become increasingly important:

> In international business, people of different cultures have difficulty communicating effectively without some caring and appreciation of each other's points of view, values, and goals. If individuals do not attempt to develop this awareness, stereotyping of people, information, and behavior takes place. This eventually can lead to systematic discrimination.[7]

NOTES

Communication between two cultures can be awkward if professionals do not conduct proper research. In the global business arena a misinterpretation can be very costly. As a result of using wrong or inappropriate words business leaders from other countries may become offended and refuse to close important business deals. For instance, Japanese firms tend to involve the senior business officials in the negotiation of major business agreements. Prior to a meeting with a Japanese firm, U.S. negotiators must identify the senior Japanese executives to avoid embarrassment. Business leaders should provide important documents only to the senior Japanese executives at the start of the meeting. If global leaders do not follow this protocol Japanese executives will perceive this as an insult and a show of disrespect.

Successful MNCs acknowledge cultural differences and adapt parts of the business to recognize the unique differences and variables in communication. Major communication variables include different meanings of words across languages, verbal communication, non-verbal communication, and context (high and low).

### Different Meanings of Words across Languages

The various languages spoken throughout the world may use similar terminology, but different meanings may exist for the same word or phrase. Differences in accent and usage can lead to misunderstandings. Cross-cultural or cross-language barriers exacerbate the misunderstandings that arise when trying to communicate a message. Different cultures and languages may not always present or interpret messages in the same context. The effective global business manager recognizes these differences and makes every effort to understand the culture, not assuming that those in the foreign culture will understand him or her. Global businesses outside of the U.S. typically operate in multilingual environments or those in which more than one language is spoken.

### Verbal

Verbal communication involves the actual speaking of words. In the United States, English is the dominant verbal language. In France, French is the dominant language. All countries have a spoken language. Effective global managers must become very familiar with the language that is spoken in the countries in which they intend to do business. Global business professionals must understand the appropriate times to use certain words and phrases in speaking the language of a host country.

Language affects communication in two ways: (1) the ability to encode our thoughts and purposes clearly, and (2) the ability to formulate those thoughts and purposes.[8] Effective cross-cultural communicators must know how to properly pronounce words, how to properly spell words, and how to use these words in proper grammatical form. Those doing business in a foreign nation may have to learn the language in order to make a respectable impression among the inhabitants of that country. This knowledge would result in more respect towards the business person and their business firm.[9]

Four distinct areas relate to verbal communication: jargon and slang, acronyms, humor, and vocabulary and grammar.[10] People use jargon in business sessions or in everyday conversation. The expression "that's par for the course" is a jargon statement that describes a particular situation where the results meet the expectations. Acronyms are letters of the alphabet that represent a series of words. "FYI" is an abbreviation that means "for your information."

When conducting international business acronyms should not be used; these letters will be confusing and misunderstood. Humor should also be avoided because what is humorous in one country may be offensive or misunderstood in another. All written communications should follow proper grammar rules, and sentences should be complete and properly punctuated. Abbreviations should not be used when dealing with vocabulary and grammar.[11]

*Nonverbal*

When conveying messages, non-verbal communication is just as important as verbal communication. Nonverbal communication includes various forms of facial expressions and body language. While in foreign locations, the global business professional must "do his homework" concerning the use of acceptable and unacceptable body language. Those interested in doing business in other cultures must realize that well-accepted body language in their home country may be perceived as offensive in the country of business.

Thus, the business professional should study the body language requirements of the culture before arrival in that culture. The use of inappropriate or wrong body language could be quite costly to a corporation. Business travelers and corporations may be unable to counteract the negative perceptions of inappropriate body language. Consequently, host country officials may decide to discontinue business relations with a MNC due to misinterpreted body language. One small incident can be very detrimental to all future business negotiations.

*High Context vs. Low Context*

Context is another major cross-cultural communication variable to consider. A high-context culture is "a culture that relies heavily on nonverbal and subtle situational cues in communication." A low-context culture is "a culture that relies heavily on words to convey meaning in communication."[12] High context refers to societies or groups where people have close connections over a long period of time. As a result of years of interaction with each other, many aspects of cultural behavior are not made explicit because most members know what to do and what to think.

Communication in high-context cultures implies considerably more trust by both parties. Despite how an outsider may perceive this type of communication, casual and insignificant conversation is important because it reflects the desire to build a relationship and create trust. Oral agreements imply strong commitments in high-context cultures.

**Characteristics of High-Context Communication**

- Less verbally explicit communication
- Less written/formal information
- More internalized understanding of what is communicated
- Long term relationships
- Strong boundaries—"insiders" vs. "outsiders"
- Knowledge is situational and relational.

Low-context refers to societies where people tend to have many connections of shorter duration. In these societies cultural behavior and beliefs may need to be spelled out explicitly so that those coming into the cultural environment know how to behave. In low-context cultures enforceable contracts will tend to be in writing, precisely worded, and highly legalistic. Low-context cultures value directness. Managers are expected to be explicit and precise in conveying intended meaning.[13]

NOTES

As can be seen by the comparison of high-context cultures and low-context cultures, many subtle nuances exist. Since the communication styles are very different,

> **Characteristics of Low-Context Communication**
>
> - Rule oriented: people play by external rules
> - More knowledge is codified, public, external, and accessible
> - More interpersonal connections of shorter duration
> - Knowledge is more often transferable

the wrong message can easily be sent, or the communication can be misinterpreted. Does this mean that high-context cultures are more effective in terms of communication than low-context cultures? The answer is no. Regardless of the cultural-communication context the differences must be understood, and proper actions must be displayed at the appropriate time.

## *Religion*

The term "religion" may mean many things to different people. When discussed across cultures the topic of religion is open for misunderstanding. This misunderstanding may originate from either a preconceived notion or a lack of knowledge concerning the topic. Global business professionals must understand and be well versed in this important cultural aspect. In general, religion has been defined as an action or conduct indicating a belief in, reverence for, and desire to please a divine ruling power; the exercise or practice of rites or observances implying a particular system of faith and worship. The following brief summaries of the major world religions may be helpful in understanding this cultural variable in the global business environment.

### *Christianity*

Jesus Christ of Nazareth is the central figure in Christianity. Jesus was conceived by Immaculate Conception and born around 3 AD to the Jewish virgin, Mary. He was fully man in that He was born to Mary, and yet he was the only begotten Son of God, living a perfect and sinless life. Jesus performed numerous miracles, taught with absolute authority about his Father in heaven, and proclaimed that He was the Christ, the Son of God. For this, he was crucified at the age of thirty three. Christ's suffering and death upon the cross paid for the sins of all mankind; and through Him, God grants salvation to anyone who believes in Christ's sacrifice. Following Christ's death He rose from the grave and returned to the earth, appearing to over five hundred of his followers and telling them of the Kingdom of God, to which He was going. He also promised His disciples that He would return one day to bring all believers with him to that Kingdom to enjoy eternal life in the presence of God.

The only authoritative Christian holy text is the Bible, which includes the Old Testament (also considered sacred to Judaism and Islam) and the New Testament. The Old Testament chronicles the history of God's plan for man through Abraham's descendants who had been promised a Savior by God and were waiting for Him. The New Testament is unique to Christianity in that it focuses on the figure of Jesus and His teachings. Christians believe that Jesus is the foretold Savior of the Old Testament; therefore, Christians are not looking for a savior but are waiting for the return of Jesus so that He can take them to his Kingdom, or Heaven. The Apostle's Creed contains the core beliefs of Christianity.

This document distinguishes Christianity from other religions and proclaims Christian doctrine in a concise manner. It reads as follows:

> I believe in God the Father Almighty, maker of heaven and earth. And in Jesus Christ, His only Son, our Lord; who was conceived by the Holy Spirit, born of the Virgin Mary, suffered under Pontius Pilate, was crucified, died and was buried. He descended into hell; the third day He rose again from the dead; He ascended into heaven and is seated at the right hand of God the Father Almighty; from there He shall come to judge the living and the dead. I believe in the Holy Spirit, the holy Christian Church, the Communion of Saints, the Forgiveness of sins, the Resurrection of the body, and the Life everlasting. Amen.[14]

## Judaism

Judaism is a monotheistic religion which believes that the world was created by a single, all-knowing divinity. God designed all things within that world to have meaning and purpose as part of a divine order. According to the teachings of Judaism, God's will for human behavior was revealed to Moses and the Israelites at Mount Sinai. The Torah, or commandments, which decreed how humans should live, was a gift from God. The beliefs of Judaism can be seen in the words of Moses Maimonides, a Spanish Jew who in the twelfth century condensed the beliefs into a concise thirteen articles of faith. It reads as follows:

1. I believe with perfect faith that the Creator, blessed be His Name, is the Creator and Guide of everything that has been created; He alone has made, does make, and will make all things.

2. I believe with perfect faith that the Creator, blessed be His Name, is One, and that there is no unity in any manner like unto His, and that He alone is our God, who was, and is, and will be.

3. I believe with perfect faith that the Creator, blessed be His Name, is not a body, and that He is free from all the properties of matter, and that He has not any form whatever.

4. I believe with perfect faith that the Creator, blessed be His Name, is the first and the last.

5. I believe with perfect faith that to the Creator, blessed be His Name, and to Him alone, it is right to pray, and that it is not right to pray to any being besides him.

6. I believe with perfect faith that all the works of the prophets are true.

7. I believe with perfect faith that the prophecy of Moses, our teacher, peace be unto him, was true and that he was the chief of the prophets, both of those who preceded and of those who followed him.

8. I believe with perfect faith that the whole Torah, now in our possession, is the same that was given to Moses, our teacher, peace be unto him.

9. I believe with perfect faith that this Torah will not be changed and that there will never be any other Law from the Creator, blessed be His name.

10. I believe with perfect faith that the Creator, blessed be His name, knows every deed of the children of men, and all their thoughts, as it is said. It is He that fashioned the hearts of them all, that gives heed to all their works.

11. I believe with perfect faith that the Creator, blessed be His Name, rewards those who keep His commandments and punishes those that transgress them.

12. I believe with perfect faith in the coming of the Messiah; and, though he tarry, I will wait daily for his coming.

13. I believe with perfect faith that there will be a revival of the dead at the time when it shall please the Creator, blessed be His name, and exalted be His Fame for ever and ever. For Thy salvation I hope, O Lord.[15]

Three branches of Judaism circulate that form the framework for the type of lifestyle and beliefs of Jewish individuals: (1) Orthodox or traditionalists who observe most of the traditional dietary and ceremonial laws of Judaism; (2) Conservatives, who do not hold to the importance of a Jewish political state but put more emphasis on the historic and religious aspects of Judaism, doctrinally falling somewhere between the Orthodox and Reform branches; and (3) the Reform or liberal wing of Judaism, which is culture and race oriented with little consensus on doctrinal or religious belief.

*Islam*

The teachings of Islam include aspects of both faith and duty. Muslims receive instruction only from those who consider themselves adequately learned in theology or law. Muslims base their doctrine on the teachings in the Qur'an (Koran), the scripture of Islam. Muhammad's disciples have said that sometime during the seventh century AD, the Angel Gabriel dictated the contents to him, infallible and without error. For Muslims, the Qur'an is the word of God and the carrier of the revelation of Muhammad who is the last and most perfect of God's messengers to mankind. Five articles of faith comprise the main doctrines of Islam. All Muslims are expected to believe the following:

1. There is one true Allah, who alone is the creator of the universe.

2. Angels exist and interact with human lives. They are made of light, and each has different purposes or messages to bring to earth. Each man or woman has two angels who record his actions; one records good deeds, the other bad deeds.

3. The four inspired books include the Torah of Moses, the Psalms (Zabin) of David, the Gospel of Jesus Christ (Injil) and the Qur'an. All but the Qur'an have been corrupted by Jews and Christians.

4. God has spoken through numerous prophets throughout time. The six greatest are Adam, Noah, Abraham, Moses, Jesus, and Muhammad. Muhammad is the last and greatest of Allah's messengers.

5. Last Days: The last day will be a time of resurrection and judgment. Those who follow Allah and Muhammad will go to Islamic heaven, or Paradise. Those who do not will go to hell.[16]

In addition to believing the Five Articles of faith, Muslims observe the Five Pillars of Faith, which are duties each Muslim must perform.

1. One must state, "there is no God but Allah, and Muhammad is the Prophet of Allah" publicly to become a Muslim.

2. Prayer must be done five times a day (upon rising, at noon, mid afternoon, after sunset, and before going to sleep) towards the direction of Mecca. The call to prayer is sounded by the muezzin (Muslim crier) from a tower (minaret) within the mosque.

3.  Muslims are legally required to give one-fortieth of their income to the needy. Since those to whom alms are given are helping the giver achieve salvation, no sense of shame results from receiving charity.

4.  During the holy month of Ramadan, faithful Muslims fast from sunrise to sunset each day. This develops self-control, devotion to God, and identity with the needy.

5.  Each Muslim is expected to make the pilgrimage to Mecca at least once in his or her lifetime, if he has the means to do it and is physically capable of the trip. This pilgrimage is an essential part of gaining salvation, so the old or infirm may send someone in their place. It involves a set of rituals and ceremonies.[17]

A sixth religious duty associated with the Five Pillars is Jihad, or Holy War. This duty requires that if the situation warrants, men must go to war to defend or spread Islam. If killed, they are guaranteed eternal life in Paradise.

*Hinduism*

Hinduism has no specific founder or theology.  It developed as the combination of religious practices of Aryan tribes, who migrated from central Asia around 1500 BC to India, and the early inhabitants of India, the Harappans. Over time both groups developed similar religious belief systems: Aryan polytheism and Harappan sanctity of fertility. The predominantly Aryan society eventually developed the caste system, which ranked society according to occupational class. The caste system is structured as follows:

1.  Brahmins or the priests

2.  Kshatriyas or the king-warrior class

3.  Vaishyas or the merchants, farmers, Sutras laborers, craftspeople

4.  Harijahns or the "untouchables".  These individuals are believed to be descended from the Harappan aboriginal people.  They are extremely poor and discriminated against.

The higher a person's caste the more that person is blessed with the benefits and luxuries life has to offer. Although the caste system was outlawed in 1948 the Hindu people of India still embrace the system and recognized it as the proper way to stratify society.

Hinduism is based on the concept that human and animal spirits reincarnate or come back to earth to live many times in different forms. The belief that souls move up and down an infinite hierarchy depending on the behaviors they practiced in their life is visible in many of the Hindu societal policies. As the caste system survives, charity towards others is unheard of, because Hindus believe that each individual deserves to be in the social class in which they were born. A person is born into the highest class because he or she behaved well in a past life. A person is born into poverty and shame because of misbehaviors in a past life.

A Hindu can be polytheistic (more than one god), monotheistic (one god), pantheistic (god and the universe are one), agnostic (unsure if god exists), or atheistic (no god) and still claim to be Hindu. This open theology makes discussing basic beliefs difficult because many ideas and definitions of Hinduism exist.

Central to Hinduism are the concepts of reincarnation, the caste system, merging with Brahman (or the ultimate reality), finding morality, and reaching Nirvana (the peaceful escape from the cycle of reincarnation). The Hindu paths to salvation include the way of works (rituals), the way of knowledge (realization of reality and self-reflection), and the way of devotion (devotion to the god that you choose to follow). If the practitioner follows the paths of these ways, salvation can be achieved.[18]

### Buddhism

Buddhism is a religion that is based on the teachings of Siddhartha Gautama, the son of a wealthy landowner born in northern India (now part of Nepal) around 560 B.C. In order to achieve spiritual peace, Gautama renounced his worldly advantages and became known as Buddha, or "the enlightened one." He preached his religious views his entire life throughout South Asia. The five precepts of Buddhism include the following:

1. Kill no living thing
2. Do not steal
3. Do not commit adultery
4. Tell no lies
5. Do not drink intoxicants or take drugs

Other precepts apply only to monks and nuns:

1. Eat moderately and only at the appointed time
2. Avoid that which excites the senses
3. Do not wear adornments
4. Do not sleep in luxurious beds
5. Accept no silver or gold[19]

### Confucianism

Confucius (K'ung Fu Tzu), born in 551 BC, wandered through many states of China giving advice to its rulers and accumulating a small band of students. His writings deal primarily with individual morality and ethics and the proper exercise of political power by the rulers. In China and other areas in Asia the social ethics and moral teachings of Confucius are blended with the Taoist communion with nature and the Buddhist concepts of the afterlife to form a set of complementary, peacefully coexistent, and ecumenical religions. Taoism originates with Tao (pronounced "Dow") meaning "path or the way." The term is basically indefinable and has to be experienced:

> [Tao] refers to a power which envelops, surrounds and flows through all things, living and nonliving. The Tao regulates natural processes and nourishes balance in the Universe. It embodies the harmony of opposites (i.e., there would be no love without hate, no light without dark, no male without female.)[20]

The adherents of Confucianism consider it to be a philosophy of life not a religion. According to Confucius the nature of man is fundamentally good and inclined towards goodness. Perfection of goodness can be found in sages and saints. Every man should attempt to reach the ideal by leading a virtuous life, possessing a very noble character, and doing his duty unselfishly with sincerity and truthfulness. He who possesses a good character and divine virtue is a princely type of man. The princely man sticks to virtue, but the inferior man clings to material comfort. The princely man is just, but the inferior man expects rewards and favors. The princely man is dignified, noble, magnanimous, and humble; but, the inferior man is mean, proud, crooked, and arrogant. In the "Great Learning," Confucius revealed the step by step process by which one attains self-development and by which it flows over into the common life to serve the state and bless mankind.[21]

The order of development that Confucius set forth is as follows:

1.  Investigation of phenomena
2.  Learning
3.  Sincerity
4.  Rectitude of purpose
5.  Self-development
6.  Family discipline
7.  Local self-government
8.  Universal self-government[22]

*Shinto*

Shinto is an ancient Japanese religion that originated about 500 BC and was originally a mixture of nature worship, fertility cults, divination techniques, hero worship, and shamanism. Its name is derived from the Chinese words "shin tao" and is translated "The Way of the Gods." Unlike most other religions Shinto has no real founder, no written scriptures, no body of religious law, and a very loosely-organized priesthood. The Yamato dynasty consolidated its rule over most of Japan in the eighth century AD. Divine origins were ascribed to the imperial family, which then established Shinto as an official religion of Japan along with Buddhism. This situation remained until after the end of World War II, which resulted in the complete separation of Japanese religion from politics. The Emperor was forced by the U.S. army to renounce his divinity at that time.[23]

Of all the dimensions of culture the religious dimensions typically provide the ethical foundations that define business relationships overseas. Those cultures that deny the existence of God through the practices of agnosticism or atheism still require standards of morality and conduct essential to the orderly functioning of society. The astute global business professional is well versed in the ethical foundations for both the home and host nations in which he or she is doing business.

*Ethics*

Ethics is the study of morality and standards of conduct. U.S. firms have developed and implemented standards of conduct for employees to serve as guidelines as to how they should comport themselves when representing the company. Some firms have employed knowledgeable consultants and subject-matter experts to teach corporate ethics, hoping to ensure that employees will conduct themselves in an ethical manner. What one culture considers moral may not be accepted as moral by another. A discussion of the concepts of ethics logically follows a discussion of religion because the two can be very related. On the other hand, one should consider the two issues separately, as ethical standards are not always a result of religious standards—although in many cases they are. One only needs to consider the founding of the U.S. The religious beliefs and faith of the Founding Fathers greatly influenced the writing of the Declaration of Independence and the U.S. Constitution. These documents continue to influence, in part, what many consider ethical conduct today. However, all cultures do not agree. Understanding the ethics of a particular culture is important when it comes to doing business in that culture.

*Definitions*

A general definition of ethics is as follows: the discipline dealing with what is good and bad and with moral duty and obligation. Business Ethics is the study of ethical dilemmas, values, and decision making in the world of business. Business ethics should not be considered a separate disciple from ethics. International business ethics examines the many practical issues that result from the international context of business. In the global context, the cultural relativity of ethical values receives more emphasis than when considering domestic business ethics. Universal values do exist to form the basis for international business ethics, such as those relating to killing, lying, cheating, etc.

The ethical differences between cultures can be both vast and complex. One example of ethical differences can be seen in the exploitation of children in the workforce in Third World nations. Other cultures do not universally accept the ethics driving specific laws that govern the employment of children in the U.S. The global business professional may encounter this ethical dilemma while working overseas and have to craft strategies that are in line with the ethical standards of the business. The trafficking of narcotic drugs provides another example of ethical differences across cultures. U.S. law prohibits the trade of these harmful substances, yet it may be legal, even ethical, in other nations to engage in such trade. One should note that no legitimate business operating overseas would engage in drug trafficking to the U.S. Those firms involved in the legitimate global business community recognize that they have a social responsibility to their trading partners, based upon mutually agreed ethical principles.

*Corporate Social Responsibility*

Ethically speaking, one of the most important issues global business professionals may face is that of being socially responsible in the cultures in which they choose to do business. Nothing will sour the relationship between a foreign business and the community in which

---

**Global Business Professionals Must be Able to do the Following**

1. Compare business ethical traditions across cultures.

2. Compare business ethical traditions from various religious perspectives.

3. Understand the ethical concerns of conducting international business transactions, including property rights and transparency.

4. Understand and respond appropriately to varying global standards, including various wage and labor practices.

5. Understand the ethics of outsourcing and other potentially controversial issues associated with globalization.

---

it operates more quickly than the perception that the company is operating in a way that is harmful to that community. Socially responsible organizations investigate ways in which to reinvest in those communities by readily contributing in terms of growth and economic development. Greed and corruption must be avoided at all costs, both by global businesses and their trading partners.

*The Issue of Corruption*

Corruption is a major concern for those engaged in global business. The issue of corruption has been addressed across the globe in numerous venues such as international conferences, policy forums, government official speeches, international organizations, including the OECD and Transparency International—an international nongovernmental organization. Government leaders increasingly cite corruption as a reason for withholding foreign aid or debt relief. Many believe that a nation's inability to pay interest on its loans is due to its leaders siphoning off national earnings into their own bank accounts. Thus, extending aid or canceling the debt may encourage further corruption. While many international initiatives to combat corruption focus on developing nations, these nations are increasingly being scrutinized by potential investors as well. "Corruption is a source of concern for governments, entrepreneurs, private individuals, nongovernmental organizations, companies and indeed for society as a whole."[24]

A strong correlation exists between poverty and corruption. This correlation reinforces the growing evidence that corruption hampers efforts to lift people out of poverty and provide them with new economic opportunities. "Corruption clearly results in the misallocation of resources and tends to be more prevalent where systems of governance and political will to combat corruption are weak."[25] Corruption helps to fuel poverty especially when high-level public officials steal from their nations or mismanage public resources intended to finance their people's aspirations for a better life. In many parts of the world government officials have lined their own pockets instead of funding development such as new roads, schools, and hospitals. Corruption eventually may lead to economic stagnation and increase economic and social disparities over time—when the high costs of providing public services and low capacities to collect taxes occur together. Investment opportunities and economic growth do not materialize easily in places where corruption is rampant. Investors are demanding a higher assurance of market integrity to mitigate potential risks from poor governance. Government leaders can address corruption more effectively when a strong political will exists to combat it—by enforcing countries' laws criminalizing bribery and prosecuting corrupt individuals at all levels of society.[26]

Transparency International (TI) is an international non-governmental organization dedicated to fighting corruption worldwide. TI provides guidelines for organizations wishing to develop anticorruption programs. These guidelines are derived from its "Survey of Best Practices for Corporate Anti-Corruption Programs."[28]

### TI Succeeds Through the Following Mission:

1.  Curb corruption through international and national coalitions, encouraging governments to establish and implement effective laws, policies, and anticorruption programs.

2.  Strengthen public support and understanding for anticorruption programs and enhance public transparency and accountability in international business transactions and in the administration of public procurement.

3.  Encourage all parties involved in international business transactions to operate at the highest levels of integrity.[27]

Because the resource materials are from U.S. companies, the primary focus of the guidelines is compliance with the Foreign Corrupt Practices Act. However, the material can also be adapted for compliance with non-U.S., anti-bribery initiatives, including those of the OECD.

As a result of Securities and Exchange Commission (SEC) investigations in the mid -1970s, over four-hundred U.S. companies admitted making questionable or illegal payments in excess of $300 million to foreign government officials, politicians, and political parties. The abuses ran the gamut from bribery of high foreign officials to secure some type of favorable action by a foreign government to so-called facilitating payments that allegedly ensured that government functionaries discharged certain ministerial or clerical duties. Congress enacted the Foreign Corrupt Practices Act (FCPA) to bring a halt to the bribery of foreign officials and to restore public confidence in the integrity of the U.S. business system.

The FCPA was intended to have and has had an enormous impact on the way American firms do business. Several firms that paid bribes to foreign officials have been the subject of criminal and civil enforcement actions. These actions resulted in large fines, suspensions, debarment from federal procurement contracting, and employee jail time. To avoid such consequences, many firms have implemented detailed compliance programs to prevent and detect any improper payments by employees and agents.

Following the passage of the FCPA Congress became concerned that U.S. companies were operating at a disadvantage compared to foreign companies. These foreign companies routinely paid bribes and in some countries were permitted to deduct the cost of such bribes as business expenses on their taxes. In 1988 Congress directed the Executive Branch to commence negotiations in the OECD to obtain the agreement of the U.S. major trading partners to enact legislation similar to the FCPA. In 1997 the U.S. and thirty three other countries signed the OECD Convention on Combating Bribery of Foreign Public Officials in International Business Transactions. The anti-bribery provisions of the FCPA make it unlawful for a U.S. person, and certain foreign issuers of securities, to make a corrupt payment to a foreign official for the purpose of securing business with or directing business to any person. Since 1998 these provisions also apply to foreign firms and persons who attempt corrupt payments while in the United States.[29]

## Values and Attitudes

The study of culture must include values and attitudes. Values are generally accepted beliefs about what is right and wrong. Values are an interpretation of culture by societal members. A society derives its culture from its history and environment. The developed values of a society influence the members of the society. The values are a basis for developing social norms and decision making. If a citizen behaves according to social norms the society accepts and respects the individual. If the citizen behaves contrary to social norms, he or she stands out and may be subject to correction. An attitude is the manifestation of values, beliefs, feelings, and states of mind.[30]

To value something is to consider or rate it highly. In a cultural context a value would then be anything that a particular culture holds in high esteem. An attitude is "a mental position with regard to a fact or state or a feeling or emotion toward a fact or state."[31] An attitude is what one thinks or feels about someone or something. Values and attitudes are interrelated, as attitudes often shape values, and vice versa.

*Variances in Attitudes across Cultures*

The astute global business professional recognizes the variances in attitudes between the home culture and the host culture. Differences in attitudes toward time, work, change, gender, social status, and social mobility impact all stages of the business relationship. Time differences effect meeting attendance as well as ongoing employee attendance. Gender differences impact female employment.

*Concept of Time*

Different cultures approach the concept of time and corresponding time management practices very differently. For example in some South American cultures, meeting might begin thirty minutes late.[32] French businesspeople are also relaxed about time but find it rude to visit unannounced.[33] Middle-Eastern nations that are predominantly Muslim do not hold a schedule tightly. Middle-Eastern businessmen prefer an open office space design. Interruptions will be frequent. Visitors who value time should invite Middle-Eastern businessmen to meet away from the business to minimize the interruptions.[34]

U.S. businesses tend to view time as a resource. Time is allocated and used to deliver maximum value to the organization. Australian, Japanese, Canadian, and British business people also see punctuality as respectable. Germans place great value on punctuality but never make decisions quickly. Many meetings may be required because negotiators typically must receive approval from an advisory board before action is taken. Italians expect visitors to be punctual, but the Italian businessperson may be acceptably late. Like the Germans, Italians make decisions slowly because of a slow bureaucracy and legal system.[35]

Some cultures view work as the purpose for life. Other cultures view work as means to support life. Global business professionals must make this important distinction as a misunderstanding in this area can be debilitating. For example, workers in some European nations, such as France and Italy, are accustomed to taking one-month-long vacations every summer. Most Italian workers take the month of August for vacation. The same occurs in France during July. The global business professional should be prepared for this eventuality. Vacation takes priority over work in some cultures. This cultural tendency will impact production during the affected month, as well as others in the supply chain who rely on the Italian and French organizations to provide resources or support. The mass vacation does not preclude Italy or France from consideration for expansion by an international manager. The cultural approach to a summer vacation requires the manager to plan for shut down so that it does not impact other operations. Another example affects time during the day. In Mexico lunch begins between 2:00 p.m. and 3:00 p.m. and may last three to four hours.[36] The impact of this attitude will be lost production time or management challenges when trying to adjust to the local culture.

*Dealing with Change*

Cultural attitudes differ in the approach to change. A culture that is open to change encourages creativity and individualism. Germany targets its children into education tracks that fit the learner, thus developing a society of technical experts instead of developers. Without the tension created in school that challenges students to be creative in how they learn, there will be little creativity in later productive years. Japan, with its group orientation, is producing experts at reverse engineering rather than design. Japanese industry has become very successful by mastering production efficiency through Total

Quality Management and Quality Circles—both team-oriented efforts. Societies readily accept change in a culture that rewards creative thinking and embraces diversity. The United States and Canada are examples of cultures that embrace change. These cultures lead the world in technological innovation, transportation, and agricultural sciences.

### The Role of Gender

Cultural attitudes differ in terms of the role of gender. Some cultures treat women as equals, while others view women as subservient. If a culture does not consider women eligible to work outside the home, an international manager knows that the workforce and diversity are limited. Women have affected German culture in powerful ways twice in the last century. Though Germany was a historically male-dominated society, women were pivotal in caring for injured soldiers during World War II and assisting in reconstruction after the war. The second instance occurred during the transition after the Berlin Wall came down. As the German economy grew, women were needed to satisfy the demand for labor.[37] Iranian women were pivotal in the revolution that overthrew the Shah in 1979; however, in the post-revolution society, many women's freedoms have been curtailed. Once again, they must wear a veil. However, Iranian women do work outside of the home, and they do have the right to vote.[38] Gender differences in Mexico have been narrowing since the 1970s. The number of women in the workforce has doubled in the last ten years. Educated women are pursuing careers. Unfortunately, wages are lower for women than men, and women are often subjected to sexual harassment.[39]

### Social Status

Cultural attitudes differ by social status structures. The cultural attitude of social status impacts business. Training and promotional opportunities from within are limited whenever a culture forbids mobility across social classes. This suppression minimizes potential motivation techniques and creativity. Four social classes exist in Iran: Upper, Middle, Working, and Lower. The upper class includes large landowners, industrialists, financiers, and high-ranking clergy. Middle-class members are professionals, business and landowners, high-ranking government officials and military officers, teachers, and low-ranking clergy. The working class is made up of skilled labor. The lower class consists of unskilled labor and the unemployed.[40] France is another country with stratified social classes. Citizens are not expected to make large jumps from one class to another.

### Business Manners and Customs across National Cultures

Etiquette, manners, and cross-cultural or intercultural communication have become critical elements required for the global business professional. As international, multinational, transnational, multi-domestic, and global business continues to expand and bring people closer, the most important element of successful business outcomes may be the appreciation and respect for regional, country, and cultural differences. Understanding cultural diversity is a critical success factor for the global business professional.

Gaining insight into the cultural dynamics of a country or region can be very helpful in understanding why people act the way they do. This insight also reveals the appropriate ways one should act while in that country.

*Social Structures*

The social structure of a culture refers to the manner in which the society is organized, including its institutions, social groups, statuses, and roles.

**Global professionals must have a knowledge and respect for the following issues:**

- General information, including population, cultural heritage, language, and religion.

- Appearances, including do's and don'ts involving dress, clothing, body language, and gestures.

- Behavior, including do's and don'ts involving dining, gift giving meetings, customs, protocol, negotiation, and general behavioral guidelines.

- Communication, including do's and don'ts involving greetings, introductions, and conversational guidelines.

An institution is an established and enduring pattern of social relationships. Traditional institutions include family, religion, politics, economics, and education. Nontraditional institutions have recently gained influence. These nontraditional institutions include science and technology, mass media, medicine, sport, and the military. Inadequacies in social institutions may engender many social problems within a culture. The educational institution's failure to prepare individuals for the job market and alterations to the structure of the economic institution significantly influence unemployment.

Institutions are made up of social groups. A social group is defined as two or more people who have a common identity, who interact, and who form a social relationship. Examples of social groups include the family and religious associations. Social groups may be categorized as primary or secondary. Primary groups tend to involve small numbers of individuals and are characterized by intimate and informal interaction. Families and friends are examples of primary groups. Secondary groups often involve small or large numbers of individuals, are task oriented, and are characterized by impersonal and formal interaction. Examples of secondary groups include employers and their employees and clerks and their customers.

Institutions consist of social groups; social groups consist of statuses. A status is a position a person occupies within a social group. The status one occupies largely defines one's social identity. Statuses may be either ascribed or achieved. An ascribed status is one that society assigns to an individual on the basis of factors over which the individual has no control: gender, race, ethnic background, and socioeconomic status, into which one is born. A society assigns an achieved status on the basis of some characteristic or behavior over which the individual has some control. Achieved status depends largely on the outcome of one's own efforts, behavior, and choices. One's ascribed statuses may affect the likelihood of achieving other statuses. In some cultures, one born into a poor socioeconomic status may find it more difficult to achieve the status of "college graduate" because of the high cost of a college education. Every individual has numerous statuses simultaneously. A

NOTES

person's master status is the status that the society considers the most significant to the individual's social identity. A society typically regards a person's occupational status as his or her master status.

Every status is associated with many roles—the set of rights, obligations, and expectations associated with a status. Roles guide behavior and allow one to predict the behavior of others. A single status involves more than one role. The status of a manager includes one role for interacting with superiors and another role for interacting with subordinates.[41]

## CROSS-CULTURAL ANALYSIS MODELS

The study of culture and personality, which many experts consider a subset of anthropology and psychology during the first half of the twentieth century, concentrates on traditional and preliterate societies. Conclusions drawn from cultural studies come from psychoanalysis.[42] From 1967 to 1973, Geert Hofstede applied the subset of cultural dimensions to the field of business management. He segregated them into independent areas to be further divided in order to get a more precise understanding.[43] Not long after Hofstede began his work, Fons Trompenaar, expanded on Hofstede's research and developed another framework for understanding the different dimensions of culture. In 1993, Robert House began a project, later called the GLOBE study, that expanded upon both Hofstede's and Trompenaar's work.

Through their employment in large multinational corporations, both Hofstede and Trompenaar conducted research that would lead each man to draw his own conclusions about the theories of cultural dimensions. Each postulated theories based on the research of a somewhat captive audience: the employees of the multinational companies. Years of research led both men to their respected cultural guidelines.

Geert Hofstede developed four initial theories and later added a fifth. Hofstede's understanding of different cultures led to the understanding that both national cultures and organizational cultures simultaneously occur within the same society. National cultures can be studied by examining the known facts. These facts will historically remain stable and very difficult, if not impossible, to change. On the other hand, organizational cultures can be quite dynamic, managed, and changed to varying degrees of difficulty. The degree of difficulty depends on how ingrained the organizational culture is within the company.

Fons Trompenaar developed a seven-cultural-factors theory model that expanded on the thinking and research of Geert Hofstede. Trompenaar's model further explored cultural diversity on a large multinational scale. His model concentrated on intercultural diversity and how well these different cultures assimilated in the workplace.

Robert House developed a model of nine dimensions that followed the research by Hofstede in many respects with regards to understanding cultural dimensions. Six out of the nine cultural dimensions identified by House are also identified by Hofstede. His model grouped countries according to similar cultural characteristics.

### Hofstede's Dimensions of Culture

National culture relates to our deeply held values and beliefs. These values and beliefs distinguish people of one nation from those of another and are acquired when we are young. These acquisitions generally occur during the first ten years of our life and they contain most of our basic values.[44] These acquisitions are obtained mostly through our experiences in the family unit, through society, and in school. Characteristics that are culturally determined include the language spoken, common customs, religious observances, acceptable gender roles, occupations, and other aspects of behavior common to a group of people. National culture assists us in our values regarding what is normal versus what is abnormal, what is good versus bad, and what is rational behavior versus irrational behavior.

Research performed by Hofstede led the way into a better understanding of what national culture is and how it plays an important and essential role in our daily lives. Even though occupants of nations can rarely be fitted into a one size fits all culture, there are certain characteristics that are similar to each nation that its inhabitants follow. The study of national culture was pioneered in the 1970s when Hofstede conducted a study of workers in IBM in over 120 countries. Hofstede originally identified four national cultural dimensions that can be used to help evaluate the differences in national cultures.[45] As mentioned, this research has since been updated to include fifth and six elements.[46]

These six distinct dimensions of culture are (1) power distance (PDI); (2) individualism (IDV); (3) masculinity (MAS); (4) uncertainty/avoidance index (UAI); (5) long-term orientation (LTO); and (6) indulgence vs. restraint (IVR). The fifth dimension which was added to Hofstede's original four dimensions of culture, was the result of a collaborative study with Michael Bond from the Chinese University of Hong Kong. The sixth dimension was added with the collaboration of Minkov who studied a person's perception of life control and importance of leisure in the respondent's life.[47] Minkov showed that measures of life control and importance of leisure are the best predictors of happiness across more than 90 nations.[48] Hofstede then invited Minkov to become part of the third edition of the book Cultures and Organizations: Software of the Mind, where the sixth dimension was duly added. These six cultural differences may help explain why some cultures favor certain things while other others do not or even why managers and employees react in certain ways. The work by Hofstede has since been augmented by work performed based on the GLOBE study to include nine national cultural dimensions which we will discuss in the next section.

**Power Distance.** Power distance is defined as the extent to which less powerful members of organizations within a country expect and accept how power is distributed throughout the organization.[49] A high power distance ranking indicates that inequalities of power and wealth are present within a society. These societies are more likely to follow a caste system that does not allow significant upward mobility of its citizens. A low power distance raking indicated the society de-emphasizes the differences between citizen's power and wealth. In these societies equality and opportunity for everyone is stressed. The United States experiences a relatively low score on this dimension which is evidenced by the principles of equal rights, liberty and justice for all that this country was founded on. Within the American organization, hierarchy is established for convenience such that communication between managers and non-managers is informal, direct and participatory. Lower power distance fosters communication and openness within members of the organization.

Countries where high scores on the power distance scale are seen are those who, as a general rule are not readily willing to discuss matters outside of their job functions because they do not believe that they have the necessary qualifications. A prime example of a high power distance country is France. In France managers are considered more knowledgeable about management due to their education. Hofstede explained that managers in the

United States tend to advocate participation by subordinates whereas in France there is little concern with participative management and more concern over who has the power within the organization.

Hierarchy is another dimension of power distance. In countries that scored high on the power distance scale, inequalities are accepted and hierarchy is viewed as needed and necessary. The ideal organization within the high power distance cultures is one where a pyramid scheme is used.[50] A pyramid scheme is one where hierarchy is clearly seen with managers on the top of the pyramid and non-managers on the bottom. This type of system is also evident in many Asian countries such as Japan and China where a high power distance score was also achieved. Exposing weaknesses of local Chinese managers in front of their own subordinates, for example, should be avoided. The concept of saving face is an important element for the Chinese. Therefore people wishing to conduct business with the Chinese need to be mindful of the high power distance that exists in China.

**Individualism.** Individualism can be defined as individuals looking after themselves and only their immediate family versus people belonging to in-groups that look after them in exchange for loyalty. Individualism focuses on the degree to which the society reinforces individual or collective achievement and interpersonal relationships. A high individualism ranking indicates that individuality and individual rights are paramount within the society. Individuals in these societies may tend to form a larger number of loose relationships. An individualistic culture stresses independence and individual initiative. A tight social framework in which people expect others in their groups to look after them and protect them when they are in trouble characterizes collectivist cultures. Individualistic cultures are more loosely knit social frameworks in which people are expected to look after their own interests. The United States ranked at the top on this cultural dimension. A low individualism ranking typifies societies of a more collective nature with close ties between individuals. These cultures reinforce extended families and collectives where everyone takes responsibility for fellow members of their group.

**Masculinity.** Masculinity focuses on the degree to which a society reinforces, or does not reinforce the traditional masculine work role model of male achievement, control, and power. The dominant values in a masculine society are achievement and success; the dominant values in a feminine society are caring for others and quality of life. In masculine societies, performance and achievement are highly valued; and achievement must be demonstrated, so status brands or products such as jewelry are important to show one's success. In masculine cultures male and female roles are differentiated, whereas in feminine cultures roles overlap. In masculine cultures, household work is less shared between husband and wife than in feminine cultures. Men also do more household shopping in the feminine cultures.

A high masculinity ranking indicates that the country experiences a high degree of gender differentiation. In these cultures males dominate a significant portion of the society and power structure, including females. Japan scored high on the masculinity scale. This ranking helps us understand why males are viewed as dominate in business interactions. This cultural dimension may need to be considered when doing business in Japan since sending over a female to conduct business negotiations or participate in management meetings may not be readily accepted by male counterparts. A low masculinity ranking indicates the country has a low level of differentiation and discrimination between genders. In these cultures, females are treated equally in all aspects of the society.

**Uncertainty Avoidance.** Hofstede discussed the dimension of uncertainty avoidance as the extent to which the members of a culture feel threatened by ambiguous or unknown situations and have created beliefs and institutions that try to avoid them.[51] Uncertainty avoidance focuses on the level of tolerance for uncertainty and ambiguity within a society. A high uncertainty avoidance ranking indicates that the country has a low tolerance for uncertainty and ambiguity. Members of high uncertainty avoidance cultures try to minimize the level of stress by creating strict laws, and rules. In countries that experience high uncertainty avoidance, feelings of "what is different is dangerous" prevails.[52]

People who are part of high uncertainty avoidant countries are less open to change and innovation than people of low uncertainty avoidance cultures. Managers are hesitant about implementing anything new. High levels of anxiety are felt within an organization where a high score in the dimension of uncertainty avoidance is felt. A low uncertainty ranking indicates the country has less concern about ambiguity and uncertainty and has more tolerance for a variety of opinions and changes. This low ranking reflects a society that is less rule-oriented, more readily accepts change, and takes more and greater risks.

**Long-term Orientation.** Hofstede's fifth dimension of national culture was derived from a values inventory suggested by Asian researchers and is reminiscent of the teachings of Confucius.[53] This dimension was added independent of the four identified in the original IBM studies conducted by Hofstede. The long-term versus short-term dimension expresses the extent that virtuous living is a goal, independent of any religious justification and is related to the ability to solve well-defined problems. The Confucian work of dynamism value that is reflected in this dimension has been identified as almost exclusively an Asian value. Long-term versus short-term orientation is the extent to which a society exhibits a pragmatic future-oriented perspective rather than a conventional historic or short-term point of view.

The long-term orientation dimensions focuses on the degree to which the society embraces or does not embrace, long-term devotion to traditional, forward thinking values. A long-term orientation implies the willingness for investment in the future. Values included in long-term orientation are perseverance, ordering relationships by status and observing this order, thrift, and having a sense of shame. High long-term orientation ranking indicates that the country prescribes to the values of long-term commitments and respect for tradition. This orientation is thought to support a strong work ethic where a society expects long-term rewards as a result of today's hard work. However, businesses may take longer to develop in this society, particularly for an "outsider."

The opposite view is short-term orientation, which includes personal steadiness and stability, respect for tradition, and the pursuit of happiness rather than pursuit of peace of mind. A low long-term orientation ranking indicates that the country does not reinforce the concept of long-term traditional orientation. In this culture, change can occur more rapidly as long-term traditions and commitments do not become impediments to change.

**Indulgence vs. Restraint.** This cultural dimension refers to the happiness, leisure, and control over one's life. The prevailing values of East Asian cultures would constrain speakers not to hurt one another's feelings and not to impose themselves on one another. As with any generalized study, the results may or may not be applicable to specific individuals or events. Although Hofstede categorized his results by country, more than one cultural group often exists within that country. Therefore, the results of a multicultural country may deviate significantly from the study's typical results. An example is Canada where the English speaking majority and the French speaking minority have moderate cultural differences. Another example would be Switzerland where the differences between the French speaking and German speaking parts of the country are as quite evident.

Hofstede's dimensions analysis can assist the business person or traveler in better understanding the intercultural differences within regions and between countries. The dimensions of national culture are not limited to research just in the social sciences. National culture has been researched and shown to be involved in many different aspects of business practices. The dimension of national culture influence management practices because the dimensions are brought to an organization by its employees and therefore become part of the organization's culture.[54] Therefore gaining an understanding of a host country's national culture would be beneficial for any organization desiring to do business internationally.  Learning local customs and beliefs while establishing managerial practices and organizational rules is vital.

Hofstede's approach to interpreting cultural dimensions is not without its share of criticism. That his research was originally conducted at IBM between 1968 and 1973 raises questions about whether the information can still be applicable today. Another criticism is the narrow scope of his research being that it involved only one company. Others have said that Hofstede's data is not concrete enough to warrant granting assumptions on societies and cultures. Hofstede responded to much of the criticism against his research by stating that even though surveys are not the only way to obtain information, they provide a solid tool for gathering data. He pointed out that cultures do not change their ways of life rapidly, so information that is a few decades old should not be dismissed as inaccurate. The addition of the GLOBE study that has confirmed Hofstede's six dimensions, should give credence to Hofstede's research.

### Trompenaar's Model of Culture

Fons Trompenaar has worked as an author and as a consultant for companies such as General Motors, Merrill Lynch, Motorola, and Nike. From 1986-1993, Trompenaar conducted extensive research on different countries, from which he developed his "Seven Dimensions of Culture Model."[55] Trompenaar believed that every culture distinguishes itself from others by the specific solutions it chooses to certain problems and dilemmas. One can categorize these problems under three headings: (1) those which arise from our relationships with other people, (2) those which come from the passage of time, and (3) those which relate to the environment. Trompenaar identified seven fundamental dimensions of culture:

**Universalism vs. Particularism.** People in universalistic cultures share the belief that general rules, codes, values and standards take precedence over particular needs and claims of friends and relations. In a universalistic society, the rules apply equally to the whole "universe" of members. Any exception weakens the rule. Particularistic cultures see the ideal culture in terms of human friendship, extraordinary achievement and situations, and in intimate relationships. The "spirit of the law" is deemed more important than the "letter of the law."

**Individualist vs. Communitarian.** In a predominantly individualistic culture, people place the individual before the community. Individual happiness, fulfillment, and welfare set the pace. Society expects people to decide matters largely on their own and to take care primarily of themselves and their immediate family. The culture sees the quality of life for all members of society as directly dependent on opportunities for individual freedom and development. People judge the community according to how it serves the interests of individual members. In a predominantly communitarian culture, people place the community before the individual. The individual has the responsibility to act in ways which serve society. By doing so, individual needs will be met naturally.

**Specific vs. Diffuse.** In specific cultures, the whole is the sum of its parts. Each person's life is divided into many components that can only be entered one at a time. Interactions between people are highly purposeful and well defined. The public sphere of specific individuals is much larger than their private sphere. People are easily accepted into the public sphere, but it is very difficult to get into the private sphere, since each area in which two people encounter each other is considered separate from the other—a specific case. Specific individuals concentrate on hard facts, standards, and contracts. On the other hand, people from diffusely oriented cultures start with the whole and see each element in perspective of the total. All elements are related to one another. These relationships are more important than each separate element. Thus the whole is more than just the sum of its elements. Diffuse individuals have a large private sphere and a small public one. Newcomers are not easily accepted into either. But once they have been accepted, they are admitted into all layers of the individual's life.

**Affective vs. Neutral.** In an affective culture, people do not object to a display of emotions. These cultures do not consider it necessary to hide feelings and keep them inside. Affective cultures may interpret the less explicit signals of a neutral culture as less important. They may ignore or not even notice these signals. In a neutral culture, people are taught to the error of showing one's feelings overtly. These people do have feelings, but they limit the degree to which feelings become manifest. Individuals from a neutral culture accept and are aware of feelings, but they maintain control over them.

**Achievement vs. Ascription.** Achieved status refers to what an individual does and has accomplished. In achievement-oriented cultures, individuals derive their status from what they have accomplished. A person with achieved status has to prove what he or she is worth over and over again; status is accorded on the basis of his or her actions. Ascribed status refers to what a person is and how others relate to his or her position in the community, in society, or in an organization. In an ascriptive society, individuals derive their status from birth, age, gender or wealth. A person with ascribed status does not have to achieve to retain his status; it is inherent.

**Sequential vs. Synchronic.** Every culture has developed its own response to time. The time orientation dimension has two aspects: the relative importance cultures give to the past, present, and future, and their approach to structuring time. Time can be structured in two ways. In sequentialism, time moves forward, second by second, minute by minute, hour by hour, in a straight line. People structuring time sequentially tend to do one thing at a time. They view time as a narrow line of distinct, consecutive segments. Sequential people view time as tangible and divisible. They strongly prefer planning and adhering to plans once they have been made. Sequential individuals take time commitments seriously. Staying on schedule is a must. In the synchronism approach, time moves around in cycles: of minutes, hours, days, and years. People structuring time synchronically usually do several things at a time. To them, time is a wide ribbon, allowing many things to take place simultaneously. Time is flexible and intangible. Time commitments are desirable rather than absolute. These people change plans easily. Synchronic people especially value the satisfactory completion of interactions with others. Promptness depends on the type of relationship.

NOTES

**Internal vs. External.** Every culture has developed an attitude towards the natural environment. The way people in a particular culture relate to their environment is linked to the way they seek to have control over their own lives and destiny. Internalistic people have a mechanistic view of nature. They see nature as a complex machine, and machines can be controlled if one has the right expertise. Internalistic people do not believe in luck or predestination. They are inner-directed—one's personal resolution is the starting point for every action. Externalistic people have a more organic view of nature. Mankind is one of nature's forces, so it should operate in harmony with the environment. Mankind should submit to nature and go along with its forces. Externalistic people do not believe that they can shape their own destiny. "Nature moves in mysterious ways," therefore one never knows what will happen to him or her. The actions of externalistic people are outer-directed—adapted to external circumstances.[56]

## The GLOBE Study

GLOBE is an acronym that stands for the Global Leadership and Organizational Behavior Effectiveness. The GLOBE study was a project conceived by Robert J. House in 1991 and begun in 1993.[57] The GLOBE study consisted of more than 17,000 participants who were middle managers from the financial services, food processing, and telecommunications services industries. The data that was accumulated from over 800 organizations in 62 countries identified nine dimensions on which national cultures differ. With 170 co-investigators in 62 countries, the GLOBE project may be the largest international management research project that has ever been undertaken.

The major premise of the GLOBE study was that leadership effectiveness is contextual and is embedded in the societal and organizational beliefs, norms, and values of the people being led. The researchers identified nine cultural dimensions: (1) power distance, (2) uncertainty avoidance, (3) humane orientation, (4) in-group collectivism, (5) institutional collectivism, (6) gender egalitarianism (similar to masculinity versus femininity), (7) assertiveness, (8) performance orientation, and (9) future orientation (similar to long-term versus short-term orientation). The nine dimensions resemble Hofstede's work regarding the understanding of cultural dimensions. The main difference is the GLOBE framework added dimensions such as egalitarianism (the degree to which an organization or a society minimizes gender role differences while promoting gender equity and equality of genders), humane orientation (the degree to which a society rewards individuals for being altruistic, generous, and kind to others), and performance orientation (the degree to which a society encourages and rewards group members for performance improvement and excellence), and assertiveness (the degree to which individuals in organizations or societies are assertive, confrontational, and aggressive in social relationships).

Two books have been written about the GLOBE study. In 2004 the first book *Culture, Leadership, and Organizations: The GLOBE study of 62 Societies* was published. This book was the result of a ten year research project that studied societal culture, organizational culture, and the attributes of effective leadership in 62 cultures. A team of 160 scholars worked together to conduct this study. A second book was published entitled *Culture and Leadership across the World: The GLOBE book of In-Depth Studies of 25 Societies* was published in 2007.[58] The second book complements the first book by providing country specific data on leadership theory and leadership behavior in 25 countries.

In the GLOBE study, countries were grouped according to similar cultural characteristics which were called clusters. Cultural similarity is greatest amongst societies that constitute a cluster. The GLOBE study has several distinguishing features that do not exist in Hofstede's or Trompenaar's work. First, the GLOBE study was a cross-cultural research project where the data collected in each country was accumulated by investigators who were either native to that culture, or had extensive knowledge and experience in the culture. Second, there were several industries selected for participation. The study was not restricted by one industry or company. Third, a large number of participants were surveyed, the largest research project of this nature, in order to get a more representative sample of each culture.[‡]

NOTES

‡ The author expresses appreciation to Angela McCaskill for providing information regarding the GLOBE study

NOTES

## **KEY CONCEPTS**

- Buddhism
- Christianity
- Communication across cultures: high context vs. low context
- Communication across cultures: verbal and non-verbal
- Confucianism
- Corporate social responsibility in global business
- Dimensions of culture: communications, language, religion, ethics, transparency, values, attitudes, social structures and organizations
- Ethics in global business

- Global business culture
- Hinduism
- Hofstede's dimensions of culture
- Islam
- Judaism
- Managerial paradigms: ethnocentric, polycentric, geocentric
- Shinto
- Trompenaar's dimensions of culture
- Values and attitudes across cultures

# Chapter 2 Exercises: Observational Analysis

*Ponder on the following key concepts and ideas as you read the chapter.*

1.  The relational complexities that potentially exist between a culture and a foreign organization seeking to do business in that culture

2.  Managerial cultural paradigms: ethnocentric, polycentric, geocentric. The dimensions of culture and the effects that communication, religion, ethics, values and attitudes, variances in attitudes, business manners and customs, and social structures have on global businesses

3.  Understanding Geert Hofstede and Fons Trompenaar work on the dimensions of culture

4.  Start a list of books, journals, and scholarly websites that would aid in the understanding of the chapter's main concepts and ideas. Start a journal for your own thoughts and ideas. What outside sources support your conclusions?

# Chapter 2 Exercises: Key Terms Analysis

*Match the answers by writing the correct letter in the space provided*

_____ 1. Dimensions of Culture

_____ 2. Culture

_____ 3. Ethnocentric

_____ 4. Roles

_____ 5. Oral agreements

_____ 6. Judaism

_____ 7. Siddhartha Gautama

_____ 8. Transparency International (TI)

_____ 9. Geocentric

_____ 10. Iranian upper class

_____ 11. Status

_____ 12. Foreign Corrupt Practices Act

_____ 13. Polycentric

_____ 14. Social structure

_____ 15. Corruption

_____ 16. Values

_____ 17. Ascribed status

_____ 18. Ethics

_____ 19. Individualism

_____ 20. Low Context

A. One's own culture is superior to all others; standard by which all other cultures should be measured

B. Founded Buddhism

C. Major concern for those engaged in global business

D. A monotheistic religion which believes that the world was created by a single divinity

E. Position a person occupies within a social group

F. Develop an integrated system with a worldwide approach

G. Promotes openness towards other cultures, opinions, and ways of life

H. Enacted by Congress to halt bribery in the U.S. Business system

I. The manner in which a society is organized

J. Set of shared attitudes, values, goals, and practices; characterize a society or an organization

K. The status assigned by society to an individual based on uncontrollable factors

L. Set of rights, obligations, and expectations associated with a status

M. Beliefs about what is right and wrong

N. Study of morality and standards of conduct

O. Example of cultural attitude on social class

P. Degree which society reinforces individual or collective achievement/interpersonal relationships

Q. Communication/religion/ethics/values/attitudes manners/customs/social/organization/education

R. Implies strong commitments in high-context cultures

S. Dedicated to fighting corruption worldwide

T. Societies where people tend to have many connections but of shorter duration

# Chapter 2 Exercises: Theoretical Analysis

*Analyze the questions and select the best answer based on the reading of the chapter material*

1. A form of verbal language includes

   a. Hand gestures

   b. Facial expressions

   c. A country's dominant language

   d. Body language

2. Regardless of the managerial-cultural paradigm in use, the business professional recognizes that an understanding of the major dimensions of culture is essential for success in doing business overseas.

   a. True

   b. False

3. From 1967 to 1973, Fons Trompenaar applied the subset of cultural dimensions to the field of business management, segregating them into independent areas to be further divided in order to get a more precise understanding.

   a. True

   b. False

4. Trompenaar believed that every culture distinguishes itself from others by the specific solutions it chooses to certain problems and dilemmas.

   a. True

   b. False

5. The Premise of the _____ was that Leadership effectiveness is contextual and is embedded in the societal and organizational beliefs, norms, and values of the people being led.

   a. Cross Cultural Analysis Model

   b. The Globe Study

   c. Model of Culture Study

   d. 7 Dimensions of Culture

6. Culture is the set of shared attitudes, values, _____, and practices that characterize a society.

   a. Goals

   b. Dreams

   c. Educational level

   d. Language

7. Which of the following is NOT a cultural paradigm?

   a. Ethnocentric

   b. Polycentric

   c. Monocentric

   d. Geocentric

8. Effective, cross-cultural communicators must know how to properly pronounce words, how to properly spell words, and how to use these words in proper grammatical form.

   a. True

   b. False

9. _____, as the opposite of _____, promotes openness towards other cultures, opinions, and ways of life.

   a. Polycentrism, Monocentrism

   b. Geocentrism, Ethnocentrism

   c. Ethnocentrism, Monocentrism

   d. Polycentrism, Ethnocentrism

10. Polycentric managers think home-country nationals are more intelligent, reliable and trustworthy than foreign.

    a. True

    b. False

11. The geocentric organization's primary objective is to develop an integrated system with a (n) _____.

    a. Worldwide approach

    b. Centrally located approach

    c. International approach

    d. None of the above

12. Which of the following is true regarding the use of words across languages?

    a. Differences in pronunciation and meaning can lead to misunderstandings

    b. Different cultures and languages may not always present or interpret messages in the same context

    c. Cross-cultural or cross-religion barriers exacerbate the misunderstandings that arise when trying to communicate a message

    d. Educational levels may cause a communication lapse within a country's own language

13. Business Ethics is the study of ethical dilemmas, values, and decision making in the world of business. Business ethics should not be considered a separate disciple from ethics.

    a. True

    b. False

14. Which of the following is a characteristic of a high-context culture?

    a. Rule oriented

    b. More knowledge is codified, public, external, and accessible

    c. More interpersonal connections of shorter duration

    d. Knowledge is situational and relational.

15. Congress enacted the Foreign Corrupt Practices Act (FCPA) to bring a halt to the bribery of foreign officials and to restore public confidence in the integrity of the U.S. business system.

    a. True

    b. False

16. The anti-bribery provisions of the OECD make it unlawful for a U.S. person, and certain foreign issuers of securities, to make a corrupt payment to a foreign official for the purpose of securing business with or directing business to any person.

    a. True

    b. False

17. Three branches of Judaism include

    a. Orthodox, Reservists, Conformists

    b. Reform, Orthodox, Conservatives

    c. Conservatives, Reservists, Reform

    d. Reservists, Orthodox, Reform

18. All of the following are part of the 5 Pillars of Faith in the Muslim religion except

    a. Prayer must be done seven times a day

    b. Give one-fortieth of their income to the needy

    c. During the holy month of Ramadan, faithful Muslims fast from sunrise to sunset each day

    d. Each Muslim is expected to make the pilgrimage to Mecca at least once in his or her lifetime

19. An ascribed status is one that society assigns to an individual on the basis of factors over which the individual has no control: gender, race, ethnic background, and socioeconomic status, into which one is born.

    a. True

    b. False

20. Which of the following is a dimension in Fons Trompenaar's Model of Culture?

    a. Diffuse

    b. Power Distance

    c. Uncertainty Avoidance

    d. Masculinity

21. In high-context cultures, enforceable contracts will tend to be in writing, precisely worded, and highly legalistic. High-context cultures value directness. Managers are expected to be explicit and precise in conveying intended meaning.

    a. True

    b. False

22. Communication between two cultures can be awkward if professionals do not conduct proper research.

    a. True

    b. False

23. People in a particularism culture see the ideal culture in terms of human friendship, extraordinary achievement and situations, and intimate relationships.

    a. True

    b. False

24. In an _____ culture, people place the individual before the community; individual happiness, fulfillment, and welfare set the pace.

    a.  Individualistic

    b.  Specific

    c.  Particularism

    d.  Internal

25. _____ culture: time moves around in cycles; people tend to do several things at a time; time is flexible and intangible.

    a.  Internalistic

    b.  Diffuse

    c.  Achievement

    d.  Synchronic

26. People in a _____culture share the belief that general rules, codes, values, and standards take precedence over particular needs and claims of friends and relations.

    a.  Universalism

    b.  Individualist

    c.  Particularism

    d.  Internal

27. _____status refers to what an individual does and has accomplished;

    a.  Achievement

    b.  Synchronic

    c.  Ascription

    d.  Independent

28. Synchronic culture tend to do one thing at a time view time as a narrow line of distinct, consecutive, segments

    a.  True

    b.  False

29. In a _____culture, people start with the whole and see each element in perspective of the total; the whole is more important than the sum of its elements. Individuals have a large private sphere and a small public one.

    a.  Communitarian

    b.  Diffuse

    c.  Universalism

    d.  Internal

30. Internalistic cultures have a mechanistic view of nature; nature is a complex machine, and machines can be controlled if one has the right expertise; people do not believe in luck or predestination;

    a.  True

    b.  False

# Chapter 2 Exercises: Practical Analysis

*Write a short essay in the space provided to each of the following questions.*
*Please use outside references for each answer to support your ideas and thoughts.*

1. It is important to understand the culture dimensions of business in order to effectively communicate and incorporate successful business operations and practices.

    a. Using the Internet access the following website: www.geert-hofstede.international-business-center.com

    b. Select 3 nations and write a brief summary of the cultural dimensions in those nations.

2. Trompenaar and Hofstede have developed models for understanding business cultures across nations.

    a. What are the similarities between the two models?

    b. What are the differences between the two models?

3. Suppose you were given a business assignment that required you to travel on a two-week business trip overseas. In the first week, you will be visiting Copenhagen, Denmark; in the second week, you will be visiting Managua, Nicaragua.

    a. Which nation has a high-context communication process and, which nation has a low context communication process?

    b. What communication differences might create difficulties as you transition from one nation to the other?

    c. How would you prepare yourself to change from one communication context to the next?

4. Corruption and business risk are interrelated. The global business professional understands that nations with higher levels of perceived corruption tend to have higher levels of business risk. Access http://www.transparency.org and locate the current corruption perceptions index. After studying the index, what surprised you the most, and what surprised you the least? Explain your reason.

# Chapter 2 Exercises: Biblical Worldview Application

*Write a short essay in the space provided to each of the following questions.*
*Please use biblical references and research, where applicable, to support your ideas and thoughts.*

1.  Read http://www.focusonthefamily.com/faith/christian_worldview/whats_a_christian_worldview.aspx. Could the Biblical Worldview be considered a cultural dimension? Why or why not?

2.  Select a model presented in this chapter and describe which parts of the model align with a Biblical World view, as well as which parts do not. Be specific in your answers.

3.  Suppose you have been assigned to a new job in another nation, and that nation does not embrace the Biblical Worldview. What would you need to do to prepare yourself for that assignment?

# Macroenvironmental Factors and Risks

## CHAPTER OVERVIEW

The global community is experiencing unprecedented integration of business, governments, and nongovernmental organizations. Multinational corporations (MNCs) and nations increasingly rely on each other to improve cross-border trade necessary for survival in the global community. Policy issues can have a major impact upon businesses in the global market. Global business professionals must be knowledgeable of the history, tradition, and laws of nations in which they wish to conduct business. Sometimes these regional aspects create dilemmas for firms wishing to do business in the region. As discussed in chapter two, a practice or tradition in one country may actually be offensive to people in another country. Complying with local guidelines can be a financial burden on a company, but the loss of business or the cost of a lawsuit would undoubtedly cause the company far more.

The decision to conduct business overseas entails determining what is an acceptable level of risk. The competent global business professional evaluates the levels of risk by carefully considering the political, legal, and economic environments for each offshore location. The purpose of this unit is to integrate the elements of these three global business environments with the realities of the types and causes of risk one might encounter internationally.

## POLITICAL AND LEGAL MACROENVIRONMENT

### Why Governments Intervene in Global Trade

International trading is very important to a nation because it generates business and government revenue and promotes varying levels of trust between trading partners. These levels of trust can have both positive and negative outcomes. Some nations are better suited for producing certain items that other countries may demand. Nations profit by trading with other nations better suited to producing products in demand. On the other hand, governmental disagreements may lead to embargoes and the cessation of international trade between the countries' businesses. Consumers are the main beneficiaries of trade, which also makes them the primary victim of embargoes. Consumers will have to pay higher prices for hard-to-find items if their government imposes an embargo on a country that is the main producer of the item.[1]

Governments may also intervene in order to protect their domestic market. A developing market is not ready to fully engage in international trading on its own and may require the protection of the government. On the other hand, domestic businesses may be ready to begin trading in the international

> **Political Issues That Significantly Impact Global Business**
> - Government intervention in trade.
> - Government promotion of trade.
> - Government restriction of trade.

market; however, they may not have the finances needed to undertake the endeavor. Some government agencies may choose to financially assist their domestic businesses in order to spur the whole nation's economic growth.

Governments are also aware of trade deficits that may develop between nations. A trade deficit occurs when a country is importing more than it is exporting. The government has the responsibility of ensuring that extreme deficits are monitored and corrected. If a trade deficit becomes excessive, then the government must correct the deficit before the entire nation's economy is at risk of faltering.

Whether motivated by the desire to improve standards of living for its citizens, the protection of domestic industries, or the management of trade deficits, a number of options are available for governments to promote cross-border trade. These include special government agencies, subsidies, export financing assistance, and foreign trade zones.

## Special Government Agencies

**Government Actions that Promote Trade**
- Special government agencies
- Subsidies
- Export Financing
- Foreign Trade Zones

In 1995, as business and policy makers alike saw the potential growth of global business, the World Trade Organization (WTO) was created by several countries in order to monitor trade around the entire world. Since then many other nations have formed regional trade agreements such as the North American Free Trade Agreement (NAFTA) and the European Union (EU), to promote regional trade in their respective areas.

The U.S. Department of Commerce developed the International Trade Administration (ITA) in order to stimulate economic opportunities for U.S. businesses and their employees. Specifically, the ITA assists U.S. companies in navigating foreign markets by teaching them about marketing, financing, logistics, etc. Consequently, the U.S. Commercial Service was developed to oversee and promote international trade.[2] The ITA has placed many offices in the U.S. and numerous other nations in order to continue to encourage international trade.

Most U.S. states have developed special government agencies to partner with constituent companies to do business overseas. The Virginia Economic Development Partnership has created the Division of International Trade. This division has developed multiple programs and services to assist both manufacturing and service firms, located within the state, to increase their exports. Services include operating overseas state offices, conducting overseas trade missions, providing a resident subject-matter expert, and advice and counseling at all levels in the exporting process. The astute global-business professional should take full advantage of these services and programs utilizing both federal and state special government agencies to expedite and supplement their global business presence.

## Subsidies

Subsidies are special privileges offered by the government in order to attract businesses to a region or to provide them with the funding to operate successfully. A nation's government may provide tax breaks, lower the cost of required land, or offer other money-saving techniques to businesses that it wishes to attract or maintain in a region.[3] Providing subsidies may allow a region to acquire a company that will bring more jobs to the area, thus increasing productivity and strengthening the economy. These subsidies are designed to attract overseas firms and their foreign direct investment into the local government's economy. This type of subsidy should not be confused with those subsidies that the government frequently offers to domestic firms in an effort to protect local industries from the effects of free trade and world-wide competition. Foreign investment funding and other outside resources have greater potential to elevate local economic well being than money that merely circulates within a local economy.

*Export Financing*

Export financing differs from commercial lending, mortgage lending, or insurance. A company increases payment time when it sells and ships a product overseas. This type of transaction requires extra time and energy, to make sure that buyers are reliable and creditworthy. Foreign buyers—just like domestic buyers—prefer to delay payment until they receive and resell the goods. Due diligence and careful financial management can mean the difference between profit and loss on each transaction. Diligence and management is especially important for small businesses engaged in exporting, as these organizations may need government assistance in obtaining finances for export activities. The Export-Import Bank (Ex-Im Bank) is the official export credit agency of the United States. The Ex-Im Bank is a valuable tool for small businesses because it does not require a minimum transaction limit. Using an organization to finance the cost of the exported goods will allow all parties involved to have more time to gather the finances needed to complete the transaction.[45]

Other institutions that operate underneath government agencies, private companies, or general organizations are available to finance exports.[5] Export credit institutions, export banks, and export finance institutions specialize not only in financing exports but also in circulating capital and providing insurance on the items being traded. Two forms of credit are associated with export financing. The first is the supplier's credit where a loan in which the exporter is covered, but the value of the cover will be less than the value of the contract. The second form is buyer's credit, which is more closely associated with long-term loans. Some international projects may take more than four years to complete; therefore, the financial institution needs the importer's credit to protect parties from potential problems that might arise during this extended time period.

While many governments have created institutions that oversee export finances, some allow the private sector to control its own financing. Because governments have different economic policies, some government-controlled credit institutions may not be successful or required. However, newly emerging governments could take advantage of financing agencies in order to assist their business community in the creation and maintenance of sustainable global trade. Financing can help protect businesses from potential losses by providing them with insurance against political and commercial risks while also increasing their international business confidence.

*Foreign Trade Zones*

The United States' capitalistic economy allows citizens to engage in a free-trade system within the country and with other countries that operate under the free-trade model. Operating under a free-trade model provides many benefits; but as with any model, the costs can be significant. The Foreign-Trade Zones (FTZ) program alleviates some of the costs associated with free trade in the rapidly increasing global economic environment.

The Foreign Trade Zones program was created with the enactment of the U.S. Foreign-Trade Zones Act of 1934.[6] This program was created during a defining moment of American history when Americans were beginning to open doors to foreign policy as well as to foreign business opportunities. U.S. policy makers hoped to encourage foreign commerce in order to spur the declining U.S. economy. The United States designated certain areas "Customs Ports of Entry" where commercial merchandise would "receive the same customs treatment it would if it were outside the commerce of the United States. Merchandise of every description may be held in the Zone without being subject to Customs duties and other ad valorem taxes."[7] These zones are supervised by the U.S. customs service through audit-inspection checks.

During the 1950s and 1960s the global trade environment underwent tremendous change. Tariff barriers were continually reduced, and international trade began to flourish. However, as more countries began to open their doors to international trade, unexpected costs hidden within the free trade system became apparent. Each country was attempting to gain as much profit as possible while spending less on imported goods. Countries spent much time deliberating on trade negotiations so that all countries involved could reap the benefits of international trade. In order to ensure the prosperity of all parties involved in global trade the National Association of Foreign Trade Zones (NAFTZ) was created in 1972. In 1980 the U.S. Customs Service issued a new ruling that allowed U.S. based manufacturers to bring foreign-sourced parts into free-trade zones without paying extra duties. This act, coupled with the continued increase in global trade, greatly spurred the U.S. economy and the U.S. Foreign-Trade Zones program. More than 230 Foreign-Trade Zone projects and nearly 400 sub-zones currently exist within the United States.

FTZs offer numerous benefits to manufacturers and distributors in the United States. Organizations investigate overseas options when deciding to locate or expand a new manufacturing or processing facility. Such location and expansion decisions must take into account all costs of manufacturing in a certain nation. As do most other nations, U.S. law may have unintended import tax penalties for firms located, or considering locating, in the United States. The FTZ program plays an important role in providing a level playing field when investment and production decisions are made. While the U.S. government might incur a reduction in Customs duty revenue through the FTZ program, these reductions are offset by the income taxes from created or existing jobs. In addition local governments benefit from sales and property taxes.

### Government Actions that Restrict Trade

Governments may attempt to restrict trade with other countries especially in circumstances of large trade deficits or excessive currency outflows. Such actions may result in protectionism—when a nation deliberately reduces the number of imports it receives. As with any government action, advantages and disadvantages may accrue. Common forms of government actions that restrict trade include, but are not limited to, tariffs, quotas, and embargoes.

### Tariffs, Quotas, and Embargoes

A tariff is a tax applied to selected categories of imports. Governments design tariffs to raise revenues and to generally provide a competitive advantage for domestic businesses. Tariffs are similar to excise taxes (taxes on cigarettes and alcohol, for example) in design and economic impact. Governments design tariffs, which they normally impose as a fixed percentage of the value of imports, to discriminate against selected imports by raising the price of imports relative to domestic prices for the same products. The tariff or duty is collected at a product's point of entry into a

| Government Actions that Restrict Trade | |
| --- | --- |
| • Tariffs | • Local content Requirements |
| • Quotas | • Administrative Delays |
| • Embargoes | • Currency Controls |

country. Since World War II, multilateral trade negotiations under the General Agreement on Tariffs and Trade (GATT) have resulted in large reductions in tariff and non-tariff barriers to international trade. A guiding principle for increasing international trade for goods and services has been the eventual elimination of all tariffs on imports.

Governments use quotas, also known as quantitative restrictions, to limit the quantity of imports allowed into a nation. Quotas typically "raise the price of imports, reduce the volume of imports, and encourage demand for domestically made substitutes."[8] Quotas and tariffs are similar in that their general purpose is to control the number of imports that enter a domestic market. While tariffs generate money for the government, because they are essentially an import tax, quotas can have some negative effects on a government. Quotas place power in the hands of customs officials. These officials determine which nations will be allowed to import goods into the domestic system while denying other nations because no room exists for their products. This refusal can cause a nation to become disgruntled with the government of the nation in which they are trying to import their goods. Customs officials may even choose a favorite exporter, rather than importing goods on an equal level. Such corruption may be harmful to a country's economy, as well as its foreign relations.

Tariffs and quotas may increase smuggling activity. If the quota is extremely low or if a tariff is unreasonably high, smugglers may attempt to push goods through a country's borders without paying the proper taxes. The incidence of smuggling may then be reduced by lowering the tariff while still collecting revenue from the taxes.[9]

Embargoes are economic and trade sanctions against targeted foreign countries, groups, organizations, and individuals. Embargoes can be motivated by political, economic, or moral reasons. The United States Department of the Treasury oversees and enforces all U.S. economic sanctions through the Office of Foreign Assets Control (OFAC). The following reveals some of the purposes behind embargoes:

- Punishing a country or group for unacceptable behavior
- Influencing the behavior of the target
- Signaling disapproval of a government's or group's behavior
- Warning the target nation that harsher measures could follow
- Limiting a target's freedom of action
- Denying resources or technology
- Increasing the cost of engaging in unacceptable behavior
- Drawing international attention to unacceptable behavior
- Challenging allies to take more forceful action themselves in support of common objectives
- Signaling to a government or group that is engaging in practices which violate core values that a "business-as-usual" approach is not acceptable
- Protecting the assets of allies from hostile actions
- Assuring that the assets of targets will be available to meet future claims

The various methods of imposing economic sanctions include the following:

- Limiting exports and re-exports to the targets (including exports to third countries predominantly for use in products for the targets)
- Limiting imports from the targets

- Blocking assets of the targeted country, company or individual
- Restricting investments in the targets
- Prohibiting private financial transactions
- Restricting government trade financing and investment assistance regarding the target

### Local Content Requirements

Local content requirements are means by which governments can block open trade within a country's borders. These requirements can hinder foreign exports from reaching a nation or from being purchased in the domestic market and place restrictions on domestic businesses. Local content requirement is a popular government policy in developing countries to regulate foreign direct investment. The World Trade Organization is striving to eliminate local content requirements, so that the global market may profit from free trading. However, the WTO has not yet been completely successful in its efforts.[10]

### Administrative Delays

Administrative delays impose a waiting period between the determination of a product's quality and the determination of when it can actually be sold in a market. This prohibits the producer of the product from improving the quality of the product during the waiting period. This delay causes the producer to miss an opportunity to gain profits. Furthermore, administrative delays do not provide any extra revenue to the nation that imposes the delay—they do not bring in any extra revenue aside from the standard tariff.[11] If a popular item becomes available in other nations while in administrative delay, then smugglers may attempt to introduce the item into the country's economy further hurting the country's revenue from the tariff. If the delay is excessive, the demand for the new item may decrease by the time the item makes the shelves of the importing country. Both countries would lose profits in this scenario. Administrative delays have the potential to be harmful to all parties involved.

### Currency Controls

Some governments practice strict control over their currency. Currency control is a system whereby a nation attempts to regulate the value of its own money within its borders. From simple to complex policy changes, such government initiated systems attempt to control currency fluctuations through the regulation of interest rates, bonds, laws, money printing, and many more. Nations that lack adequate currency control tend to experience hyper-inflation or depression.

## Types of Law

The astute global business professional understands the impact of political issues and regulations on commerce. In addition to the political issues a keen awareness of the legal aspects of doing business overseas is essential for success. Legal aspects of international business focus on the types of laws and legal issues used across nations and borders. The basic legal issues include standardization of laws, property rights, and copyrights.

NOTES

Laws are essential to the efficient and effective operation of business establishments and corporations within a society. They provide standard rules, regulations, and protocols necessary for fairness and ethical treatments of customers, employees, and suppliers. Each sovereign nation has the right to establish laws that govern the conducting of business within its borders. Such laws typically fall into one of three categories: common, civil, and theocratic.

### Common Law

The common law was originally developed in historical England and is the result of judicial decisions that were based in tradition, custom, and precedent. Common law may be unwritten or written in statutes or codes. The common law as applied in civil cases (as distinct from criminal cases), was devised as a means of compensating someone for wrongful acts—known as torts—including both intentional torts and torts caused by negligence, in order to develop the body of law that recognizes and regulates contracts. In a common law system an adversarial approach is used to investigate and adjudicate guilt or innocence. The adversarial system assumes that truth is most likely to result from the open competition between the prosecution and the defense. Primary responsibility for the presentation of evidence and legal arguments lies with the opposing parties, not with a judge. Each side is acting in its self-interest and is expected to present facts and interpretations of the law in a way most favorable to its interests. The approach presumes that the accused is innocent, and the burden of proving guilt rests with the prosecution. Through counterargument and cross-examination each side is expected to test the truthfulness, relevancy, and sufficiency of the opponent's evidence and arguments.[12]

### Civil Law

Civil law has its origins in Roman law and is the predominant system of law in the world. It sets forth a comprehensive system of rules that are usually codified then applied and interpreted by judges. Historically, the original difference between common law and civil law was that common law was developed by custom, beginning before any written laws existed and continuing to be applied by courts after they were written. Civil law developed out of Roman law. The difference between civil law and common law is grounded in the methodological approach to codes and statutes. Civil law nations view legislation as the primary source of law. Courts base their judgments on the provisions of codes and statutes from which they derive their particular solutions to cases. Courts must reason extensively on the basis of general rules and principles of the code, often drawing analogies from statutory provisions. By contrast in the common law system, cases are the primary source of law while statutes are seen only as incursions into the common law and interpreted narrowly.

### Theocratic Law

Theocratic law refers to laws which are derived from religion. Due to the numerous religions in the world, such as Christianity, Islam, Buddhism, and Hinduism, nations find difficulty coming to agreements over theocratic laws. Because of the increase in globalization within the marketplace as well as communities, a common secular law is needed in order to ensure the prosperity of international trade.

### Standardization of Laws

Each nation has its own distinct set of laws that govern its people. While some nations rely on civil law others focus on either common or theocratic law. As globalization continues to grow the efforts to form a set of standardized international laws continue to increase. Theocratic law presents an especially difficult challenge in global trade because of the wide variance of religious groups in the world whose theocracies can vary greatly. Another issue with international law is that ultimately an economically independent country can refuse to follow international law without fear of economic sanctions. This refusal to observe international law could become dangerous and potentially lead to physical war between two nations. International laws will be difficult to enforce unless all participants can come to an agreement on the laws and appoint a governing body to settle disputes.

A widely used tool in law and development programs is the supply of well-designed laws from the outside. This method of law development has now been embraced by international organizations as a way to improve the legal framework for global markets. The International Monetary Fund (IMF) has endorsed attempts by various organizations to develop legal standards with special emphasis on corporate and financial institution laws. The common idea behind these attempts is that the supplied laws once incorporated into domestic legal systems will improve the existing legal framework, furthering economic development.[13]

### Property Rights

Protecting property is an important part of promoting the global trade. Trade, simply put, is the trading of property in order to receive monetary value. Property can be classified as both physical and intellectual. Ideas spur innovation which spurs the development of new goods that will be available for trade. The World Trade Organization (WTO) allows for a minimum level of property rights to provide its members with a global standard of protection.

> **The WTO's System of Property Covers the Following Issues**
>
> - How basic principles of the trading system and other international, intellectual property agreements should be applied.
>
> - How to give adequate protection to intellectual property rights.
>
> - How countries should enforce those rights adequately in their own territories.
>
> - How to settle disputes on intellectual property between members of the WTO.[14]

*Intellectual property.* The WTO defines intellectual property rights as "the rights given to persons over the creations of their minds. They usually give the creator an exclusive right over the use of his/her creation for a certain period of time."[15] Examples of intellectual rights include patents, trademarks, and copyrights.

*Industrial Property.* (patents and trademarks). Industrial property rights protect specific signs and trademarks that distinguish specific goods and services from other goods and services. The property on a trademark can last as long as the trademark is easily distinguishable. Patents protect individuals who are in the process of creating a new invention. Individuals can receive a patent protection for approximately twenty years.[16] This protection allows the individual enough time to develop the product into a working invention without threat of competition. After the patent expires, other persons or companies may attempt to reproduce a similar product.

### Copyrights

Copyrights are a form of intellectual property rights designed to encourage and reward creative intellectual work by protecting the author's work. Copyrights protect the rights of authors in regards to literary and artistic works. These works include all books, songs, compositions, paintings, films, and computer programs. Authors are protected by copyright for at least seventy years after their death. The modern copyright system can be traced back to the Berne Convention (1886). The Berne Convention provides a minimum protection of property rights that are independent of the nation in which the work originated. The agreement made at the Berne Convention protects the artistic domain of authors in regards to literary works, such as novels, songs, and compositions. The following is a list of rights authorized for protection by the Berne Convention:

- The right to translate

- The right to make adaptations and arrangements of the work

- The right to perform in public dramatic and musical works

- The right to recite in public literary works

- The right to communicate to the public the performance of such works

- The right to broadcast (with the possibility of a contracting State to provide for a mere right to equitable remuneration instead of a right of authorization)

- The right to make reproductions in any manner or form (with the possibility of a contracting nation to permit, in certain special cases, reproduction without authorization, provided that the reproduction does not conflict with the normal exploitation of the work and does not unreasonably prejudice the legitimate interests of the author; and with the possibility of a contracting State to provide, in the case of sound recordings of musical works, for a right to equitable remuneration)

- The right to use the work as a basis for an audiovisual work, and the right to reproduce, distribute, perform in public, or communicate to the public that audiovisual work[17]

The Berne Convention allows authors to possess moral rights in which they can object to anyone using their work in a manner that would dishonor the reputation of the author.[18]

## ECONOMIC SYSTEMS

The global economy involves complex national and regional economic systems with many variables. These economic systems span developed and newly industrialized nations and include centrally planned, market, and mixed systems. Organizations such as the United Nations and the International Monetary Fund (IMF) use various measurement tools to determine the economic status of all nations. These tools include the Human

Development Index (HDI), Gross National Product (GNP), Gross Domestic Product (GDP) and Purchasing Power Parity (PPP). An understanding of the economic systems of the world must be preceded by an understanding of the beliefs and values of various cultures.

### *Individualist vs. Collectivist Economic Values*

As cultures converge across the globe, companies must be engaged in learning the converging patterns that underlie a vast array of societies. The U.S. economic value system has developed from the Puritanical belief that endorsed individualistic values and characteristics.[19] Other nations, such as Great Britain, Australia, and Canada also have similar value systems. Cultures such as China, North Korea, and Cuba believe that an economic value system should be founded on cumulative efforts and controlled by greater entities or governments. A distinction between individualist and collectivist societies is crucial to the proper understanding of cross-cultural beliefs and values.[20]

Individualism refers to a self-orientation, an emphasis on self-sufficiency and control, the pursuit of individual goals, which may or may not be consistent with the in-group goals, a willingness to confront members of the in-group to which a person belongs, and a culture where people derive pride from their own accomplishments. In an individualistic environment, people are motivated by self-interest and achievement of personal goals. Individualists are hesitant to contribute to collective action unless their own efforts are recognized, preferring instead to benefit from the efforts of others.[21]

The benefits of individualism include the following:

- Employee develops stronger self-concept and more self-confidence

- Consistent with achievement motivation

- Competition among individuals encourages greater numbers of novel concepts, ideas, and breakthrough innovations

- Stronger sense of personal responsibility for performance outcomes

- Linkage between personal effort and rewards creates greater sense of equity

The drawbacks of individualism include the following:

- Emphasis on personal gain at expense of others; selfishness, and materialism

- Individuals have less commitment/loyalty and are more "up for sale"

- Differences among individuals are emphasized

- Interpersonal conflicts are encouraged

- Greater levels of personal stress; pressure for individual performance

- Insecurity can result from overdependence on one's self

- Greater feelings of loneliness and alienation

- Stronger incentive for unethical behavior, expediency

Collectivism involves the subordination of personal interests to the goals of the larger work group, an emphasis on sharing, cooperation, and group harmony, a concern with group welfare, and hostility toward out-group members. Collectivists believe that they are an indispensable part of the group and will readily contribute without concern for being

NOTES

taken advantage of or whether or not others are doing their part. They feel personally responsible for the group product and are oriented towards sharing group rewards.[22] The following list contains the benefits of collectivism:

- Greater synergy from combined efforts of people with differing skills

- Ability to incorporate a diverse perspective and achieve a comprehensive view

- Individuals treated as equals

- Relationships more personalized, synchronized, harmonious, while interpersonal conflicts are discouraged

- Greater concern for welfare of others; network of social support available

- More consensus regarding direction and priorities

- Credit for failures and successes equally shared

- Teamwork produces steady, incremental progress on projects[23]

The subsequent list includes the drawbacks of collectivism:

- Loss of personal and professional self to group/collective

- Greater emotional dependence of individuals on the group or organization

- Less personal responsibility for outcomes

- Individuals "free ride" on efforts of others; rewards not commensurate with effort

- Tendency toward "group think"

- Outcomes can represent compromises among diverse interests, reflecting need to get along more than need for performance

- Collectives can take more time to reach consensus: may miss opportunities[24]

### Types of Economic Systems

The three primary types of global economic systems are centrally planned economy, market economy, and mixed economy. Depending on a nation's governmental control, combinations of economic systems usually emerge making it difficult to accurately analyze their economic system. In most instances, one global economic orientation tends to dominate.

### Centrally Planned Economic System

A centrally planned economy most often refers to an economic system that is under comprehensive control and regulation by a government, in accordance with the plan of economic development. The centrally planned economy is in contrast to a market economy, in which market forces dictate supply, demand, production, pricing, etc. In a centrally planned economy, an overriding hierarchy (usually the government) attempts to control supply, demand, production, distribution, and pricing. Most centrally planned economic systems are associated with communism. Several governments including Cuba and North Korea still adhere to its practices.

Cuba became a member of the Council for Mutual Economic Assistance (CMEA), which was a part of the Soviet trading bloc in 1972, as it transformed from a capitalist economic system to a centrally planned economic system, led by President Fidel Castro. Prior to its revolution in 1959, Cuba, because of its great resources, strategic location, and trade relationship with the United States, was a major economic force in the Caribbean. During the period of 1945 through 1958, Cuba was able to double its gross national product, ranking third among Latin American countries. Economists estimate that Cuba's GSP or gross social product—Cuba's measure of economic production—decreased 30 percent from 1989 through 1992.[25] In addition to the dissolution of the CMEA in 1990 several items have contributed to the distress of the Cuban economy since the late 1980s:

- The failed system of ownership, where collective ownership has proven to be a disastrous economic policy

- Artificially valuing the peso and continuing to issue money into circulation

- Production of sugar beyond what is economically rational, thus causing low productivity in other areas

- Misallocated investment resources into large projects with no economic basis

- Technological retrogression in that rather than adopting economic reform, they have reverted back to ox carts and bicycles[26]

To stimulate growth and trade Cuba attempted to introduce economic reform in the early 1990s. These reforms included the establishment of a new "unofficial" exchange market to replace the black market, transformation of many state farms into co-operatives, and steps towards decentralization of economic management.[27] Although these initial reforms were thought to be the beginnings of a transition to a market economy, subsequent events have shown that the reforms were no more than Cuban officials' claims of an increased use of market mechanisms within a framework of continued state ownership and economic control.

*Market Economic System*

A market economy is also known as a free-market economy and a free-enterprise economy, which is an economic system where the production and distribution of goods and services takes place through the mechanism of free markets. The market is guided by a free price system rather than a planned economy controlled by the state.[28] The free-market economy is controlled by the supply and demand of goods and services rather than a hierarchy control such as government. Many nations, most notably the U.S., are considered free market economies; however, no nation operates with a true free-market economy. All economies have some governmental control, and none are completely free to operate unrestricted. Nations that primarily functioned under the centrally planned economic system prior to the 1980s, such as China and Russia (formerly know as the Soviet Union), have migrated to a quasi-market economy. While within this strategy their overall economies have improved, they continue to face many challenges in the transition from a fully centrally planned economy to a truer market economy focus.

Throughout the 1990s Russia has worked to transition from a centrally planned economy to a market economy and has seen the explosion with new markets of previously neglected services and consumer goods. In 2013 services accounted for approximately 58.3 percent (est.) of GDP compared to only 36 percent in 1990. Although Russia has experienced increased markets and a higher GDP, from 1998 through 2008 the economy had averaged 7 percent growth rate, the post-communist government inherited an economic catastrophe: a GDP decline in 1991 of 12 percent, a budget deficit at 26 percent

NOTES

of GDP, and inflation rates that advanced to triple digits. Several underlying factors caused this transitional collapse:

- Long-standing political commitment to expanding heavy industry with little consideration for its impact on the new market system

- The dissolution of the Council for Mutual Economic Assistance (CMEA) disrupted many supply chains

- The government's inability to financially assist the agricultural market without raising food prices beyond the reach of its citizens

- The Russian people were trained to operate under the disciplines of the planned, economic system and struggled with the disciplines needed to succeed under the market system

- The old political elite resisted even the most moderate of economic reforms[29]

Though Russia experienced greater success as result of the transition, they were one of the hardest hit countries from the global economic crisis in 2008 and 2009 due to lowering fuel prices and drying up of foreign credits. They also have experienced difficulty in attracting foreign direct investment. As a result, GDP growth rate slowed to 3.4 percent In 2012 (est.) and 1.3 percent in 2013 (est.). In addition, The Russian Economic Development Ministry reduced its growth forecast to 2.5 percent through 2030 which is down from its previous forecast of 4 to 4.2 percent.[30]

### Mixed Economic System

A mixed economy is an economic system that allows for the simultaneous operation of publicly and privately owned enterprises. Mixed economies combine the purest forms of the market system and the centrally planned system. Countries such as Cuba are typically defined by economists as centrally planned systems, which could be considered a mixed economic system, as characteristics from both planned and market systems contribute to its makeup. Hong Kong, while being considered closely resembling a free market system, should technically be classified as a mixed system because both planned and market system characteristics are a part of its functionality.

## Classification of Nations

The United Nations, the World Bank, the International Monetary Fund (IMF), and the Central Intelligence Agency (CIA) have developed classifications for all nations. These organizations have broken the classification of nations into three distinct groups: developed, newly industrialized, and developing. Of the 193 nations currently in existence, developing countries make up one-third of this number.

### Developed Nations

A developed nation is a nation that has great wealth and resources as well as the knowledge to properly manage its resources to take care of the well being of its people. Developed nations have a high per capita income. Industrialized countries and First World countries are also used to refer to developed nations. A United Nations Human Development Index score of 0.8 or higher would indicate that a nation is developed.

The 2013 Human Development Report classify the following nations, listed alphabetically, as developed:[31]

- Andorra
- Argentina
- Australia
- Austria
- Barbados
- Belgium
- Brunei Darussalam
- Canada
- Chile
- Croatia
- Cyprus
- Czech Republic
- Denmark
- Estonia
- Finland
- France
- Germany
- Greece
- Hong Kong, China
- Hungary
- Iceland
- Ireland
- Israel
- Italy
- Japan
- Korea( (Republic of)
- Latvia
- Liechtenstein
- Lithuania
- Luxembourg
- Malta
- Netherlands
- New Zealand
- Norway
- Poland
- Portugal
- Qatar
- Seychelles
- Singapore
- Slovakia
- Slovenia
- Spain
- Sweden
- Switzerland
- United Arab Emirates
- United Kingdom
- United States

### Newly Industrialized

According to the Organization for Economic Cooperation and Development (OECD), many formerly third world countries are entering into the arena of newly industrialized nations.[32] Mainly because of the technology boom of the last twenty-five years, many Asian countries, such as Hong Kong, Singapore, South Korea, and Taiwan have seen considerable economic growth. Many consider newly industrialized nations as those transitioning from the status of developing nations (sometimes referred to as "third world") to that of a developed nation. A regional variation of newly industrialized nations include Caribbean nations such as Barbados, Guyana, Jamaica, Trinidad, and Tobago where per capita incomes, access to healthcare, education, and technology are significantly greater than in regions such as Africa, Asia and Latin America.[33] Because tourists from around the globe can access these island nations, they are progressively becoming classified as industrialized or developed nations.

As technology improves and the movement of people between nations becomes blurred, more nations will transition from developing to the developed or newly industrialized category of nations.

### Developing

The United Nations and other global monitoring agencies classify nations with the lowest economic status as developing nations. Developing nations typically have a Human Development Index of less than 0.5 according to the Human Development Reports office.[34] Economists also consider developing nations third world nations where poverty and disease run rampant, education is nearly nonexistent, and life expectancy is very low. Approximately two-thirds of the world's population lives in developing countries as population growth is high versus the population growth of developed nations.

For decades governmental and nongovernmental agencies have attempted to help poverty-stricken nations move towards true development through various programs of financing, agricultural training, and basic-needs focus. Due to the high cost to sustain the programs, the agencies have not deemed the programs universally successful. Many experts believe the answer to truly developing third world nations is through the small business venue.[35] Small businesses have traditionally played a vital role in the success of developed nations, such as the United States, Japan, Israel, and the United Kingdom. In time small business could be the answer to developing impoverished nations. Several challenges exist in promoting small business in third world nations. The first challenge centers on the significant difference in economic data that is available in the developed countries, as opposed to developing countries. Although this information is becoming increasingly available for developing nations, it is still far short of the quantity of data available for a developing nation. The second challenge centers on the lack of consideration of current models of entrepreneurship development. The factors of success for entrepreneurial ventures in developing countries differ significantly from those faced in developed countries.[36] Small business development has always been a catalyst for improved employment and transforming agrarian economies. While obstacles such as lack of technology, obtaining financing, unskilled and uneducated workforce, lack of infrastructure, and price volatility are present in developing nations, small business development is crucial to developing economies.[37]

### Basic Issues in Economic Development

One way to properly analyze data in order to help develop solutions for economies that are newly industrialized (or in the developing stage) is the use of reliable economic data. Such data is often organized into meaningful categories, or indices. These indices provide indicators that can be used to forecast development trends. Such indicators include Gross National Product (GNP), Gross Domestic Product (GDP), Purchasing Power Parity (PPP) and the Human Development Index (HDI).

### National Production—GNP vs. GDP

Gross Domestic Product (GDP) is the total market value of all the goods and services produced within the borders of a nation during a specified period. GDP is the more common measure of income and production for countries around the world. Gross National Product (GNP) is the total market value of all the goods and services produced by a nation during a specified period. GNP includes the income produced in other countries to GDP. GNP per person is often used as a measure of the welfare of the citizens of a country. Countries with higher GNP often score high on other measures of welfare, such as life expectancy. However, there are serious limitations to the usefulness of GNP as a measure of welfare. GNP does not take into account several key factors: (1) unpaid economic activity such as domestic work; (2) inputs used to produce the output; (3) movements in exchange rates; and (4) factors that may be important to quality of life, such as the quality of the environment (as distinct from the input value) and security from crime. Because of these limitations other measures such as Purchasing Power Parity and the Human Development Index should be used in any economic development analysis.

*Purchasing Power Parity (PPP)*

Purchasing Power Parity is based on the idea that changes in exchange rates should balance the price of a basket of traded goods in a foreign country. Once the foreign prices are converted to domestic currency at the exchange rate, the traded goods in the foreign country should roughly equal the price of the same basket in the domestic country.[38] The Big Mac Index is often used as an example for PPP in that the product is the same wherever you are in the world and involves several commodities such as agriculture, labor, advertising, real estate cost, and transportation. Suppose one purchases a Big Mac in the U.S. for $3 (USD) and a Big Mac in Great Britain for £2 (GBP). The exchange-rate Purchasing Power Parity is $3 (USD) to £2 (GBP). While PPP seems to make sense on the surface, this simplistic approach creates several problems:

- Even the most homogeneous goods have different degrees of quality

- Even products sold with the most rigorously controlled distribution will be different (e.g., the Big Mac)

- Even if two identical items were sold in two different places with one at a lower price, it would not make sense to buy the cheaper item and ship to the more expensive area (consider cost of shipping and distribution channels at arrival)[39]

*Human Development Index*

Understanding the Human Development Index (HDI) is essential to comprehend how various organizations including the United Nations, the World Trade Organization, and the World Bank classify nations. The HDI includes a number of human development indicators that provide a global assessment of country achievements in different areas of human development. The table on the following page shows the breakdown of nations and their HDI score. Nations with a score of 0.8 or higher are typically considered developed nations. Nations with a score of 0.5 or lower indicate developing nations while nations who score in the range of 0.5 and 0.8 characterize newly industrialized nations. The 2012 HDI is provided on the next page as an example.[40]

# INTERNATIONAL BUSINESS RISK

Knowledge of the political and economic environments of international business can empower the global business professional in their pursuit of global markets. From a practical perspective, this knowledge is valuable in terms of assessing and confronting the numerous risks associated with doing business overseas. Operating a domestic-only business can have many risks. Due to the increased complexity, engaging in global business has more and greater levels of risk that must be identified and managed for success.

Global business risk is any worldwide factor outside the laws of supply and demand that could impact the success or failure of any venture moving into the international arena.[41] The three types of risk for global international business are ownership risk, operation risk, and transfer risk.

**NOTES**

| HDI rank | Human development index (HDI) value 2012 | Life expectancy at birth (years) 2012 | Gross National Income (GNI) per capita 2012 | Mean years of schooling 2010 |
|---|---|---|---|---|
| **High Human Development** | | | | |
| 1 Norway | 0.955 | 81.3 | 48,688 | 12.6 |
| 2 Australia | 0.938 | 82.0 | 34,340 | 12.0 |
| 3 United States | 0.937 | 78.7 | 43,480 | 13.3 |
| 4 Netherlands | 0.921 | 80.8 | 37,282 | 11.6 |
| 5 Germany | 0.92 | 80.6 | 35,431 | 12.2 |
| 6 New Zealand | 0.919 | 80.8 | 24,358 | 12.5 |
| 7 Ireland | 0.916 | 80.7 | 28,671 | 11.6 |
| 7 Sweden | 0.916 | 81.6 | 36,143 | 11.7 |
| 9 Switzerland | 0.913 | 82.5 | 40,527 | 11.0 |
| 10 Japan | 0.912 | 83.6 | 32,545 | 11.6 |
| 11 Canada | 0.911 | 81.1 | 35,369 | 12.3 |
| 12 Korea (Republic of) | 0.909 | 80.7 | 28,231 | 11.6 |
| 13 Hong Kong, China | 0.906 | 83.0 | 45,598 | 10.0 |
| 13 Iceland | 0.906 | 81.9 | 29,176 | 10.4 |
| 15 Denmark | 0.901 | 79.0 | 33,518 | 11.4 |

*Ownership Risk*

Ownership risk ranges from property title uncertainty, property line encroachment, squatting, and even government expropriations, such as capital levies and unexpected export or excise taxes.[42] Ownership risk may be categorized as follows: (1) the risk of a claim from a previously dispossessed owner, and (2) the risk that the current owner will be dispossessed.

*Operation Risk*

Operation risk appears to be one of the main risks that companies can actually do something about. Operation risk is defined by the Bank for International Settlement (BIS) as "the risk of loss resulting from inadequate or failed internal process, people and systems or from external events."[43] Operation risk can include differences in language, cultures, accounting methods, and data entry between different branches of a company located across the globe.

*Transfer Risk*

Transfer risk occurs when debtors in a country are unable to ensure timely payments of foreign currency debt service. This is due to either transfer or exchange restrictions or a general lack of foreign currency.[44] Transfer risk can range from governmental regulations that restrict the flow of dollars to governments taking over funds or industries to civil disturbances that make it impossible for borrowers or lenders to make wire transfers or send mail.

## Sources of Risk

The findings of a survey of international risk managers by the Economist Intelligence Unit, indicates that the most significant issues facing business are reputation risk (defined as the threat of any event that can damage a company's reputation), regulatory risk (defined as problems caused by new or existing regulations), and IT network risk, which encompasses network security breaches and IT systems failure. These are perceived as more significant issues than market risk, foreign exchange risk, and country risk. Other categories of risk that typically have high exposure in the media, such as terrorism and natural hazard risk (e.g., earthquakes or hurricanes), received negative scores in the survey, indicating that they are a low or very low priority for most risk managers in the survey.

"The focus for risk managers is shifting from financial risk to less understood areas, with reputation and regulatory issues topping their list of priorities," says Daniel Franklin, editorial director of the Economist Intelligence Unit. "By regularly tracking changes in the risk environment, the Risk Barometer will help risk professionals understand how their peers are responding to these new trends and challenges."[45]

Global-business risk has many sources: corruption and bribery, unstable political systems, excess involvement of military or religious leaders in government, internal conflict among ethnic and religious groups, and unstable relations with other nations. Astute business professionals should always monitor any threat to the success of their business.

NOTES

### Corruption and Bribery

"Corruption is the misuse of public power for private profit or political gain—represents a hazard to free trade and investment, a threat to democracy and development, and, in collusion with international crime, a danger to national security."[46] The Organization for Economic Cooperation and Development (OECD), the World Trade Organization, the World Bank, and the International Monetary Fund have all indicated that corruption is the greatest single barrier to economic development worldwide.[47] Two things have contributed to global business corruption over the past twenty years: the end of the Cold War and the explosion of democracy and markets.[48] As more economies move from planned economies to market economies, each society must confront the specter of corruption. A bribe is "an inducement that influences a public official to perform his/her duties in a manner contrary to the course that would otherwise be adopted."[49] International bribery is disguised in various forms and hinders global, economic development, disrupting the flow of distribution channels, destroying any incentives to compete solely on quality and price, distorting market efficiency and predictability, and eventually denying people the right to a fair standard of living.[50]

### Unstable Political System

Because of political unrest in the countries of Eastern Europe, the Middle East, Latin America, Africa, and Southeast Asia, many companies looking to enter or expand in the international arena are not willing to commit resources to these and other similarly afflicted areas of the world. Companies cannot afford even the smallest of investments to risk a potential overnight change in a political regime that would force new laws and regulations upon the management of a new international venture. Before entering the market of any foreign country, businesses must properly investigate and analyze the political climate to assure themselves of no threats from political instability.

### Excess Involvement of Military or Religious Leaders in Governments

Because historians have only recorded three-hundred war-free years, a good look at the military status of a country would be an important consideration before establishing a business in a foreign country. Even though civilian regimes have become powerful and effective in many Latin American countries, a number of these countries, such as Columbia, Ecuador, and Venezuela, are still heavily influenced by military leaders.[51] Amid the influence of military leaders in Latin America, countries such as Argentina, Chile, Brazil, and Uruguay are thriving economically from less military control.[52] Whether the influence is in the U.S., the Middle East, or India, religious leaders play a very powerful part in the economic success of any country. The Saudi Arabian government has recently faced challenges in attempting to open its economy—a result of Islamic leadership on the Saudi Arabian government and economy for generations.[53] As its population continues to grow and economic growth remains flat, Saudi Arabia is more willing to invite new markets into its economy. As foreign influence arrives with the new markets the traditional rule of Islamic leaders in the school systems, government agencies, and judicial systems may need to be adjusted to accommodate economic growth.[54] Any company considering moving into a foreign economic market must consider the powerful influence of the military and religious leadership.

## Internal Conflict among Ethnic and Religious Groups

Religious beliefs among ethnic groups have always been a source of internal conflict in countries around the world. This conflict frequently arises when one ethnic group wants to ethnically cleanse its country from another ethnic group. After the end of the Cold War in the early 1990s, Bosnia experienced civil war because the Bosniaks (Muslims), the Serbs (Eastern Orthodox Christians), and the Croats (Roman Catholics) had differing opinions as to the establishment of Bosnia as a state.[55] The Serbs and Croats wanted to partition Bosnia and establish ethnically pure states; however, the Bosniaks were seeking a unified multiethnic Bosnia.[56] The war ended in 1995 with the Dayton Agreement, establishing Bosnia as a multiethnic state; nevertheless, the tragic consequences of this ethnic religious conflict still exist today.[57]

## Unstable Relations with Other Nations

Relations among nations appear to be an extension of ethnic religious group conflicts that have crossed borders and involve two or more nations. Usually, when two nations are in conflict, a heightened sense of alarm extends around the globe, negatively impacting the global economy. When terrorists destroyed the World Trade Center in New York in 2001, the stock market, as well as the U.S. economy, suffered The ripple effect was felt on economies around the world. Although no one can predict unstable relations among nations, astute business managers must be aware of and prepared for the risk.

### Causes of Risk

Many sources of risk are associated with conducting domestic business. This is amplified with international business because of added pressures caused by sovereign governments, geography, and culture. The successful global business professional identifies the potential risks, assesses the potential profits, and puts the appropriate risk mitigation tools into place. A number of causes of risk are associated with international transactions including violence and conflict, terrorism and kidnapping, confiscation, expropriation, and nationalism. Understanding the causes of global business risk helps managers properly address risk before it becomes detrimental to the success of the organization.

## Violence and Conflict

Violence and conflict in overseas markets can occur at a moment's notice, disrupting business operations for anyone involved in global trade. Companies can experience violence and conflict, resulting from foreign governments and third parties, potentially leading to forced shutdowns, relocations, and other unforeseen expenses. The origin of the conflict and violence could be legislative, executive, judicial, popular revolt, or various combinations of these factors. In formulating a definition of country risk the difference between risk and uncertainty is paramount. Uncertainty is an unknown chance that an event will occur.

## Terrorism and Kidnapping

Terrorist acts in modern times have impacted the global business environment by temporarily disrupting economic gain and the pursuit of capitalism. At the same time these acts have backfired on those against free-market economies, as an entire industry

NOTES

has emerged that is devoted to antiterrorism. In addition, "thanks to good economic crisis management (monetary and fiscal policy adjustments) including international cooperation, the short-term adverse economic impact of the September 11 attacks was far less serious than initially feared."[58] The U.S. economy bounced back as the strength of capitalism proved to be more resilient than the terrorists who were willing to destroy innocent people.

Kidnapping is another action that increases global business risk, and protection from this action has emerged as a reality of doing business in a global economy.[59] The problem can be compounded when managers do not know how to handle the risk of employee kidnapping. Expatriates and those working overseas should be aware of the following protective measures:

1. Avoid any country that has potential for this kind of behavior.

2. Plan for it to occur if you must do business in a hostile country, and be sure to have an extraction plan in place.

3. Communicate and develop relationships inside and outside the company and continue to communicate after an incident occurs.[60]

Terrorism, kidnapping, and extortion are all common occurrences around the world. The best way to handle them is to be prepared.

### Confiscation, Expropriation, and Nationalism

A mutual mistrust exists between international companies and the government of hostile foreign countries in which they enter.[61] From the perspective of the company, this mistrust is based on government actions, such as the rise of confiscation, expropriation, and nationalization. These have become a great concern for the business community.[62] Confiscation is the seizure of private property for the public treasury. Expropriation is to deprive of possession: a government could take away a private business from its owner. Nationalism converts ownership from private to governmental control.

## **KEY CONCEPTS**

- Administrative delays
- Cause and effect risk factors in global business
- Central, market, and mixed economic systems
- Common, civil, and theocratic law
- Developed, newly industrialized, and developing nations
- Export financing
- Foreign trade zones
- GNP vs. GDP
- Human development index
- Import/export subsidies
- Individual vs. collectivist economic values across nations
- Industrial property rights across nations

- Intellectual property rights across nations
- Local content requirements
- Methods of imposing economic sanctions
- Ownership, operation, and transfer risk
- Purchasing power parity
- Sources of risk in global business
- Special government agencies for international trade
- Standardization of international law
- Tariffs, quotas, embargoes
- Why governments intervene in global trade

# Chapter 3 Exercises: Observational Analysis

*Ponder on the following key concepts and ideas as you read the chapter.*

1. Consider the political issues impacting global business: how governments intervene in global trade, what actions they do to promote trade, and why trade is important to nations, businesses, consumers, and workers.

2. Analyze the types of laws used across nations that help govern and handle people and business. The need to form a set of standardized international laws due to the increase and spread of globalization. The importance of protecting property rights in order to promote global trade.

3. The types of economic systems, classification of nations, and the basic issues in economic development. The impacts and effects of global business risk and their effect on global trade and international business success.

4. Start a list of books, journals, and scholarly websites that would aid in the understanding of the chapter's main concepts and ideas. Start a journal for your own thoughts and ideas. What outside sources support your conclusions?

# Chapter 3 Exercises: Key Terms Analysis

*Match the answers by writing the correct letter in the space provided*

——— 1. Ownership Risk

——— 2. Developed Nation

——— 3. Mixed Economy

——— 4. Common Law

——— 5. WTO

——— 6. Centrally planned economy

——— 7. Local content requirement

——— 8. Civil law

——— 9. Human Development Index (HDI)

——— 10. Quotas

——— 11. Transfer Risk

——— 12. Big Mac Index

——— 13. Developing nation

——— 14. Administrative delays

——— 15. Gross domestic product (GDP)

——— 16. Buyer's credit

——— 17. Theocratic law

——— 18. Protectionism

——— 19. Supplier's credit

——— 20. Industrial property

A. Created to monitor trade around the world

B. System that allows for the simultaneous operation of public/private owned enterprises

C. Comprehensive control/regulation by a government in accordance with the plan of economic development

D. Is the predominant system of law in the world

E. Lowest Economic Status; HDI less than 0.5

F. Closely associated with long-term loans

G. Quantitative restrictions

H. A nation reducing number of imports it receives

I. Used as an example of PPP in that a product is the same wherever you are in the world

J. Total market value of goods/services produced within a nation in a year

K. Risk of a claim from a previously disposed owner and risk that the current owner will be disposed

L. Impose a waiting period between the determination of a product's quality and when it can be sold

M. Governments block open trade within a country's borders

N. Loan: exporter is covered; value of cover<contract value

O. Refers to laws which are derived from religion

P. Greatest wealth and resources; HDI of 0.8 or higher

Q. Occurs when debtors in a county are unable to ensure timely payments

R. Patents and Trademarks

S. Used as a means of compensating someone for wrongful acts known as torts

T. Assessment of nations based upon certain achievements

# Chapter 3 Exercises: Theoretical Analysis

*Analyze the questions and select the answer based on the reading of the chapter material*

1.  Nations that primarily functioned under the centrally planned economic system prior to the 1980s, such as China and Russia, have embraced the market economy.

    a.  True

    b.  False

2.  Global business risk is any worldwide factor—outside the laws of supply and demand—that could impact the success or failure of any venture moving into the international arena.

    a.  True

    b.  False

3.  _____ imposes a waiting period between the determination of a product's quality and the determination of when it can actually be sold in a market

    a.  Local content requirements

    b.  Tariff

    c.  Currency controls

    d.  Administrative delays

4.  Which type of risk do managers have some control over?

    a.  Organizational

    b.  Operational

    c.  Transfer

    d.  Ownership

5.  Operation risk occurs when debtors in a country are unable to ensure timely payments of foreign currency debt service because of either transfer or exchange restrictions or a general lack of foreign currency.

    a.  True

    b.  False

6.  The WTO was designed to

    a.  Stimulate economic opportunities for U.S. businesses and their employees.

    b.  Monitor trade around the entire world

    c.  To promote regional trade

    d.  Develop international monetary standards

7.  The Organization for Economic Cooperation and Development (OECD), the World Trade Organization, the World Bank, and the International Monetary Fund have all indicated that unstable political systems are the greatest single barrier to economic development worldwide.

    a.  True

    b.  False

8. Which of the following is an economic trade sanctions against targeted foreign countries, groups, organizations, and individuals, which can be politically, economically, or morally motivated?

    a. Tariffs

    b. Quotas

    c. Embargoes

    d. Foreign Trade Zones

9. Any company considering moving into a foreign economic market must consider the powerful influence of the military and religious leadership.

    a. True

    b. False

10. Political issues that significantly impact global business include

    a. Government prevention of trade

    b. Government control of trade

    c. Government restriction of trade

    d. None of the above

11. Which of the following is NOT a way that Governments promote trade?

    a. Special government agencies

    b. Subsidies

    c. Import Financing

    d. Foreign Trade Zones

12. _____ are special privileges offered by the government in order to attract businesses to a region or to provide them with the funding to operate successfully.

    a. Subsidies

    b. Bribes

    c. FTZs

    d. Tariffs

13. Which of the following is designed to raise revenue for governments and provide a competitive advantage for domestic businesses?

    a. Tariffs

    b. Quotas

    c. Embargoes

    d. Foreign Trade Zones

14. Cultures such as China, North Korea, and Cuba believe that an economic value system should be founded on cumulative efforts, controlled by greater entities or governments.

    a. True

    b. False

15. Which of the following are designated areas in Customs Ports of Entry that allow commercial merchandise to receive the same customs treatment it would receive if it were outside the commerce of the United States.

    a. Tariffs

    b. Quotas

    c. Embargoes

    d. Foreign Trade Zones

16. A market economy most often refers to an economic system that is under comprehensive control and regulation by a government, in accordance with the plan of economic development.

    a. True

    b. False

17. Supplier's credit is

    a. Loan in which the exporter is covered, but the value of the cover will be less than the value of the contract.

    b. Loan in which the importer is covered, but the value of the cover will be less than the value of the contract.

    c. Loan in which the exporter is covered, but the value of the cover will be more than the value of the contract.

    d. Loan in which the importer is covered, but the value of the cover will be more than the value of the contract.

18. Quotas typically

    a. Decrease the price of imports, increase the volume of imports, and encourage demand for foreign made substitutes.

    b. Raise the price of imports, reduce the volume of imports, and encourage demand for domestically made substitutes.

    c. Raise the price of exports, reduce the volume of imports, and encourage demand for domestically made substitutes.

    d. Decrease the price of exports, reduce the volume of exports, and encourage demand for domestically made substitutes.

19. Which of the following is NOT a purpose behind embargoes?

    a. Protecting the assets of allies from hostile actions;

    b. Assuring that the assets of targets will be available to meet future claims.

    c. Increasing resources or technology

    d. Punishing a country or group for unacceptable behavior

20. The three types of global business risk include ownership, operational risk, and transfer risk.

    a. True

    b. False

21. Which of the following are types of risk companies are exposed to in International transactions?

    a.  Violence and Conflict

    b.  Terrorism and Kidnapping

    c.  Confiscation and expropriation

    d.  All of the above

22. In 1975, as business and policy makers' alike saw the potential growth of global business, the World Trade Organization (WTO) was created by several countries in order to monitor trade around the entire world.

    a.  True

    b.  False

23. Which of the following places power in the hands of customs officials?

    a.  Tariffs

    b.  Quotas

    c.  Embargoes

    d.  Foreign Trade Zones

24. The U.S. Department of Commerce developed the International Trade Administration (ITA) in order to stimulate economic opportunities for U.S. businesses and their employees.

    a.  True

    b.  False

25. The United States Department of the Treasury oversees and enforces all U.S. economic sanctions through the Office of Foreign Assets Control (OFAC).

    a.  True

    b.  False

# Chapter 3 Exercises: Practical Analysis

*Write a short essay in the space provided to each of the following questions.*
*Please use outside references for each answer to support your ideas and thoughts.*

1. The World Trade Organization (WTO) is an international organization created to help deal with trade and trading rules between nations. The WTO intention is to promote trade that is free and prosperous and that promotes an economic world that is peaceful and accountable. Conduct an internet search on the World Trade Organization; based on your research:

   a. How does the WTO help to promote trade relations and communications between nations? Do they do an effective job of monitoring and effectively negotiating and sorting out trade problems between member nations?

   b. Does the WTO necessarily help the conduct of business while at the same time help governments effectively deal with social and environmental objectives and issues? Explain your answer.

2. Each nation has its own distinct set of laws to govern its people. This aspect makes it very difficult when trying to effectively form a set of standardized international laws for each nation to abide by, especially with the growing aspect of globalization.

   a. Give an example of each type of law that a country uses to govern its people. How are these laws useful for international trade and growth? What challenges do they present?

   b. Conduct an Internet search on international property rights or intellectual property. Give some examples of property rights that are unique and difficult to control on an international basis? How do property rights help promote or hinder global trade? How has the WTO helped to deal with the problems of property rights? Is their system adequate in dealing with the problem?

3. Each corporation or nation is going to face much global business risk when interacting on an international or global scale; Global business risk can impact the success or failure of any venture that is entering the global arena.

   a. What are the three types of risk for global international business and give a brief description of what it means and the risk associated with it. How and why is it important to understand each aspect of risk when operating on a global level?

   b. List some sources and causes of global business risk. Though it is impossible to eradicate global business risk, what would be some helpful and useful ways to monitor, assess, and possibly mitigate Global Business Risk?

   c. What could be done on a national, organizational, or corporate level to help with some of sources and causes of global business risk?

# Chapter 3 Exercises: Biblical Worldview Application

*Write a short essay in the space provided to each of the following questions.*
*Please use biblical references and research, where applicable, to support your ideas and thoughts.*

1. Matthew 22:36-40 states, *"Teacher, which is the greatest commandment in the Law?" Jesus replied: "'Love the Lord your God with all your heart and with all your soul and with all your mind.' This is the first and greatest commandment. And the second is like it: 'Love your neighbor as yourself.' All the Law and the Prophets hang on these two commandments."* What would be the implications for nations to follow the above, when considering tariffs, quotas, and embargoes? Write a short essay for each consideration.

2. Psalm 24:1 states: *"A Psalm of David. The earth is the LORD'S, and all it contains, The world, and those who dwell in it".* 1 Corinthians 10:26 states: *"... for, "The earth is the Lord's, and everything in it."* Job 41:11 states: *"Who has a claim against me that I must pay? Everything under heaven belongs to me."* Consider the above scriptures and write a short essay on the biblical worldview response to ownership, operation, and transfer risk. Give equal response to each type of risk.

3. Ecclesiastes 11:11 states: *"Cast your bread on the surface of the waters, for you will find it after many days."* As mentioned in the text, Solomon was deeply involved in cross-border commerce. Consider the trade of grain. When the Israelites would trade their grain with other nations, they were essentially "casting [their] bread upon the water." But notice that with Solomon, the word is plural: "cast your bread on the waters."

    a. Write a short essay explaining the implications from a business perspective regarding diversification of money, assets, and investments of "casting you bread upon the waters"?

    b. Write a short essay on the biblical worldview response to dealing with business risk within the context of cross-border commerce. What are some proper ways to approach business risk while at the same time being responsible with investments? How is being responsible with investments different than a business gamble since both involve the risk of losing?

# International Trade
# and Investment

NOTES

# CHAPTER OVERVIEW

International Trade and Investment is the trading of goods, services, or funding that crosses international borders. Funding may be in the form of Foreign Direct Investment (FDI), the amount invested in property, equipment, or services capability in a foreign country. The expansion of international trade and investment in the last half century has helped to create a global economy, affording increased opportunity to investors and manufacturers, both foreign and domestic.[1]

A primary indicator of a nation's status, in terms of international trade, is its balance of payments. The national balance of payments is a gauge to track the coming and going of international trade dollars. The ideal is that a nation's net income from trade in goods and services would be positive. A nation's capital account defines the net change in foreign ownership of domestic and foreign assets and records the purchase and sale of domestic and foreign assets. Governments attempt to attract foreign direct investment and promote those industries that will use national endowments most intensely, increasing a nation's competitiveness and the competitiveness of the region for FDI. Therefore, the global business professional has a keen awareness of the benefits of international trade and knowledge of international trade patterns.

# THEORETICAL FOUNDATIONS

International trade and investment theory can be used to forecast levels and consequences of export and import activities within specific economic, geographic, and political circumstances. This allows for the prediction and prescription concerning the content, direction, and size of international trade flows. The history of modern economic theory can be traced to the sixteenth century, emerging at approximately the same time as the modern nation-state. Early economic theory, though later debunked by Adam Smith and others, likely facilitated the drive for growth and expansion of nation-states worldwide for the next three-hundred years. The historical development of international trade and investment theory serves as a framework for understanding global trade patterns and the underlying reasons for the growth of trade between nations. The following sections of this chapter will trace the major international trade theories from mercantilism to new trade theory.

### Pre-Industrial Revolution—Mercantilism

Mercantilism was the prevailing thought in terms of international trade theory during the Pre-Industrial Revolution period. Although mercantilism does not meet the above criteria established for a trade theory, many consider it can be considered an economic policy whereby governments accumulate wealth in the form of gold bullion. The gold is then used in efforts to control the domestic economy, invest in other wealth-building enterprises, and expand into other global markets. Mercantilism was a typical idea during the era of nation building, which preceded the Industrial Revolution. Mercantilism allowed the development of the notion that the principal source of wealth was global trade, thus shifting European political power from feudal lords and the church to national sovereigns.

The trade-policy implication of this concept was the generation of a national trade surplus paid for by accumulation of gold reserves. Before fully developed financial systems, international credit was scarce. Therefore, a current-account surplus was not matched by net capital outflow (net loans or investment overseas); rather, it was matched by a net inflow of gold to pay for the excess of goods exported from the country. Some of this gold found its way to overseas investment by the ruling monarch. Mercantilism, as a national economic policy, collapsed because nations cannot export without another nation's willingness to import.[2] The United States Declaration of Independence in 1776 listed the "cutting off our trade with all parts of the world" as one of the reasons for declaring a separation from Britain.[3] These actions of Great Britain's King George were no doubt a reflection of the then waning economies of mercantilism. It is no coincidence that the founders of the United States of America were clearly influenced by the new economic theories of the eighteenth century, specifically Adam Smith's Absolute Advantage.

### Absolute Advantage Theory

A nation is said to have an absolute advantage when it is able to produce more output than any other nation. In order to achieve an economic advantage, a nation should specialize, produce, and export only those products where the nation holds an absolute advantage. Adam Smith first proposed the theory of absolute advantage in his *An Inquiry into the Nature and Causes of the Wealth of Nations* (1776) by pointing out that an individual would not make anything that would cost him less to buy. A farmer would not spend a whole day sewing a pair of pants when he could buy a pair of pants from the tailor with only a half day's worth of corn (his farm output). Absolute Advantage Theory says that the farmer should specialize where he has an advantage—in this case corn—and the corn output will "buy" more of other goods, where the farmer does not have a production advantage:

> What is prudence in the conduct of every private family can scarce be folly in that of a great kingdom. If a foreign country can supply us with a commodity cheaper than we ourselves can make it, better buy it of them with some part of the produce of our own industry employed in a way in which we have some advantage. . . . According to the supposition, that commodity could be purchased from foreign countries cheaper than it can be made at home. It could, therefore, have been purchased with a part only of the commodities, or what is the same thing, with a part only of the price of the commodities.[4]

Any domestic resource that a nation can buy at a lower price than it would cost to produce domestically should be purchased and not produced. Smith proposed that nations should specialize to increase overall output and productivity, and his theory altered economic thought sufficient to promote the concept that governments should allow free trade and efficient allocation of resources. This would raise the general welfare and standard of living of trading nations.

### Comparative Advantage Theory

Adam Smith's Theory of Absolute Advantage served to demonstrate the benefit of nations specializing in producing outputs where it had an absolute advantage over all other nations. However, the theory was too simplistic. Nations can benefit from trade even when one trading partner does not have an absolute advantage on any of the products being traded. Thus, there was a need for a somewhat more sophisticated international trade theory. David Ricardo developed this when he proposed the Theory of Comparative Advantage in his 1817 work *On the Principles of Political Economy and Taxation.*[5]

In an effort to demonstrate Ricardo's theory, one should consider the possibility of trade that exists between a lawyer and an automotive mechanic. Both the lawyer and the mechanic are capable of performing automotive repairs or writing a will. In fact, the lawyer once worked as a mechanic and was exceptionally efficient in that trade. From the table below,

| | Time Required | |
|---|---|---|
| | **Repair Car** | **Write a Will** |
| Lawyer | 2 | 3 |
| Mechanic | 3 | 15 |

suppose each task requires a different length of time to complete, and that the lawyer, because of his proficiency in the trade, has an absolute advantage over the auto mechanic in terms of hours (or units of time) required to complete each task.

To know whether the lawyer should repair his own car, or in order for the mechanic to know if he should write his own will, each must consider the opportunity cost and the cost of the object. Opportunity cost is the value of what had to be given up, or foregone, to consume or achieve the object. The table below presents the opportunity cost for the lawyer and the mechanic.

| | Opportunity Cost To: | |
|---|---|---|
| | **Fix Car** | **Write a Will** |
| (@ $100 / Hr) Lawyer | $200 | $300 |
| (@ $30 / Hr) Mechanic | $90 | $450 |

The lawyer has absolute advantage in fixing the car and writing a will in terms of hours (or units of time) and has opportunity costs of $200 and $300 respectively for these tasks. The mechanic has an opportunity cost of $90 and $450 respectively. If the lawyer chooses to repair his own car, he would not be able to earn money as a lawyer while repairing the car, and thus he would forego $200 (2 hours at $100) in lawyer revenue. This example represents the lawyer's opportunity cost to perform the repair. If the mechanic chooses to write his own will, he will forego $450 dollars in mechanic revenue (15 hours at $30 per hour) while writing the will.

The lawyer and mechanic easily make the best decision once they know their opportunity cost. Though the mechanic does not have an absolute advantage in either repairing the car or writing a will, he does have a relative advantage when fixing the car—in that his disadvantage is the least with this task. Both lawyer and mechanic would be better off working in their specialty and buying the services that they do not specialize in. To conclude, the mechanic saves $150 ($450 opportunity cost MINUS $300 lawyer fee) by paying the lawyer to write the will, and the lawyer saves $110 ($200 opportunity cost MINUS $90 mechanic fee) by paying the mechanic to fix the car.

The following is a direct application of Ricardo's Comparative Advantage theory to international trade. Ricardo provided the example of England and Portugal to clarify his theory. Specifically, both nations were compared in terms of the production of two commodities (cloth and wine), with labor being the only input of production. Ricardo assumed productivity of labor—defined as the quantity of output produced per worker—to be varied between industries and both nations. While Adam Smith's theory assumed that England would be more productive in producing one good and Portugal in producing the other, Ricardo's theory assumed that Portugal would be more productive in both goods.

Consider the following tables to help explain David Ricardo's Theory of Comparative Advantage. The first table shows that Portugal can produce both wheat and wine more cheaply than England—it has an absolute advantage in both commodities. Ricardo noted that it could still be mutually beneficial for both countries to specialize and trade. A unit of wine in England costs the same amount to produce as 2 units of wheat. Production of an extra unit of wine means foregoing production of 2 units of wheat. In other words, the opportunity cost of a unit of wine is 2 units of wheat. In Portugal, a unit of wine costs 1.5 units of wheat to produce; therefore, the opportunity cost of a unit of wine is 1.5 units of wheat. Some might wonder why it would be mutually advantageous for both countries to trade, even though Portugal has an absolute advantage in both commodities. The answer lies in the difference between the relative or comparative costs for each nation would be improved if trading occurs.

| Cost per Unit in Man-Hours | | |
|---|---|---|
| | **Wheat** | **Wine** |
| England | 15 | 30 |
| Portugal | 10 | 15 |

Because Portugal is relatively better at producing wine than wheat, it has a comparative advantage in the production of wine. England is relatively better at producing wheat than wine, thus it has a comparative advantage in the production of wheat.

The second table (see below) provides the example of how trade may be advantageous, according to Ricardo's theory. This table makes the following assumptions:

- England has 270 man hours available for production. Before trade takes place, it produces and consumes 8 units of wheat and 5 units of wine.
- Portugal, having fewer labor resources, has 180 man hours of labor available for production. Before trade takes place, it produces and consumes 9 units of wheat and 6 units of wine. Total production between the two economies is 17 units of wheat and 11 units of wine.

| Production Levels | | | | |
|---|---|---|---|---|
| | Before Trading | | After Trading | |
| | **Wheat** | **Wine** | **Wheat** | **Wine** |
| England | 8 | 5 | 18 | 0 |
| Portugal | 9 | 6 | 0 | 12 |
| **Total** | **17** | **11** | **18** | **12** |

If both countries specialize—Portugal producing only wine and England producing only wheat—total production is 18 units of wheat and 12 units of wine. Specialization has enabled the global economy to increase production by 1 unit of wheat and 1 unit of wine. In other words, the result of each nation specializing where they have a comparative advantage is a total gain in output from the same labor inputs. The standard of living in each nation would be improved if trading occurs.

Ricardo's theory is very simple and is based on the following assumptions:

- Transport costs are not considered.

- Costs are constant with no economies of scale.

- Only two nations are producing two goods.

- Traded goods are homogeneous – identical.

- No tariffs or other trade barriers are considered.

- Perfect knowledge exists – merchants and customers know where the least-cost goods are located.

NOTES

*Factor Proportions Theory*

The presupposition of Absolute Advantage and Comparative Advantage is that differences in productivity determine patterns of international trade. This, too, was a simplistic view of trade; therefore, the need for another, more sophisticated theory of trade arose. The sophistication lies in the idea that factor endowments, not differences in productivity, determine the patterns of trade. One of the first theories to address this issue was the Factor Proportions Model developed by two Swedish economists in the 1920s: Eli Heckscher and his student, Bertil Ohlin. The monograph "Interregional and International Trade" was published in 1933.[6]

Where the earlier theory of Comparative Advantage considers differences in productivity, the Factor Proportions Model considers also the dimensions of capital—equipment and machines—and the proportion—mix of technology and capital—along with the intensity that the factors of production are used. Technology in this context is the application of specialized knowledge to work. Factors of production include the following:

- Land—natural resources used in the production process, including timber, minerals and water resources

- Labor—physical and mental work (intelligence) brought to bear in the production of goods and services

- Capital—machinery and equipment, including facilities, used to manufacture and deliver products

The Factor Proportions Theory recognizes nations as having different amounts of capital and labor, called endowments, and the ratio of those labor to capital endowments. Nations endowed with abundant labor can produce agricultural products using labor-intensive methods, just as nations with abundant capital–using, capital-intensive methods can also abundantly produce agricultural products. Examples might include Canada, using capital-intensive agricultural methods, and India, using labor-intensive methods in the production of wheat. The Factor Proportions Theory, as a model of production, attempts to explain that nations will produce and export goods that use the highest proportion of those factors of production that are most abundant to a nation.[7] For example, Japan, as a nation with abundant capital, skilled labor, and little land, will be a heavy importer of raw materials and an exporter of capital-intensive products, which only a highly capable labor force could produce.

Comparative Advantage and Factor Proportions are the foundational concepts of the traditional or neoclassical theory of international trade. In simple terms neoclassical theory seeks to determine how one should proceed in trade if the goal was to maximize world production (the goods and services available to citizens of each country). This theory assumes that the (1) factors of production are immobile, (2) goods are mobile, and (3) technology is stable and ubiquitous. World production and the goods and services available to each country are thus maximized by using resources for the production of goods that face the lowest opportunity cost within each nation, trading locally unneeded products for other goods produced with the lowest opportunity cost for resources in other nations. The neoclassical theories provided the important theoretical frameworks for understanding international trade up until the 1950s, which ushered in the so-called "Space Age." New developments in technology and transportation required the formation of new theories to understand and predict emerging global trade patterns. The emerging theories assisted marketers to move beyond the previously predominant emphasis on production in their efforts to create and sustain competitive advantage across global markets.

## *International Product Life Cycle Theory*

Raymond Vernon developed and published the International Product Life Cycle Theory in 1966. Vernon's three-stage theory proposes that new products are first (stage one) invented and produced to satisfy a domestic, (local) high-income customer in a highly developed nation. Products are also manufactured with higher-cost, local labor. In stage two, a maturing product begins to saturate the domestic market, while exports are growing to meet demand in foreign markets of high-income customers. Production capacity is added in these foreign markets with both domestic and foreign production satisfying a local, high-income customer. In stage three, the product demand world wide has been steady enough that the producer, now facing low demand uncertainty and a need to maintain or increase profit, is able to make investment in specialized equipment, to take advantage of economies of scale, building what is now a standard product. An investment in specialized equipment allows the producer to now use cheaper low-skill labor, which is abundantly available in less developed nations. Production moves to a less developed nation, and the cycle is complete as highly developed nations become importers of this product.[8]

## *New Trade Theory*

New Trade Theory, introduced in 1979 by Paul Krugman, shifted economic thinking by proposing that certain industries should not be modeled using the perfect-competition assumption, frequently used in economic theory. Today, the World Trade Organization acknowledges this assumption, noting that where producers exist with high fixed costs, perfect competition will not be the result.[9] Krugman recognized that increasing returns to scale in certain industries would lead to a few firms engaging in competition, growing larger, and obtaining not constant, but increasing returns to scale. Nations that vigorously pursue the quick development of economies of scale in a given export may gain comparative advantage in that export. Such nations can produce the product more efficiently, relative to other products, than can their trading partners, but not necessarily due to factor endowments. It is due to the development of industry support such as skilled labor, specialized infrastructure, networks of suppliers, and localized technology. In this case governments play a major role in support of technology by crafting industry-specific measures, such as tax credits for research and development of new technologies and trade policies that support essential technology sectors.

The New Trade Theory Model demonstrated that in certain industries, government protections of an industry prove advantageous. The implications of New Trade Theory may suggest protecting the same "infant industries" of classical economics.

Michael Porter's, The Competitive Advantage of Nations (1990) proposed that the role of government is as an indirect determinant, equal with chance. Porter's Diamond has four determinants that indicate the level of competitiveness of a national industry—in addition to the two indirect determinants of Government and Chance. The relationship between the four determinants or Diamond (see figure on next page)[10] model a nation's competitive environment for an industry The determinants are (1) factor conditions, (2) demand conditions, (3) firm strategy, structure, and rivalry, and (4) related and supporting industry.[11]

NOTES

Factor conditions are not to be confused with factors of production, such as land, labor, and raw materials. Factor conditions refer to specialized or value-added factors that are developed because they do not naturally occur. Examples might include industry–specific, highly skilled people or processes of production that are the result of continuing industry investment. Demand conditions that increase the competitiveness of an industry are the result of demanding domestic customers that push, pull, and prod for innovation to occur. Satisfying demanding customers requires high-quality, innovative products. Firms in such a domestic industry are better prepared to meet the demands of customers in the global market. Factor Conditions and Demand Conditions are the horizontal components on Porter's Diamond model.

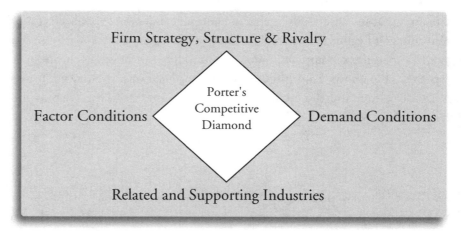

The interaction between the vertical components of rivalry and related and supporting industry drives a nation's national competitive advantage. The rivalry and related industry relationship stimulates a firm to achieve the capability necessary to take advantage of special factor conditions which are available in order to meet the expectations of demanding customers. As this occurs within an industry and on a national level, industry "clusters" in a geographic concentration increase the interactions represented in the Porter's Diamond and expand and transform the diamond into an interrelated system. Porter's Diamond provides a systematic explanation and guide for developing national competitiveness.

Global trading systems evolved in a parallel manner to the theoretical frameworks. The astute global business professional understands this parallel development and seeks to apply the theoretical to the practical. The next few sections of this chapter will discuss these global trading systems and how they interact in terms of Foreign Direct Investment and Balance of Payments.

## GLOBAL TRADING AND INVESTING SYSTEMS

A global trading system should be without discrimination, freer, predictable, more competitive, and more beneficial for less developed countries. Trading systems, by definition, consist of multilateral agreements between several, and sometimes many, nations. Trade agreements are negotiated, legal documents pertaining to all manner of trade between nations. As a result, these documents are very complex. Trade agreements are the foundation for a common understanding of the rules governing trade. These agreements guide the trading conduct of nations that may not have similar legal foundations or business customs.[12]

A guiding principle of the ideal global trading system is equality between trading partners, when partners do not prefer domestic products, services, people, or the products of their trading partners over others. When trade operates under standard rules, it is more predictable, free, and competitive—positively impacting the economies of all participants. When the rules encourage lesser-developed nations to produce and trade, they also facilitate participation in the global economy, increasing their economic prosperity—which would not have been likely without a trading system. Synthesizing the dictionary definitions of the term "system" provides a working definition for the modern global trading system: an interdependent group acting as a unified whole, following shared principles, performing activities to achieve a common goal.[13] The common goal is to increase the global economy and raise the standard of living for all people.

### *General Agreement on Tariffs and Trade (GATT)*

The historical development of GATT can be traced through the international trade theories, from mercantilism to new trade theory. Mercantilism posits a country could only gain at the expense of its rival, i.e., a country grew rich by the amount of gold that it amassed through the sale of domestic goods to foreigners and constraining the amount of foreign goods sold on the home market. Protection of the domestic market was the prime objective. Mercantilism gave way to the neoclassical theories of Adam Smith and David Ricardo. They argued that international trade could be a win-win proposition. This outcome was possible if each country specialized in producing and selling the goods that it could produce the most efficiently relative to another country. The flow of goods also had to be free and unregulated among and between countries. While the era of free trade had begun, protection of domestic markets was still important to national economies. The dawn of the twentieth century ushered in modern wars—most notably the two World Wars. International trade was severely disrupted as nations sought to secure and protect domestic industries from the economic ravages of war. At the conclusion of World War II, the Allies recognized that nations might be able to prevent war if they were allowed to trade freely. Such free trade would require nations to adapt standards of free trade, which provide the legal foundations for global trade and the need for a general agreement among participating nations.

The General Agreement on Tariffs and Trade (GATT) was signed on January 1, 1948. Originally created by the Bretton Woods Conference as part of a larger plan for economic recovery after World War II, its primary purpose was to reduce barriers to international trade. Representatives from twenty-three nations accepted what would later be considered the precursor to the World Trade Organization (WTO). This first attempt at setting international trade rules covered forty-five thousand tariffs and 20 percent of the world trade.[14] The goal of this conference was to create a body called the International Trade Organization, which the United Nations was to organize. Not wanting to jeopardize the work that had already been accomplished in the new agreement, the signatory nations accepted the GATT draft provisionally. Even though this agreement was accepted as provisional, it existed as an international trade agreement until 1995. The Uruguay Round and the Marrakesh Declaration followed which lead to the creation of the World Trade Organization.[15]

NOTES

## World Trade Organization (WTO)

Though the World Trade Organization (WTO) has officially existed since 1995, the foundation for the rules in this trading system originates in the GATT. Like the GATT, the WTO deals with the rules of trade between nations at a global or near-global level. Where the primary focus of GATT was trade in goods, the WTO agreements include intellectual property and trade in services. The WTO provides a forum for negotiation between members concerning the lowering or elimination of trade barriers, and freedom of trade. The WTO is not exclusively about lowering or reducing trade barriers, but "in some circumstances its rules support maintaining trade barriers—for example, to protect consumers or prevent the spread of disease."[16] The WTO encourages trading under the guiding principle of trading fairly by treating other nations equally under the concept of most-favored-nations (MFN) status. This discourages excessive import duties that act as trade barriers, though exceptions can be made to favor developing nations. WTO rules emphasize and promote expanding and increasing trade between nations.

The WTO encourages nations to practice the Golden Rule on a national level, pointing out that foreigners and foreign industries should be treated just like the locals and domestic industries. The WTO refers to this as extending the "national treatment," and the application of any WTO rule assumes that developing nations will change and comply increasingly with time.[17] Rules in the WTO system serve to provide stability by guiding the conduct of agents operating in the system and by helping members in the system know what to expect as they follow the rules. Trading partners should not expect hidden trade policies, quotas, and other trade barriers, knowing that quotas and import duties are allowed in limited and controlled situations—and usually when a less-developed nation is involved.[18]

## Foreign Direct Investment

As organizations become more involved in the global community, they may opt to purchase land or other resources in other nations. This activity, known as foreign direct investment (FDI), is commonly used to purchase real estate and existing properties. The idea is to buy physical assets or a significant amount of ownership of a firm in another nation to gain a measure of managerial control. While no standard percentage of ownership exists, most nations consider the threshold to be within the range of 10 to 25 percent. The U.S. Department of Commerce's FDI ownership threshold is 10 percent. In the event that the financial objective is not to gain a measure of managerial control, the investment is considered "portfolio investment." FDI typically takes two forms. The first, Greenfield Investment, involves the development of an entirely new operation in a foreign nation. The second entails acquiring or merging with an existing operation in a foreign nation. These forms of FDI allow the firm to achieve strategic goals, including (1) establishing a presence in a new geographic market, (2) creating and maintaining global competitiveness, (3) filling gaps in global product lines, and (4) reducing production and logistical costs.

*Why Companies Engage in FDI*

As companies become affluent, they begin looking globally for economic development potential. Additionally, they seek out foreign investment for a better value for their money in terms of labor or material costs. The trend of foreign companies making foreign direct investments in the U.S. is increasing. An example would be Canada, who attracted by U.S. technology firms, has sought to align itself with the creativity being generated in high-tech places, such as Silicon Valley. While FDI is a great enabler of international trade and competition fuels the U.S. economy, U.S. companies hesitate to join the increasing trend of FDI. The dramatic increase of foreign investment dollars in the United States has mixed results. Foreign dollars are good for U.S. companies looking to sell assets because the price of these assets will likely rise. However, U.S. companies looking to expand their businesses may see an increase in prices because of the increased competition brought on by FDI.[19]

Foreign Direct Investment can also take place by injecting marketing dollars into the economy of a given country. Companies that are looking to gain brand awareness have turned to international sporting events as a means of self-promotion. Hyundai, the Korean auto-manufacturer, made a foreign direct investment in Athens, Greece, during the 2004 summer Olympic Games. Hyundai promoted its brand heavily by providing cars, buses, and signage at facilities.[20] Their focus was not media coverage or the tourists attending the events, but on the Grecian market itself. Hyundai is currently the second best-selling brand in Greece, and the sponsorship was designed to solidify their grip on the Grecian auto market. By investing their marketing capital in Athens during the Olympics, Hyundai not only promoted their brand to millions but also strengthened their position in the market.

## GOVERNMENT'S ROLE IN INTERNATIONAL BUSINESS

Keeping track of the activity surrounding international trade and investment is done by maintaining a record of all international transactions, otherwise known as the balance of payments (BOP). The balance of payments is the sum of all monies that flow in and out of a given country including imports, exports, goods, services, and financial investments. Usually calculated on a yearly basis, the balance of payments acts as a gauge to track the coming and going of international trade dollars. In a perfect world the balance of payments accounting columns would cancel each other out. In theory each dollar given in trade for goods or services goes to some source in the country providing the goods. In terms of recording the balance of payments, if a country has received money it should be recorded as a credit. For example, a credit is placed in the U.S. balance of payments if Japan purchases wheat from the U.S. Reciprocally, if the U.S. purchases Japanese cars, a debit is shown in the U.S. balance of payments.

### *Components*

Similar to any accounting spreadsheet, the balance of payments is determined by measuring different factors to determine a result. The balance of payments for a country is the sum of the current account and the capital account. The current account is sometimes known as the financial account.

*Current Account*

The current account, sometimes called the financial account, is the sum of one country's net income from trade in goods and services. This includes what is known as net factor income, or interest payments from foreign debt, and also net unilateral transfers from abroad. Positive net income from abroad corresponds to a credit in the current account. Negative income from abroad corresponds to a debit in the current account. A current account surplus is usually associated with positive net exports because a country's exports are usually the largest source of income they will receive from abroad.

*Capital Account*

The capital account is the net change in foreign ownership of domestic assets. These assets can include liquid, real estate, stock, or intellectual property. If foreign ownership increases faster than domestic ownership, then the country is said to have a capital account surplus. Conversely, if domestic ownership of foreign assets increases faster than foreign ownership of domestic assets, then the country has a capital account deficit.

The capital account entity records the purchase and sale of domestic and foreign assets. The assets are separated into categories such as Foreign Direct Investment, Portfolio Investment that include stock and bond transactions, and Other Investment that include bank deposits and cash assets.

*The Issue of Surpluses and Deficits*

An inequity between the current account and the capital account will create a trade surplus or deficit depending upon whether the inequity is positive or negative. For example, a trade surplus will be generated if a nation's exports outweigh its imports. In contrast, a trade deficit will be generated if the imports outweigh the exports. Surpluses and deficits will affect the current account holdings, which affect the overall balance of trade. Assume for a moment that the current account was much like a personal checking account. In order to purchase goods or services, funds must be available in the checking account before the transaction will be successful. If, however, funds are not available the transaction can still occur if the consumer is willing to borrow the capital needed. Essentially, a trade deficit is created in the same way. If a nation wished to import goods or services (in excess of what it is exporting), it does so by borrowing the capital necessary, which creates a trade deficit in the current account. If the nation that financed the transaction invests the money in the trading nation's economy, then the deficit will again disappear.[21] Assuming that the financing nation did not reinvest the money in the borrowing nation's economy, the financing nation now has a surplus in the current account. In mathematical terms,

Exports – Imports = Savings – Investments

The equation represents the relationship between trade deficits and surpluses. For example, if a country wanted to reduce its trade deficit, it would need to reduce the disparity between its savings and investments. Several factors can affect the international BOP and either create or reduce surpluses and deficits. A few of these factors are detailed below:

- Prices of domestic goods—typically the prices are affected by the raw materials required to produce the final products. A low supply in any one raw material required in the production of a particular commodity will cause an inevitable need to increase the cost of the final product.

- Trade agreements (or lack of trade agreements)—if a nation has an international trade agreement to purchase a particular commodity from another nation, this agreement will affect the ability for a third party nation to successfully compete in that market; furthermore, if a nation has established a trade barrier against a particular nation, the capacities for exports have been curtailed.

- Taxes and Tariffs—if a nation chooses to impose heavy taxes or import tariffs on goods from another nation, the furnishing nation will likely reduce exports into that nation.[22]

While these are just a few examples of factors that affect surpluses and deficits, one can see that nearly everything that affects the import or export of goods can generate lasting economic effects for a nation. The final sections of this chapter will discuss how governments and businesses deal with these issues relating to global trade.

## Government and Global Management Issues in FDI

The relationship between government and multinational corporations can be mutually beneficial, promoting economic development and prosperity in the host country and business advantages for the multinational corporation. Successful FDI raises employment and the standard of living for nationals in the host county. From a business perspective a successful FDI can secure access to customers in the host nation and increase sales or access to lower cost resources that will lower production costs of goods, which will be exported from the host nation. Successful FDI can be a win-win situation for governments and business.

## Government Interventions

While governments do attempt to attract foreign direct investment with tax breaks, power subsidies, and reduced cost or no cost facilities, evidence shows that these incentives can be ineffective, bringing doubt about what most influences the location decision—incentives or adequate political stability and infrastructure.[23] After reviewing various FDI incentives, the WTO expressed the concern that it would be hard to make a case in support of investment incentives and that most of the world would be better off with limited use of them.[24] Though the result of intervention with incentives may be mixed, the government has a role concerning FDI. Government interventions, in the positive sense, can increase global competitiveness for their businesses, keep the balance of payments under control, and help acquire new technologies and managerial skills from foreign firms entering their markets. In a negative sense government interventions may promote protectionism.

### Increase Global Competitiveness

Government interventions may be used to increase global competitiveness. Nations have unique factors of production and unique proportions in the mix of technology and capital. The intensity of these national factors of production can be used to enhance cross-border trade. In other words governments seek to specialize in specific industries that will use national endowments most abundantly and intensely. Because a nation offers unique and valuable factors of production to certain industries, the nation will be competitive in attracting those industries and increasing competitiveness of the region for future FDI.

### Keep Balance of Payments under Control

Governments may intervene to keep the balance of payments under control. Prior to the mercantilism era, the balance of payments was not a major concern to nations. Commodities and currencies were allowed to flow without restriction. The primary concern for governments was tracking who controlled the gold. Since gold was the standard backing all currency, governments watched to ensure that potential threats did not control a large supply of the nation's gold, because a well-financed enemy posed a higher threat than one without proper financial backing. Hence, the term "war chest" was coined. If the "war chest" of a potential threat grew too large, then the government would be concerned. This idea gave way to mercantilism, one of the earliest economic theories, which sought to maintain a balance of payments of gold and silver in order to keep it out of the hands of the enemy.

Currently, the task of managing the balance of payments is primarily concerned with maintaining the surpluses and deficits owed to any nation for any commodity or currency that can be tracked. If a nation's surpluses far exceed its deficits, then the balance of payments is out of control, or more simply stated, out of balance. The same is true if the balance is reversed. Countries keep detailed accounts of the balance of payments and usually publish the findings at the end of each year. Nations should control the balance of payments so that deficits do not climb too high. This rise in deficits would indicate that a nation is merely paying (currency outflow) to other countries and not receiving investments in return (currency inflow).

### Acquire New Technologies and Managerial Skills from Foreign Firms Entering their Markets

Many countries today can benefit from the acquisition of new technologies and managerial skills from foreign firms. The acquisition of new technologies can be seen as a by-product of the international product life cycle. Although the international product life cycle theory does not describe acquiring new technology in this way, it remains a viable means for acquiring new technology. Most firms entering a foreign market try to send seasoned managers to the new market. These expatriates use their excellent management skills and know-how to train the managers and workers in the host countries.[25]

Technological change and economic development seem to go hand in hand in today's society. In an effort to stay competitive in the world market, nations have been pouring money into researching and developing new and advanced technologies. Nations can effectively tap into this resource for information by utilizing the management skills of foreigners operating in their country. In addition nations can extract the new and existing technologies from foreign firms and capitalize on an already existing technology, saving millions of dollars in research and testing. This investment also allows domestic companies to remain globally competitive in the technological arena.

### Protectionism—Restrictions in Ownership

Protectionism is the economic policy of restraining trade between nations. Methods to impose such restraints include high tariffs on imported goods, prohibitive quotas, restrictive government regulations on foreign imports and foreign ownership of domestic assets, and anti-dumping laws that are meant to protect domestic industry from foreign take over or competition. Protectionism contrasts free trade where such protective barriers are not used.

Nations use protectionism as a means of controlling foreign direct investment. For example China employs strict protectionism as a means of controlling foreign involvement in its economy. Censorship and restriction of certain business types are the norm in China. Recently the Chinese authorities have changed the rules on foreign investment in real estate. According to the China Daily the new restrictions require that in order to own property in China, a foreign business must have offices in China or have officers who have lived or worked in China for at least one year. There is also the added restriction that foreign business can only own land that they themselves are currently or immediately plan on using.[26] This example of protectionism is meant to slow the influx of western culture into China.[27]

In a historic sense protectionism is the economic policy of applying tariffs on imported goods for government funding to reduce or eliminate the need for taxation on domestic industries. One can view this traditional protectionism as a type of sales tax on foreign goods in order to relieve the need for taxation on domestic products. Some critics of protectionism say that this economic shelter of domestic industry ultimately hurts the economy by discouraging competition and allowing the weaker products to remain on the market. Opponents of protectionism say that by increasing the cost of imported goods through tariffs, the government instituting the barrier penalizes the sending country as well as the citizens it is trying to protect. Like many other issues, economic ideas are often tied to political ideologies.

### Business Managers

Issues for business managers may include degrees of ownership control, the need for "make or buy" decisions, consideration of labor and production costs, and seeking economic development incentives. Managers in large corporations may encounter international opportunities that require making a FDI decision. The United Nations Conference on Trade and Development defines FDI as investments outside the investor's home economy where the investor holds a 10 percent stake. The investment can be higher or lower, depending not necessarily on whether the investor has absolute control, but some level of influence over the foreign enterprise. The distinguishing characteristic between a portfolio of investments and a foreign direct investment is whether or not the investor's purpose in making the investment is to influence or control the target enterprise.[28] Business managers consider foreign direct investment in the effort to secure entry into nations with large markets for their goods and services. A business manager may also consider foreign investment to secure resources important to the production of domestic products, or in the case of services, access to knowledge and human resources.

*Ownership Control*

When considering FDI the most important consideration facing a corporation is the type of ownership and control the investing corporation will have over the foreign entity. While in the case of alliances and joint ventures, the degree of ownership and control may be lower—significant potential benefits exist that may not be possible otherwise. These benefits include access to markets where the government restricts foreign ownership in certain industries, the lower risk associated with having a local partner to navigate the political environment, or by not being considered an "outsider" by the market or government.

Ownership in foreign entities can be a complete or a controlling stake in the form of either a wholly owned subsidiary or through mergers and acquisitions of existing corporations. Some nations use ownership control as a way of protecting their most valuable industries. Mexico, for example, relies heavily on the tourism industry. The hundreds of miles of pristine beaches are some of its greatest natural resources. The Mexican government restricts any foreigner from owning land within 100 kilometers of the border or 50 kilometers of the coast. These areas are known as Restricted or Prohibited Zones, which are designed to protect Mexican's rights to these valuable resources. The loophole that allows for the giant hotels that line popular destinations like Cancun or Acapulco to be owned by foreigners is a fiduciary trust, known as a *Fidelicomiso*. This is similar to a U.S. beneficiary trust. The owners can be foreigners, but they must own the property through a corporation that is formed in Mexico. This protects Mexico's tax interest in the property.[29]

*Make or Buy Decisions*

If the goal is complete ownership in a foreign entity, the next business decision is to "make or buy." In the case of "buy," the investing corporation will seek an existing corporation in the target industry or market as a candidate for merger or acquisition. Frequently, the goal of having a wholly owned subsidiary leads management to make a Greenfield investment decision. Greenfield investments are investment in new assets. The Greenfield method is named literally from "green field," or what a grassy non-built up area would look like where a potential building could be built.[30] In some cases a purchasable operation may not exist, so the only option is a Greenfield investment decision.

*Labor and Production Costs*

Labor and production costs are typically lower in less developed nations. These cost savings attract international corporations desiring to increase profits while maintaining competitive prices in the global market. This is frequently the case for corporations with products in stage three of the international product life cycle. At stage three, corporations are able to leverage economies of scale through investment in specialized equipment that will facilitate production processes able to make use of cheaper, low-skill labor resources abundantly available in less developed nations.

*Economic Development Incentives*

The business manager must consider any and all economic development incentives in the FDI decision. When nations compete for FDI, the incentives can be significant. The WTO classifies investment incentives into three broad categories: equity capital, reinvested earnings, and other capital.

Equity capital is the value of the MNC's investment in shares of an enterprise in a foreign country. This category includes both mergers and acquisitions and "Greenfield" investments (the creation of new facilities). Mergers and acquisitions are an important source of FDI for developed countries, although the relative importance varies considerably. Reinvested earnings are the MNC's share of affiliate earnings not distributed as dividends or remitted to the MNC. Such retained profits by affiliates are assumed to be reinvested in the affiliate. This can represent up to 60 percent of outward FDI in countries such as the United States and the United Kingdom. Other capital refers to short or long-term borrowing and lending of funds between the MNC and the affiliate.[31]

There is an increasing global trend among nations to participate in the global economy as governments see FDI as an important component to increasing economic prosperity and raising the standard of living for their citizens. This potential for prosperity is a nation's primary reason for offering significant incentives to attract FDI.

In addition to attracting FDI on the national level, the United States' FDI incentives are often offered on the state level to lure businesses and jobs to the local economy. Examples would be Hyundai's plan to build a plant in the United States and the response by Alabama, the state where one of the proposed sites would be located. In order to win the FDI from the Korean car manufacturer, the Alabama governor had to make a sales pitch of FDI incentives. If the offer was too low, then the business would go to another state; if it was too high, the FDI incentives would offset the benefit to the state. After much negotiation and much cost-benefit analysis, the Alabama executive agreed to "grant Hyundai a $252.8m incentive package including $76.7m in tax breaks, $61.8m in training grants and $34m in land purchase assistance."[32] The incentives were enough to win the business.

The global environment has increased competition. Today, every state, county, and city in the country has an economic development agency with funds available for incentive packages that will help their particular agency compete for business. The increased competition is particularly evident in the automobile sector. Incentives in the auto industry have grown to $13.9 billion since 1985, according to the Center for Automotive Research. Public records indicate that G.M. is currently the top beneficiary of economic incentives receiving at least $1.7 billion in local incentives in the last five years. Additionally, the construction industry is notorious for enjoying various economic incentives. An example is in 2012 when Caterpillar announced a new plant in Georgia, which offered $44 million in incentives. Local counties contributed in free land and other aid including $15 million in tax breaks and $8.2 million in road, water and sewer repairs.[33]

**NOTES**

## KEY CONCEPTS

- Absolute advantage theory
- Comparative advantage theory
- Factor proportions theory
- Foreign direct investments
  - Balance of payment
  - Current account
  - Capital account
- General Agreement on Tariffs and Trade (GATT)
- Government and global management issues in FDI
  - Government interventions
  - Business management issues
  - Economic development incentives
- International product life cycle theory
- International trade patterns
- Mercantilism
- New trade theory
- The benefits of international trade
- World Trade Organization (WTO)

# Chapter 4 Exercises: Observational Analysis

*Ponder on the following key concepts and ideas as you read the chapter*

1. The benefits of international trade and investment and international trade patterns and its effect on the growth and benefits of global trade to participating countries.

2. The importance of understanding the historical development of international trade theory: Mercantilism, absolute advantage theory, comparative advantage theory, factor proportion theory, international product life cycle theory, and new trade theory.

3. Modern global trading systems (GATT and WTO); Foreign Direct Investment (FDI); balance of payments; government and global management issues in FDI; and economic development incentives.

4. Start a list of books, journals, and scholarly websites that would aid in the understanding of the chapter's main concepts and ideas. Start a journal for your own thoughts and ideas. What outside sources support your conclusions?

# Chapter 4 Exercises: Key Terms Analysis

*Match the answers by writing the correct letter in the space provided*

|    |  |    |  |
|----|--|----|--|
| ____ | 1. Factor conditions | A. | Developed the Theory of Absolute Advantage |
| ____ | 2. Exports-Imports=Savings-Investments | B. | Determines the actions needed to be taken if the goal is to maximize world production |
| ____ | 3. Eli Heckscher & Bertil Ohlin | C. | Developed the Theory of Comparative Advantage |
| ____ | 4. Adam Smith | D. | The value of what had to be given up to consume or achieve the objective |
| ____ | 5. Opportunity cost | E. | Developed the Theory Competitive Advantage of Nations |
| ____ | 6. Capital Account | F. | Sum of all monies that flow in/out of a given country |
| ____ | 7. David Ricardo | G. | Interdependent group acting as a unified whole, performing activities to achieve a common goal |
| ____ | 8. Paul Krugman | H. | Development of a new operation in a foreign nation |
| ____ | 9. Balance of payments | I. | Specialized or value-added factors that are developed because they do not naturally occur |
| ____ | 10. General Agreement on Tariffs & Trade | J. | Sum of a country's net income from trade in goods and services |
| ____ | 11. Porter's Diamond | K. | Governments accumulate wealth in form of gold bullion |
| ____ | 12. Capital account surplus | L. | Developed New Trade Theory |
| ____ | 13. Mercantilism | M. | Signifies the relationship between trade deficits and surpluses |
| ____ | 14. Modern global system | N. | Used as a means for controlling Foreign Direct Investment |
| ____ | 15. Michael Porter | O. | Precursor to the World Trade Organization |
| ____ | 16. Neoclassical theory | P. | Developed International Product Life Cycle Theory |
| ____ | 17. Protectionism | Q. | Developed Factor Proportions Theory |
| ____ | 18. Current Account | R. | When foreign ownership of domestic assets increases faster than domestic ownership |
| ____ | 19. Greenfield Investment | S. | Net change in foreign ownership of domestic assets |
| ____ | 20. Raymond Vernon | T. | The four determinants indicates the level of competitiveness of a national industry |

# Chapter 4 Exercises: Theoretical Analysis

*Analyze the questions and select the answer based on the reading of the chapter material*

1. Though the World Trade Organization (WTO) has officially existed since 1975, the foundation for the rules in this trading system originates in the GATT.

    a. True

    b. False

2. In order to achieve economic advantage, a nation should specialize, produce, and export only products where the nation holds an absolute advantage. (Circle the correct answer)

    a. International Product Life Cycle Theory

    b. Absolute Advantage Theory

    c. Comparative Advantage Theory

    d. Factor Proportions Theory

    e. New Trade Theory

3. If a nation's _____ far exceed its _____, then the balance of payments is out of control, or more simply stated, out of balance.

    a. Imports, FDI

    b. Surpluses, imports

    c. Imports, deficits

    d. Surpluses, deficits

4. As organizations become more involved in the global community, they may opt to purchase land or other resources in other nations. This activity, known as foreign direct investment (FDI), is commonly used to purchase real estate and existing properties.

    a. True

    b. False

5. Nations can benefit from trade even when one trading partner does not have an absolute advantage on any of the products being traded.

    a. International Product Life Cycle

    b. Absolute Advantage Theory

    c. Comparative Advantage Theory

    d. Factor Proportions Theory

    e. New Trade Theory

6. The General Agreement on Tariffs and Trade (GATT) was signed on January 1, 1948

    a. True

    b. False

7. Keeping track of the activity surrounding international trade and investment is done by maintaining a record of all international transactions, otherwise known as the balance of payments (BOP).

   a. True

   b. False

8. The activity, known as _____ is when companies opt to purchase land or other resources in other nations.

   a. Foreign Direct Investment

   b. Foreign Direct Inventories

   c. Frequent Domestic Investment

   d. Frequent Direct Investment

9. The equation represents the relationship between trade deficits and surpluses is expressed as: Exports – Investments = Savings – Imports

   a. True

   b. False

10. Operations of production are moved to a less-developed nation and the cycle is complete as highly-developed nations become importers of this product.

    a. International Product Life Cycle Theory

    b. Absolute Advantage Theory

    c. Comparative Advantage Theory

    d. Factor Proportions Theory

    e. New Trade Theory

11. Government interventions may be used to decrease global competitiveness.

    a. True

    b. False

12. Which of the following is NOT true regarding GATT?

    a. Originally created by the Bretton Woods Conference as part of a larger plan for economic recovery after World War II

    b. Its primary purpose was to reduce barriers to FDI

    c. Representatives from twenty nations accepted what would later be considered the precursor to the EU

    d. The first attempt at setting international trade rules covered forty-five thousand tariffs and 20 percent of the world trade.

13. The WTO encourages nations to practice the Golden Rule on a national level, pointing out that foreigners and foreign industries should be treated just like the locals and domestic industries.

    a. True

    b. False

14. The two ways companies can engage in FDI include

    a. Capital Investments and Joint ventures

    b. Mergers and foreclosures

    c. Greenfield investments and acquisitions

    d. None of the above

15. Which of the following is NOT a strategic goal of FDI?

    a. Establishing a presence in a new geographic market

    b. Creating and maintaining global competitiveness

    c. Filling gaps in global product lines

    d. Reducing capital and labor costs.

16. Socialism is the economic policy of restraining trade between nations.

    a. True

    b. False

17. The Balance of Payments

    a. Is the sum of all monies that flow in and out of government run programs

    b. Includes imports, goods, land, people, and financial investments

    c. Acts as a gauge to track the coming and going of international trade dollars

    d. Is usually calculated on a semi-annual basis

18. All of the following are factors that can affect the international BOP and either create or reduce surpluses and deficits except

    a. Prices of domestic goods

    b. Mergers and acquisitions

    c. Trade agreements

    d. Taxes and Tariffs

19. Government interventions may

    a. Be used to increase global competitiveness.

    b. Intervene to keep the balance of payments under control.

    c. Promote protectionism.

    d. A and B only

    e. All of the above

20. When considering FDI, the most important consideration facing a corporation is the type of _____ and _____ the investing corporation will have over the foreign entity.

    a. Ownership, control

    b. Partnership, political sway

    c. Ownership, authority

    d. Control, authority

21. Equity capital is the value of the MNC's investment in shares of an enterprise in a foreign country.

    a. True

    b. False

22. Governments play a major role in support of technology by crafting industry-specific measures, such as tax credits for research and development of new technologies and trade policies that support essential technology sectors.

    a. International Product Life Cycle Theory

    b. Absolute Advantage Theory

    c. Comparative Advantage Theory

    d. Factor Proportions Theory

    e. New Trade Theory

23. Ownership in foreign entities can be a complete or a controlling stake in the form of either a joint venture or through stock purchases and acquisitions of existing corporations.

    a. True

    b. False

24. Attempts to explain that nations will produce and export goods that use the highest proportion of those factors of production that are most abundant to a nation.

    a. International Product Life Cycle Theory

    b. Absolute Advantage Theory

    c. Comparative Advantage Theory

    d. Factor Proportions Theory

    e. New Trade Theory

25. In mathematical terms the current account is expressed as

    a. Exports – Investments = Savings – Imports

    b. Exports – Imports = Savings – Investments

    c. Exports + Imports = Savings + Investments

    d. Exports - Imports = Savings + Investments

# Chapter 4 Exercises: Practical Analysis

*Write a short essay in the space provided to each of the following questions.*
*Please use outside references for each answer to support your ideas and thoughts.*

1.  Is there a relationship between peace and prosperity and free trade among nations? According to Thomas Friedman in, The World is Flat, have any two nations in which McDonald's franchises exist gone to war with each other? If so, explain the details surrounding the conflict; if not, explain why this may be so.

2.  Why should one studying international business understand the historical development of international trade?

3. Foreign Direct investment is a major consideration for Multinational Corporations (MNC). In what ways is it important for small Import/Export companies?

4. Conduct an Internet search on Global Economic Development Incentives; Identify a few non-government organizations (NGO) that are involved in economic development and briefly describe their activities.

# Chapter 4 Exercises: Biblical Worldview Application

*Write a short essay in the space provided to each of the following questions.*
*Please use biblical references and research, where applicable, to support your ideas and thoughts.*

Consider the trade theories discussed in the chapter. From a Christian perspective the persistence of social and spiritual poverty and economic deprivation throughout the development of discussed theories is a strong indication that there may be something spiritually wrong with or missing from the economic theories and practices that either perpetuate or fail to ameliorate such disturbing conditions. The persistence of unmet needs and wants runs contrary to Jesus's promise of blessing that flows from the power of God and that is increased on Earth when people live and conduct themselves by the Spirit founded on a biblical worldview. Although the problem may be viewed as one resulting from individual choices (dominated by greed, selfishness and a failure to love) made in the exercise of free will, people concerned with ameliorating the situation should consider how best to reform the economic theories and institutions in order to better reflect a biblical worldview where both the social and spiritual needs are met.

1.  Consider the neoclassical trade theories: Mercantilism, Absolute advantage, Comparative advantage, Factor proportions theory, International product life cycle. Select one of them and determine what are the Biblical Worldview shortcomings of the selected theories and what if any recommendations would you make to do away with these shortcomings.

2. Provide the same answer required above to International Trade Theory.

3. Provide the same answer required above to New Trade Theory.

# Global Financial Markets
## and Monetary Systems

# CHAPTER OVERVIEW

Global financial markets promote the exchange of goods and services across national borders. The price of goods and services exchanged is based on supply and demand in the global markets. In addition to numerous industrial products exchanged within the global financial market, various types of commodities and resources are bought and sold including food, shares of stock, national currencies, gold, and even labor services. Buyers and sellers negotiate the quality and quantity of a particular product, what buyers are willing and able to pay for the product, and the commissions paid for conducting the transactions.[1]

Global Financial Markets include both physical and virtual market places that make the cross-border exchange of goods and services between buyers and sellers possible. This exchange is accomplished by using a monetary unit of account to pay for various transactions. In most cases, these transactions are executed via the foreign exchange market—a global market in which people trade one currency for another. Major financial markets are located in cities throughout the world. The most prominent are located in New York City, Tokyo, and London.

## *The Importance of Global Financial Markets*

The economies of the world have become highly interdependent because of improvements in communication and transportation technologies and the lowering of barriers to trade. This increase in the marketing of goods and services has contributed to standard of living improvements across national economies, most notably in developing nations. Specific goods produced in one nation are offered for sale in the world market and compete against products produced in other nations. This competition allows buyers and sellers to juxtapose quality and prices in their respective currency to other national currencies.[2] The end result of the global competition is higher quality products and lower prices for consumers. Mechanisms, such as the foreign exchange market, facilitate global financial market activities. Global financial markets involve both borrowers and lenders.

## *Importance to Borrowers*

Global financial markets are important to borrowers for two reasons such as (1) to expand the supply of money, and (2) reduce the cost of money. The supply and cost of money has a powerful effect on economic activities. Borrowers use the lending options of financial institutions to make major purchases of goods, property, and business ventures. The increased capital that borrowers acquire from financial institutions supplements disposable income, which encourages increased spending. Businesses react to increased spending by ordering more raw materials to increase the production of goods. This stimulation of business activity increases the demand for labor and raises the demand for capital goods.[3]

The quantity of money in a nation can affect the price of goods and services and employment. In the United States, the Federal Reserve Bank is responsible for regulating the growth of the economy, which is accomplished by the increase or decrease of money supply.[4] Other nations and economic unions have similar institutions such as the Bank of England, the Bank of Japan, and the European Central Bank.

The overspending of money by borrowers (both consumer and industrial) helps perpetuate the expansion of the money supply. The public begins to experience the effects of inflation with an expanding money supply. Inflation essentially decreases a consumer's purchasing power by making goods and services more expensive, which leads to wage-price spirals because too much money is circulating. Consumers attempt to offset inflation by exchanging the lower-value currency for something that is perceived to hold a value better such as property, gold, or foreign currencies.

### *Importance to Lenders*

Global financial markets are important to lenders for two major reasons: (1) expanding lending opportunities and (2) reducing risk. Financial institutions (commercial banks, credit unions, life insurance companies, and investment companies) are, simply put, in the business of making money. These institutions make money by accepting customers' deposits and using these funds for purchasing investments, such as government securities, or offering loans to businesses and individuals for business start-ups and real estate purchases. Earnings from the interest and fees charged to business and individuals on loans, in addition to purchased government securities, enable a financial institution to pay interest on depositors' accounts for the use of their funds. Conversely, this permits a financial institution to expand their activities and services to make more money.[5]

Lenders expand lending opportunities by offering borrowers different lending options. Typical options include the following:

- Variable Interest Rate Loans—the borrower and lender share the interest rate risks. Initially, the lender offers a lower interest rate with the premise of rising along with the prime interest rate over the term of the loan
- Secured Loan—interest rates on loans secured by some type of collateral property or savings account shares
- Short-Term Loan—traditionally, short-term loans bear lower interest rates by comparison to long-term loans
- Up-Front Cash[6]

### *Reducing Risk*

Minimizing economic risk is a major consideration and task across global financial markets. In ideal functioning markets, speculation and insurance assist in the reduction of unavoidable risks associated with uncertainties, such as unemployment, catastrophic losses, and diminished business revenue. Speculators buy and sell commodities with the intention of making profits on price differentials across global markets. They are in the business of moving goods across regions where the price is low to markets where the price is high. Investors often will buy insurance to reduce the potentially disastrous declines in utility from natural disasters, death, and the like. Insurance helps spread large risks, to the extent that they become acceptable to a greater number of investors.[7]

# FOREIGN EXCHANGE MARKETS

The Foreign Exchange Market is a physical and virtual institutionalized structure through which the currency of one country is exchanged for the currency of another country. It is a market place where the exchange rate is determined and where transactions take place. The progress of trading relations between nations has enabled international trade to evolve into a multifaceted operation where conversion of one currency to another is possible. International trade has evolved into the development of a market through which any currency can be traded or exchanged. After the Gold Standard was discontinued in 1971, the Foreign Exchange (FX) Market followed the rule of supply and demand, and currencies started to flow freely between sellers and buyers in currency markets.

The FX Market has gradually evolved into the largest, fastest, and most flexible currency trading market in the world. Operations continue around the clock every day with minimal breaks for weekends. According to the Bank for International Settlements 2013 Triennial Survey, turnover in traditional foreign exchange instruments is $5.3 trillion per day, which is up from $4.0 trillion in 2010.[8] The largest trading centers of the FX are located in Tokyo, London, and New York. Integration of modern technology and globalization of financial markets provides real-time information and real-time trading; this enables traders, investors, banks, multinational corporations, and governments to participate in FX daily trading operations from all over the world. Traders actively use modern technology to their advantage and to the advantage of their clients. Actual currencies do not change hands in FX Markets transactions,, but are completed electronically. The FX Market is best described as an over-the-counter (OTC) market place, meaning negotiations include the amount, date, and price of the transaction.

Since the world thrives to trade and does not have a uniformed international currency, the exchange rate from one currency to another is determined by supply and demand on a given day on the FX Market. The main principle of trading on FX Markets is to select a pair of currencies and measure profit or loss by the fluctuation of one currency's market activity compared to the other. The most popular currencies traded in Foreign Exchange Markets including daily average turnover percentage are the U.S. Dollar (87 percent) the Euro (33.4 percent), the Japanese Yen (23 percent), and the British Pound Sterling (11.8 percent).[9] The majority of participants in the FX Market are central banks, banks, pension funds and insurance companies, hedge funds, proprietary trading firms, as well as multinational corporations. In addition, the market is still open to individual investors through investment companies..[10]

*Functions*

The FX Market serves many functions. These functions enable investors, banks and governments to facilitate and conduct international trade. The functions allow (1) hedging of currency for protection from unexpected fluctuations in exchange rates, (2) exchanging of currency and international investments, and (3) stabilization of weak currencies by purchasing more stable or "strong" currencies. Additionally, FX investment opportunities permit transactions to acquire profit by speculating the movements of exchange rates between different currencies. The major functions include conversion, hedging, arbitrage, and speculation.

## Conversion

Many currencies can easily be exchanged for other currencies, which are referred to as convertible currencies. If a currency is converted, regardless of the circumstance to another currency, this currency is unrestricted. However, many nations restrict convertibility of their currencies due to their national and international policies and interests. A nation with a large and stable economy is able to trade freely and possess hard or reserve currency in addition to non-restricted currency. By comparison, smaller nations that have limitations and restrictions on their currencies, are considered to possess weak currencies. Large banks that are trading on FX, usually use reserve currencies as a part of their transactions; or, they refer to reserve currencies when quoting the exchange rates. Conversion rates are spot rates (or the day's rate offered by a dealer or a bank) and are quoted in pairs against one another. FX vendors often quote the values of currencies against the value of the U.S. Dollar.

## Hedging

Hedging is described as measures taken by a company or corporation to protect itself from the loss that may occur because of fluctuations in the exchange rate of currency. International corporations that operate globally conduct the majority of hedging in global markets. An example would be a major U.S. automotive firm that manufactures vehicles in Europe. The firm desires to protect its yearly gross earnings in Euros by entering into a hedging transaction. This transaction is accomplished by forecasting auto sales and approximating the gross amount of Eurocurrency that will be accumulated on a quarterly basis. The U.S. firm can enter into a hedging contract where four times a year it will exchange earned Euros to U.S. Dollars using a set exchange rate. Since hedging allows locking of future exchange rate fluctuations of Euros during the fiscal year, the U.S. firm's profits are unaffected. While hedging may protect against loss, it may eliminate a potential for unexpected gain.

## Arbitrage

Arbitrage generally means buying a commodity when its price is low and then reselling it after prices rise in order to make a profit. Currency arbitrage means buying a currency in one market at a low price and reselling moments later in another market at a higher price. However, because of the liquidity of the FX market and the number of transactions that occur each second, making a profit from arbitrage has become almost impossible.

## Speculation

Speculation on the Foreign Exchange Market is a gamble. Traders who speculate are taking risks (staying open) because they buy and sell currencies based on the predicted rise and fall in price of a given currency. For instance, if investors expect a rise in the price of the U.S. Dollar (USD), traders go long, which means purchase the rising currency. However, if predictions indicate a fall of the USD, speculators go short by selling the falling currency. As in arbitrage only few opportunities exist to make a large profit though the potential still exists.

*Currency Quotations and Terminology*

The USD remains the world's leading currency. The majority of transactions on the FX include operations with U.S. Dollars, (87 percent of all deals included the USD on one side of the transaction) where one party sells or buys dollars using other world currencies. Therefore, prices are quoted as "Currency A is worth X units of Currency B" or "Currency 1 in units of Currency 2."

Reuters is the largest informational platform that international traders use to communicate FX exchange rates. The Reuters codes for currencies are three-letter abbreviation codes. For instance, the value of one dollar in units of Japanese Yen would appear as "USD-JPY." This value may also be expressed as a fraction and will appear as JPY/USD, which causes confusion for some inexperienced traders. Professionals immediately recognize that the "U.S. Dollar is being quoted in Japanese Yen." Quotations may be delivered as being direct or indirect. Rates may be stated as spot, forward, or cross. Fluctuations may be calculated using percent change calculations. Finally, contracts may be written as spot, forward and futures, swaps and options.

*Direct vs. indirect quotation*

Direct and Indirect quotation are also referred to as American and European Quotes. Direct (American) quotation is the exchange rate of a foreign currency in domestic currency units. Only the USD and British Sterling are quoted by one unit price; all other currencies are quoted in one hundred units. Indirect quotation (European) is exactly the opposite and expresses the value of domestic currency in foreign currency and is not as common as direct quotations. Most currencies are quoted in relation to the U.S. Dollar.

*Spot, forward, and cross rates*

Spot rates indicate the exchange rate of one currency in units of another currency immediately and "on the spot." Spot FX trades settle two business days after the trade date, with the exception of the Canadian Dollar, which is settled the next day. A large percentage of all FX market transactions are spot transactions. The following table contains data that is typical of what is provided by major trading vendors, such as Reuters. Two rates are depicted per each currency: the buying price and selling price. The buying price is referred to as a "bid" rate, and the selling price as an "ask/offer" rate.

The forward exchange rate represents the rate at which a currency can be purchased in the future. Forward exchange rate dates when delivery (settlement) occurs, usually 30, 90, or 180 days from the date of the trade. Forward rates are calculated using a formula that influences the time in

| Real Time Spot Rates for April 6, 2013 | | |
|---|---|---|
| Currency | Bid | Offer |
| EUR/USD | 1.3112 | 1.3116 |
| USD/JPY | 98.85 | 99.04 |
| GBP/USD | 1.5569 | 1.5577 |
| USD/CAD | 1.0074 | 1.0080 |
| USD/CHF | 0.9348 | 0.9358 |
| EUR/GBP | 0.8418 | 0.8425 |
| ERU/CHF | 1.2261 | 1.2271 |
| GBP/JPY | 154.07 | 154.27 |

Source: http://www.oanda.com/currency/live-exchange-rates/

which settlement will take place and market expectations of fluctuations in the price of a particular currency. Forward rates are typically cheaper than spot rates. The difference between a spot rate and a forward rate is termed a forward discount. If a currency price is expected to rise in the future, a buyer pays a higher price, which is considered a forward premium. Forward rates are not quoted directly; rather, a discount or premium is quoted and expressed in decimals. Forward transactions are used in hedging to protect profits of companies operating internationally.

## Cross rates

Cross rates have to be calculated when parties are conducting a trade in currencies other than USD. For example, when customers trade EUR (Euro) against JPY (Yen), a cross rate is established based on the middle rates between EUR and USD and JPY and USD. An example of percent change calculations of cross rate using the middle rates for JPY against EUR is represented in the spot rate table on previous page:

JPY = EUR 1, if EUR 1= USD 1.3112 and USD 1=JPY 98.85
Answer: EUR 1= 1.3112 x 98.85=JPY 129.61.

## Currency swaps

There are several types of swaps with the most popular being the FX swap. An FX swap is the simultaneous purchase and sale of a currency for different delivery dates. The FX swap of currency amounts is normally fixed. The time between swaps may vary. Swaps with a far date less than a month from a near date are called short-dates swap, and swaps with far dates longer than a month are called forward swap. FX swaps are popular for several reasons. Investors use this type of swap as "an alternative to borrowing and lending in the Eurodollar and other offshore markets."[11] Another reason for FX swap popularity is the opportunity for the temporary shift of one currency into another, simultaneously avoiding the risk of exposure to daily fluctuation in exchange rates.

## Futures markets

Of the futures markets that trade currencies, the most common is International Monetary Market (IMM). It was established and launched in 1972 by the Chicago Mercantile Exchange for the purpose of developing future trade in financial products. The futures market allows smaller traders to participate in a trade. According to Swiss UBS Investment Bank, "Futures positions require a margin deposit to be posted and maintained daily. If a loss is taken on a contract, the amount is debited from the margin account after the close of trading. All contract specifications such as expiration time, face amount, and margins are determined by the exchange via the individual trading parties. Finally, the standard expiration dates for futures are each third Wednesday of March, June, September, and December."[12] The major difference between the currency futures market and the OTC market is that futures settle gains and losses on a daily basis through the margin mechanism.

The global business professional is aware that the relationships existing between currencies are volatile in terms of actual buying power of each currency in each nation. Buying power is an important principle in terms of currency trading and is related to the differences in standards of living across nations. Exchange rate theories can be used to understand these differences.

*Purchasing Power Parity (PPP)*

PPP is a widely accepted and cited exchange rate theory, which states that the difference in currency values between countries is related through Purchasing Power Parity (PPP). According to the theory of one price, similar goods or products in different countries should have a similar process after the conversion of currencies into the same one. If the currency of one country has more purchasing power than the currency of another country, the level of imports and exports is expected to change. Therefore, demand and supply for currency will be affected. For example, if a box of apples is cheaper in country X than in country Y, then market forces will start to buy apples in county X for use in country Y, where apples will be sold for monetary profit. This situation will call for demand of the currency of country X in order to purchase the apples and import them to country Y. PPP has an impact on exchange rates and indicates the current level of inflation of one currency against another. According to this theory, all the above factors impact exchange rates until relative purchasing powers of all currencies in the world are the same. The theory of PPP has few limitations because of the factors that directly involve the international trade; those factors include costs of transportation, government price controls, customs and tariffs costs, social perception of commodities, as well as cultural differences that will impact demand for products.

*Law of one price*

The "law of one price" provides the basis for PPP. In the absence of transportation and other transaction costs, competitive markets will equalize the price of an identical good in two countries when the prices are expressed in the same currency. Thus, the law of one price states that similar goods or commodities in different countries should remain at the same price after conversion of currencies according to current exchange rates. Sophisticated versions of PPP compare a large number of goods and services across nations. However, a problem arises in that people in different countries consume very different kinds of goods and services, making it difficult to compare the purchasing power between countries. A simpler way to calculate purchasing power parity between two countries is to compare the price of a "standard" good that is in fact identical across countries, such as a hamburger.

*The "Golden Arches Standard"*

In 1986 the British Magazine, The Economist, introduced the "Big Mac Index," which correlates the cost of a Big Mac in different countries, based on the theory of purchasing power parity and the conversion of prices using actual, current, up-to-date exchange rates. McDonald's has opened its restaurants in more than 120 countries around the globe and uses the same ingredients in each country to produce the famous Big Mac hamburger sandwich. The Economist took the price of the Big Mac as a unit of measurement of PPP of each currency in each country a Big Mac is sold. The index displays undervaluation or overvaluation of one currency against another, regarding the price of the same Big Mac hamburger.

According to The Economist, "the cheapest burger in our [table] is in Ukraine, where it costs $1.86, compared to $4.33 in the United States.[13] This implies that the Yuan is 49% undervalued. The index was never intended to be a precise predictor of currency movements, simply a take-away guide to whether currencies are at their "correct," long-run level. Burgernomics has an impressive record in predicting exchange rates: currencies that show up as overvalued often tend to weaken in later years, yet you must always remember the Big Mac's limitations. Burgers cannot sensibly be traded across borders, and prices are distorted by differences in taxes and the cost of non-tradable inputs, such as rents."[14]

The Foreign Exchange Market is a physical and virtual institutionalized structure whereby currency of one country is exchanged to currency of another country. It is a market place where the exchange rate is determined and where transactions take place, enabling investors, banks, and governments to facilitate and conduct international trade. However, the FX markets do not operate autonomous of governments. Governments have created institutions to regulate and control monetary policies.

| The Economist's Big Mac Index 2012 | Big Mac Price In USD | Implied PPP of the Dollar | Under (-)/Over(+) Valuation against the Dollar, % |
|---|---|---|---|
| United States | 4.33 | - | - |
| Norway | 7.06 | 9.94 | 63 |
| Switzerland | 6.56 | 1.50 | 52 |
| Israel | 2.92 | 2.27 | -33 |
| Denmark | 4.65 | 6.59 | 7 |
| Russia | 2.29 | 17.33 | -47 |
| Egypt | 2.64 | 3.70 | -39 |
| South Africa | 2.36 | 4.61 | -46 |
| Ukraine | 1.86 | 3.47 | -57 |
| China | 2.45 | 3.62 | -43 |
| Malaysia | 2.33 | 1.71 | -46 |

## Institutions

Central Banks and Governments are primarily the guardians of national currencies and are usually responsible for setting monetary policy and exchange rate policy. In many countries, including the U.S., the finance ministry (Treasury) sets exchange rate policy. Central banks may directly intervene in the currency market by buying or selling currency. When governments become involved in currency markets, they can either use their central bank or directly use market institutions. Government direct involvement in the FX market can be explained by an economic need, such as the establishment of hedges on foreign funding, debt conversions, and defense contracts.

Commercial banks and investment banks are generally the market makers on the foreign exchange. Traditionally commercial banks serve corporations who need access to currency markets to conduct their international business. Commercial currency transactions cover imports, exports, remittances, and transfers.

Corporations use the FX market predominantly to facilitate their international business activities. Hedging currency exposure from the day-to-day business is known as exposure management, while hedging against balance sheet items, such as manufacturing plants abroad, is known as managing translation exposure. Coincidentally, some corporations trade currencies for profit besides trading them for hedging purposes.

Professional money managers work on diversifying the portfolios of their clients by treating currencies as a separate asset class. Many times money managers play active roles on the FX market by establishing hedges for clients' money and lifting currency hedges—when it is deemed appropriate. International investors also depend on the FX market by purchasing foreign currency needed for investments abroad. It is not uncommon for these investments to be hedged back into the home currency of the investor.

Brokers usually facilitate a connection between two anonymous parties that are willing to trade. Successful brokers know the main sellers with the best prices of desirable currency. A broker receives the call with the request for an amount of a currency, dials the seller, negotiates the price, and only after agreement on the broker's commission, connects the seller and a buyer over the phone. However, with the proliferation of Internet trade and the Electronic Broking System (EBS), many brokers are being forced out of the FX business.

### Interbank markets

The term Interbank (trade between two banks) is often used in FX terminology regarding wholesale conditions of pricing between major financial institutions, as well as to the circle of the largest banks that participate in FX trade under wholesale conditions. Banks are major market enablers on the Foreign Exchange Market—so major, in fact, that the amount of currencies being moved in just one transaction may well exceed several billion units of a currency. The pricing of such transactions is usually different from smaller transactions and is priced at wholesale. Some of the largest players on the interbank market include Citigroup, UBS, JPMorgan Chase, Barclays, HSBC, and Deutsche Bank[15]

### Securities exchanges

Equities and securities are traded on securities exchanges. In this sense, securities refer to futures, options, stocks, bonds, treasury bills, etc. When a company releases its stock for sale, owners of purchased stocks are able to make a profit from reselling stocks they hold on a security exchange market. The value of a company's stock may rise or fall in accordance with its performance, creating opportunity for acquiring profits. The two most popular products traded on security exchange markets are stocks and futures. Hence, a security exchange market is a physical market place where securities are traded for speculative monetary profit. A securities exchange is one of the safest and most popular places where companies raise money for their operations.

Stocks represent shares of equity that a company releases for sale. Anyone who has a stock of a company is considered its shareholder or part owner. If a party owns a significant amount of stock in a company, it has a powerful input in decisions regarding the present and future of the organization. The company's value on the market is determined by the amount of stock that is traded.

Bonds are an alternative way for an enterprise to raise money. A bond is a certificate with a certain monetary value. By purchasing a bond, an investor practically loans money to the company issuing the bond. A company must have enough equity or assets to guarantee the value of all bonds issued. On a corporate balance sheet, bonds appear in a column under liabilities. Bonds are classified as fixed rate bonds and floating rate bonds. Companies must pay their bond holders a return that was promised on the bond to a purchaser. Both companies and governments issue bonds. If a company needs to expand its operations and does not have enough capital for the expansion, instead of obtaining a substantial amount of credit or a loan from the bank, it issues bonds and sells them through investment banks. The yearly interest on bonds is paid monthly or quarterly; however, instead of one bank receiving the money, it is paid to the individuals or parties holding the bonds of a company.

The two most popular products that are traded on security exchange floors are stocks and futures. Futures, like currencies on the FX market, represent contracts for future delivery of a commodity. An example would be a company that produces oil-trades futures for delivery in 20, 90, and 180 days for 1000 barrels of oil. The oil producing company guarantees that the purchaser of this future will receive delivery of this product on the due date of the future. A bank, investor, or corporation may acquire this future, keeping in mind that the price of oil is on the rise and opportunity for speculative profit exists. In this case, a trader for an investment bank will purchase the oil future and then resell the future before the actual delivery date comes due. The majority of futures traded on security exchange markets are traded for speculative profits.

Activities on the floor of the exchange also include speculative trading of securities. Investors purchase the securities of an organization and hope that the price of the security rises, so they can sell it for a profit. Some of the terms used in speculative trading include "bulls" and "bears." When securities turn "bulls," their values are on the rise, and when they turn "bears," their values are dropping. Stockbrokers are responsible for managing and trading securities in the securities exchanges. Investors utilize several devices to monitor the activity of their investments and performance. One of these devices is the Trade Alert, which notifies the investor of the price movement of shares he or she holds in the security exchange. This permits an investor to give instruction to his stock broker on what to sell or buy.

Several securities exchanges are in operation, most notably the Hong Kong stock exchange, the New York stock exchange, and the London stock exchange. Every country has its own security exchange. The first U.S. stock exchange market was founded in Philadelphia. The New York stock exchange was opened in 1792 after the traders of federal bonds and traders of New York Bank stocks agreed to operate jointly.[16] In the early part of the security exchange era, trade activity was widely unregulated. However, when companies began issuing their stocks for sale to individual investors, federal regulations mandated that annual reports would be made available for stockholders. The New York stock exchange is a voluntary association with a written constitution and by-laws, which include rules for the transaction of business and fix rates of commission to be charged by members. The New York Stock Exchange (NYSE EURONEXT) is considered a publicly traded company after its 2005 merger with a Dutch company called Archipelago Holdings, Inc. Where previously, seats to the NYSE were sold or leased to member companies by existing member companies, now trading licenses are made available by means of a Dutch auction process called Stock Exchange Auction Trading System or "SEATS." Members who hold a trading license will have access to the NYSE facilities. The splitting of commissions with nonmembers is prohibited and is one of the most strictly enforced rules of the exchange. The exchange itself does no business and keeps no record of transactions; it merely provides facilities for its members and regulates their conduct.[17]

Today securities exchange commissions monitor the activities of all securities exchange markets. The Securities Exchange Commission monitors the various companies and organizations that are quoted on the security exchange and make sure they meet the requirements for being listed. The Federal Exchange Commission is the main authority issuing regulations over the American securities exchange markets. "The mission of the United States Securities and Exchange Commission is to protect investors, maintain fair, orderly, and efficient markets, and facilitate capital formation."[18]

### Over-the-counter markets

Many innovations have evolved from the securities exchange to protect the investor, while others allow more participants in security trading. One significant innovation is Over-The-Counter Market (also called OTC market). OTC market evolved through development and growth in the information and communication technology. OTC market is a decentralized market of securities that are not listed on an exchange market. The majority of securities traded on the OTC market usually do not meet listing requirements. However, it is not uncommon to see a company that trades its securities on the OTC market, as well as on the trading floor of a security exchange. OTC participants trade over a telephone, a fax machine, or an electronic network, not a physical trading floor.

Trading in the OTC market occurs through a network of dealers unlike in securities exchanges where the broker conducts trading by ordering matchmaking service on the floor on behalf of the investor. These dealers carry inventories of securities to affect the buying and selling orders of investors. In addition, they negotiate directly with one another over computer networks and telephones. In the U.S., the National Association of Securities Dealers (NASD) monitors activities of exchange markets and OTC markets. NASD is a voluntary association of securities firms formed by the Maloney Act of 1938 to regulate the affairs of securities exchange investor firms and to promote fair and ethical practices in the securities business.[19] The NASD is a self-regulated association and is the largest self-regulated securities organization in the U.S.

### Eurocurrency markets

The Eurocurrency market is a money market wherein Eurocurrency is borrowed and lent by banks in Europe. The main function of the Eurocurrency market is to facilitate the international flow of capital and provide trade assistance between countries and Multinational Corporations (MNC) by allowing for more convenient borrowing. Corporations and national governments usually deposit Eurocurrency in banks away from their home countries. These banks are called Eurobanks. Despite the name, Eurocurrency and Eurobanks do not necessarily mean the currencies or the banks are European. Although the Eurodollar is the most prevalent currency, other currency held in Eurobanks includes the USD, Swiss Francs and English Sterling pound.

The first Eurocurrency markets were developed in Europe during the 1950s. Eurocurrency markets are very active in today's modern, global economy because they are able to avoid a country's domestic interest rate regulations and reserve requirements and other barriers to the free flow of capital. Eurocurrency markets play a significant role in a global economy because they allow for easier flow of money around the world. The capital deposited in Eurobanks is used by organizations and governments to finance projects all over the world.

### Effect of Exchange Rates on Global Business

Exchange rates have both a positive and negative effect on global business. The most important issue in understanding the effects of exchange rates on business is its volatility. Volatility is expressed as a percentage and represents the possibility of a change in exchange rates projected over a year. A a better understanding of the concept of volatility is gained by comparing it to a degree of uncertainty expressed in numbers. The larger the degree of uncertainty of behavior for a certain currency, the higher the risk of dealing with this currency and operating business in the currency's country of origin. As an example, one should consider the case of a U.S. automotive manufacturer. If a price of the Euro goes up in respect to the U.S. Dollar, then more profit can be made from the sale of each vehicle. However, if the manufacturer is buying or manufacturing parts for its cars in Europe, the price of cars will increase or decrease relative to the fluctuation in exchange rates, potentially draining profit from the sale of each car.

Exchange rate fluctuation also has an effect on domestic production and agriculture by inciting the competitiveness of exports of domestic goods to other countries. If the price of the USD is falling, U.S. agricultural goods will be more attractive to Japanese importers than to European exporters if the Euro is rising. Global exchange rate fluctuations affect every sector.

### Currency devaluation and revaluation

Global monetary policies vary by nation. Countries with large, stable, free-market economies and strong currencies allow exchange rates to freely float and change according to market supply and demand. This type of monetary policy is termed a floating exchange rate system. However, nations with unstable and emerging economies and weak currencies mostly use a fixed exchange rate system. "Under a fixed exchange rate system, only a decision by a country's government or monetary authority can alter the official value of the currency. Governments do, occasionally, take such measures, often in response to unusual market pressures. Devaluation, the deliberate downward adjustment in the official exchange rate, reduces the currency's value, but a revaluation is an upward change in the currency's value."[20] The devaluation of one unit of a nation's domestic currency decreases in value against other currencies; thus, the Purchasing Power Parity (PPP) of the devaluated currency decreases. In turn, inflation rises and affects prices on exported commodities. Foreign companies take advantage of currency devaluation in unstable countries by buying more goods for the same amount of money and exporting the goods to other countries for resale and monetary profit. Devaluation also affects prices on commodities imported from other counties by making them more expensive than before. Devaluation is also considered a benefit to a country. The lowered currency helps the country to reduce its current trade deficit. However, a government may raise interest rates in order to control increased inflation, which may slow economic growth. Many investors consider devaluation a sign of danger and often restrict flow of their investments into countries with unstable currency.

Revaluation, on the other hand, makes the currency of a country more expensive compared to other currencies and has a direct inverse effect on exports and imports, respectively. Imports become cheaper because current exchange rates allow consumers to buy more foreign goods for the same amount of domestic currency. This foreign spending raises the PPP of domestic currency. Analysts often consider revaluation a sign of economic recovery and stabilization. Foreign investors are usually attracted to currency revaluation because it results in less risk.

### Why stable exchange rates are desired by business

Stable exchange rates are a sign of less volatility, meaning that the risk of conducting business with a stable foreign currency is reduced. If there is less uncertainty in an exchange rate, then the opportunity to make plans for doing business operation rises. Even though there are several tools to protect a business from a high degree of volatility, entering into forward contracts can bring into play additional costs for business operations. Stable exchange rates serve as a straightening factor for a country's economy by encouraging domestic production while keeping imports and exports under control. Stable exchange rates attract investors and allow foreign capital to flow in a country. Businesses flourish under such conditions because it offers stability and lowers prices on operating costs, acquisition of raw materials, and labor costs.

*Impact of unstable exchange rates on business*

Unstable exchange rates are a sign of a struggling economy or an economy in crisis. Small and medium businesses usually are incapable of withstanding radical fluctuations of exchange rates, especially if an enterprise depends on purchases of imported raw parts and materials. If sudden devaluation occurs, imported parts and raw materials go up in price, making business costly. Large, stable companies, backed by significant foreign capital or foreign investors, comprise the majority of businesses capable of surviving under unstable fluctuations of exchange rates. The development of a free-market economy slows down under instability of exchange rates. Large companies take advantage of these opportunities by freely monopolizing unstable markets under such conditions.

## MONETARY SYSTEMS

The onset of World War I sparked an overabundant supply of money, as antagonistic nations printed money at an alarming rate in order to finance their war efforts. The gold standard was violated, a trend which continued through the 1920s. However, change was on the horizon, beginning with the election of Franklin D. Roosevelt as U.S. President in 1932. Reforms instituted during this election—and the three subsequent Presidential reelections—impacted the way the world conducts financial transactions. One of Roosevelt's sweeping agendas was an effort to avoid a return to the near-fatal economic chaos of the 1930s by no longer permitting U.S. paper currency to be redeemable in gold.[21] In fact, much of the successful recovery of Western Europe following World War II was made possible by U.S. aid.[22] The U.S. did not suffer aerial bombings on its industrial centers unlike Europe and Japan, and was the major post-war victor capable of manufacturing much of the world's products. Furthermore, with the help of receptive governments, the establishment of the World Bank and International Monetary Fund was made possible under the United Nation (UN) backing.[23] What series of historical events led to these developments? The story begins centuries ago with the use of gold and other precious metals as a medium of exchange for cross-border trade.

### The Gold Standard

Governments issued gold and other precious metals as a source of money as far back as Biblical times. When governments started issuing currency in the form of paper money, it was usually convertible into a predetermined amount of gold. This practice came to be commonly known as the "gold standard" by participating countries. In 1834 the U.S. fixed the price of gold at $20.67 per ounce and maintained this rate until 1933. Guaranteeing the convertibility of paper currency into gold was a way to maintain confidence in a country's currency value at home and overseas. The gold standard regulated the quantity and growth rate of a nation's money supply. Between 1880 and 1913, inflation in the United States averaged 0.1 percent per year. Because exchange rates were fixed, gold was directly related to the price of goods around the world; thus, the price of goods increased when the price of gold increased.[24]

### 1880s to World War II

Many nations backed their currencies with gold well before 1880. However, this practice became more widespread during this period; therefore, the 1880s are generally accepted as the beginning of the gold standard. Additionally, 1880 to 1914 is considered the "classical" gold standard era, because countries fixed values of their currency in gold. Prior to the onset of World War I, 1880 to 1914 was a period of dynamic economic growth, especially with regard to free trade in goods, capital, and labor. Unfortunately during World War I, the gold standard was nonexistent because of rogue nations' abundant printing of paper currencies in order to finance their war efforts. Following World War I, a Gold Exchange Standard was reinstated, which lasted between 1925 and 1931 and permitted countries to hold gold, dollars, or pounds as reserves. The only exceptions were Great Britain and the United States, which held reserves only in gold. Great Britain departed from gold in 1931 because of massive gold and capital withdrawals. In 1932, in an attempt to move the economy out of the Great Depression, U.S. officials called for reduced government spending and an end to Prohibition. President Franklin D. Roosevelt (FDR) acted on both, because Congress granted him more legislative powers to devalue the United States dollar in an effort to manipulate inflation. FDR took the U.S. off the gold standard where paper currency was no longer redeemable in gold. In January 1934, FDR fixed the price of gold at $35 an ounce, against the old price of $20.63, which inflated the dollar 40 percent.

### Demise of the Gold Standard

The demise of the gold standard was due to a variety of circumstances. World War I and the Great Depression were two of the major contributing circumstances. The first sign of the demise of the gold standard began with the outbreak of World War I, as war financing was funded by increases in money supplies of hostile nations. It became evident that these nations' gold reserves were not capable of supporting such a rapid increase in money supply. The mid 1920s saw a return to the gold standard as currencies emerged from hyperinflation in the 1920s and 1930s. European investment from the U.S. stimulated a worldwide recovery of trade and manufacturing; but, was undermined by the effects of the Versailles treaty. The treaty caused Germany to became the sacrificial lamb by assuming all reparations as punishment for starting World War I. Hence, Germany's economic recovery was stifled as a result. Further, countries resorted to implementing restrictions, tariffs, and exchange controls in an effort to maintain momentum for economic growth.

Although the U.S. was willing to provide financial backing to Europe, it was not as eager to accept goods from Europe. Consequently, Europe and the world were at the mercy of a prosperous U.S. economy. But the U.S. lost this control when the stock market collapsed in October 1929, followed by the Great Depression of the 1930s. The U.S. notified debtor nations that the balances were due. The debtor nations responded by cutting imports in order to settle affairs with other nations. The result-of this created a ripple effect worldwide. In the midst of a financial crisis, struggling nations deflated their currencies to stay steady in relation to gold, resulting in the decreased demand for their exports. In addition to notifying debtor nations that trade balances were due, the U.S. further exacerbated the situation by enacting the Smoot-Hawley Tariff Act.

The Smoot-Hawley Tariff Act of June 1930 raised U.S. tariffs to historically high levels. The original intention behind the legislation was to increase the protection afforded domestic farmers against foreign agricultural imports. Massive expansion in the agricultural production sector outside of Europe during World War I led, with the postwar recovery of European producers, to massive agricultural overproduction during the 1920s. This in turn led to declining farm prices during the second half of the decade. During the 1928 election campaign, Republican Presidential candidate Herbert Hoover pledged to help the beleaguered farmer by, among other things, raising tariff levels on agricultural products. However, once the tariff schedule revision process got started, it proved impossible to stop. Calls for increased protection flooded in from industrial sector special interest groups. Soon a bill primarily meant to provide relief for farmers became a means to raise tariffs in all sectors of the economy. When the dust had settled, Congress had agreed to tariff levels that exceeded the already high rates established by the 1922 Fordney-McCumber Act. This new policy represented among the most protectionist tariffs in U.S. history.[25]

The Smoot-Hawley Tariff was more a consequence of the onset of the Great Depression than an initial cause. Though the tariff might not have caused the Depression, it certainly did not make it any better. This tariff provoked a storm of foreign retaliatory measures and came to stand as a symbol of the 'beggar-thy-neighbor' policies (policies designed to improve one's own lot at the expense of others) of the 1930s. Such policies contributed to a drastic decline in international trade. U.S. imports from Europe declined from a 1929 high of $1,334 million to just $390 million in 1932. In addition, the U.S. exports to Europe fell from $2,341 million in 1929 to $784 million in 1932. Overall, world trade declined 66 percent between 1929 and 1934. In general, the Smoot-Hawley Tariff did nothing to foster trust and cooperation among nations in either the political or economic realm during a perilous era in international relations.[26]

Another result of this situation was unemployment, which was at unprecedented levels globally—nearly thirty million by some accounts. This crisis continued through World War II, and no organized system for exchange rates existed. Investment, foreign trade, and economic recovery declined because of the war. The gold standard was no longer viable in the post World War II global economy.[27]

### The Bretton Woods Agreement—1944 to 1971

Following World War II, implementation of a currency exchange system for the promotion of growth in international trade that linked monies, similar to the gold exchange, received worldwide political support. In 1944, delegates from forty-four nations met in Bretton Woods, New Hampshire, to discuss the initiative. Three major events resulted: (1) the establishment of a fixed exchange rate system, (2) the International Monetary Fund, and (3) the World Bank.

At the conclusion of the Bretton Woods meeting, an exchange rate agreement was made, often referred to as the gold exchange standard. Just as before, under the gold standard, each nation was to fix its currency value in relation to gold. The United States' fixed standard was $35 per ounce, and the U.S. was the only nation capable of producing and supplying goods to the rest of the world, which resulted in goods being priced and traded in dollars. Consequently, the U.S. dollar became the reserve currency for the new gold exchange system. Trade contracts were essentially executed in United States dollars.[28]

## Fixed Exchange Rates

Fixed exchange rates evolved from the gold standard. In order for nations to conduct cross-border trade, a fixed rate of exchange had to be established and generally maintained by intervention from governments in the foreign exchange markets. Fixed exchange rates, also known as pegged exchange rates, occur when a government or central bank ties the official exchange rate to another country's currency or the price of gold. The purpose of a fixed exchange rate system is to maintain the nation's currency value within a very narrow band. Fixed exchange rates offer the provision of greater certainty for exporters and importers, which allows governments to maintain low inflation. In other words, fixed exchange rates assist in minimizing interest rates, thus stimulating increased global trade and investment.

## Establishment of the International Monetary Fund (IMF)

The International Monetary Fund (IMF) was one of the results of the Bretton Woods Agreement. The role of the IMF is to supervise the exchange rate practices of member countries and to encourage the free convertibility of any national money into the monies of other countries. In simple terms, the IMF was created to maintain order in the global monetary system. The IMF assists nations in their development through capital loans to undeveloped nations. The purpose was to achieve higher standards of living among its citizens, resulting in an increased market for more goods. The overall motivation for existence of the IMF was that the development of less-developed countries is in the interest of more developed countries.[29] While the IMF and World Bank mandate stern lending criteria for undeveloped countries, the IMF inevitably lends money to countries that are experiencing problems and meets their international payment obligation as well. The IMF conducts lending practices using the annual contributions of its 188 member nations, based on quota obligations. "Quotas are denominated in Special Drawing Rights (SDRs), the IMF's unit of account. The largest member of the IMF is the United States, with a current quota of SDR 42.1 billion (about $65 billion), and the smallest member is Tuvalu, with a current quota of SDR 1.8 million (about $2.78 million)."[30]

## Establishment of the World Bank

The World Bank, another result of the Bretton Woods Agreement, was established to help finance economic development in poor countries. Simply put, the World Bank was created to promote general economic development. The World Bank also provides loans—in addition to technical expertise,to developing countries at more favorable terms than commercial lenders. The World Bank is one of the world's major borrowers and obtains its funding by issuing and selling bonds.

## Demise of the Bretton Woods Agreement

With the condition and promise of the U.S. government to redeem other central banks' holdings of dollars for gold at the fixed rate of $35 per ounce, most countries settled their international business balances in U.S. dollars under the gold exchange system. However, this agreement led to persistent payment deficits with reduced U.S. gold reserves, jeopardizing confidence in the ability of the United States to maintain this standard. Americans could import more than they exported with the willing cooperation of Europe and Japan. During the 1960s, the U.S., suffering severe inflation from the deficit financing of the Vietnam War and an expanding agenda of social programs, racked up enormous budget deficits and trade deficits. The Bretton Woods system reached a crisis when it became clear that there was a run on the U.S. gold supply as foreigners sought to exchange their dollar reserves, which were convertible to gold, at the fixed price established by the Bretton Woods system. On August 15, 1971, President Richard Nixon announced that the U.S. would no longer redeem currency for gold, the final step in officially removing the U.S. from the gold standard. The system collapsed when Nixon suspended convertibility by "closing the gold window." The current monetary order, which stems from the demise of the Bretton Woods system, consists of market-determined exchange rates between floating fiat currencies, entirely lacking any commodity backing.

### Floating Exchange Rates—1973 to Present

A floating exchange rate is an exchange rate that is freely determined by the interaction of supply and demand. Floating exchange rates allow nations to formulate macroeconomic policies independently of other nations. In 1971, major governments adopted a floating system, otherwise known as a floating exchange rate. The floating exchange rate is determined by the private market through supply and demand. Differences in open market supply and demand will "self-correct" a floating exchange rate. For instance, if demand for the U.S. dollar is low, its value will decrease, which makes imported goods more expensive and exported goods less expensive.

### Managed Float System

A managed float system is very similar to a floating exchange rate system, with one exception: the value of a currency is determined by market demand for and supply of a country's currency, with no predetermined target for the exchange rate as set by the government. Governments attempt to directly affect their exchange rates by buying or selling foreign currencies or indirectly by raising or lowering interest rates through monetary policy.

*Pegged exchange rate.* A fixed exchange rate, sometimes called a pegged exchange rate, is a type of exchange rate regime wherein a currency's value is matched to the value of another single currency, to a basket of other currencies, or to another measure of value, such as gold. As the reference value rises and falls, so does the currency pegged to it.[31] The adoption of a pegged exchange rate evolved at the conclusion of the Bretton Woods Agreement; hence, the U.S. dollar was pegged to gold at $35 an ounce, and the value of other foreign currencies was linked directly to the U.S. dollar. For example, if one needed to buy British Sterling, the value of the Sterling would be expressed in U.S. dollars, which would be expressed in gold.

The primary reason to peg a currency is for stability, which explains why a pegged rate is attractive to developing nations who want to create a stable atmosphere for foreign investment. The peg aided in the creation of global trade and monetary stability but was used only when all the major economies were part of the policy to peg. Unfortunately, the peg was discontinued in 1971 when the U.S. dollar could no longer maintain the pegged rate of $35 an ounce.[32]

*Currency board.*  A currency board is a monetary authority for a country that operates similarly to a central bank. It has the authority to issue notes and coins; but unlike a central bank, a currency board is neither the government's bank nor is it capable of bailing out a failing bank. A currency board has the capacity to operate either independently or parallel with a central bank. Currency boards have been in existence as long as central banks and have their roots in the English Bank Act of 1844. A currency board has the capacity to issue notes and coins and the conversion of local currency into the anchor currency at a fixed rate of exchange. The anchor currency is usually a stable currency: the U.S. Dollar, Euro, or British Pound. Generally, a currency board must have 100 percent of reserve currency available and a long-term commitment to the local currency. This requires a fixed rate of exchange for the issuance of notes and coins. Since a currency board is not in the business of lending money to banks or the government—like a central bank—the only means a government has in raising capital is through taxation or borrowing.[33]

Interestingly, there is no ideal monetary authority for a nation to use regarding a central banking system or a currency board system. Executing sound economic decisions through the proper management of a nation's monetary system is the primary medium for building credibility amongst global investors.

### European Monetary System—1979 to Present

As far back as World War II, a number of European nations desired a unified Europe that could compete with the economic strength of the United States. Disagreements in how this unified Europe would compete and operate under the auspices of a leading nation resulted in a contentious debate, especially between Great Britain and France. However, during the early 1980s, as European nations battled with unemployment figures in excess of 11 percent or higher throughout the region, foreign affairs became more significant in rallying support for tighter economic cooperation. Jacques Delors was appointed president of the European Economic Community (EEC) in 1985, and he became the key innovator for marshaling a plan for the European Union. One of his prior successes as finance minister in France included major economic improvement for his country by reducing inflation and cutting foreign debt. Delors set about introducing sweeping initiatives designed to expand internal trade further by convincing EEC members to pass the Single European Act (SEA) of 1987. The SEA bounded member countries to the goal of a single European market by January 1, 1993. However, not surprisingly, the major disagreement was over the European Monetary Union's management of financial unity and one common European currency—although the European Monetary Union did not yet exist. The creation of a unified European economy would require financial unity, but member countries like Great Britain and Denmark were not as eager to replace their own currency with a European currency that was yet to be tested.[34]

### Exchange Rate Mechanism
The European Community established its Exchange Rate Mechanism (ERM) in 1979 and formed the initial steps for the creation of a single European currency. The

purpose of the ERM was to control the exchange rates within the European Monetary System. Member currencies of the ERM were fixed against each other with smaller fluctuations for change as compared to a floating exchange rate among nonmember states. The euro area has one currency, the Euro, which became the official currency of 11 member states on January 1, 1999. However, there are countries outside the Euro with their own currency. Therefore, on January 1, 1999 the Exchange Rate Mechanism (ERM II) became the successor to the ERM so that the economic stability within the single market is not disrupted by exchange rate fluctuation between the euro and other EU currencies. Participation is voluntary, but before qualifying to adopt the Euro, a country must participate in the ERM II as one of the convergence criteria for entry.[35]

### Maastricht Treaty

The SEA was a major catalyst for economic integration. The fall of the Berlin Wall and Germany's subsequent unification brought to light benefits that could be accrued through improved political cooperation. Chancellor Helmut Kohl of Germany was convinced that a more politically integrated Europe was crucial to the acceptance of a combined and larger Germany. His conviction compelled other nations to press forward toward developing a monetary union, cooperation on European affairs, and a common foreign and defense policy. Discussions were underway in the latter part of 1990 and came to a head in Maastricht, Netherlands in December 1991. These negotiations resulted in the consensus of two treaties on Economic, Monetary, and Political Union—more commonly known as the Maastricht Treaty. The Maastricht Treaty called for the development of a European Union that utilized the existing offices of the European Community, supplemented by new intergovernmental offices on foreign and security policy, home affairs, and justice.[36]

*Provisions.* The Maastricht Treaty arranged for additional cooperation in the creation of an economic and monetary union—in judicial and internal affairs and in foreign and defense policy. However, the ultimate achievement of the Maastricht Treaty was the Economic and Monetary Union (EMU). The agreement to adopt a single currency and central banking system for Europe has placed the Euro as a major competitor with the U.S. dollar. The Euro was launched in global financial markets for electronic use on January 1, 1999, and was subsequently accepted as the unit of exchange for all European Union (EU) nations, with the exception of Sweden, Denmark, and Great Britain. Consequently, the U.S. dollar has been on the decline against the Euro (down 27 percent) since the then twelve Euro-area countries officially issued the Euro as a form of currency for daily consumer transactions in 2002.[37]

*EU membership requirements.* Strict requirements exist for membership in the European Monetary Union (EMU). Member states must demonstrate that they can manage their economy without recourse to excessive currency fluctuation; this mimics the conditions when the nation joins the euro area and the European Central Bank (ECB) assumes control of the monetary policy. The exchange rate stability criterion is based on 5 convergent criterion.

1. Price Stability:  Consumer price inflation rate should not be more than 1.5 percentage points above the rate of the three best performing Member States,
2. Sound Public Finances: annual government budget deficit not more than 3 percent of GDP,

3.   Sustainable Public Finances: the total outstanding government debt is not to exceed 60 percent of GDP,

4.   Durability of Convergence: The long-term interest rate must not be more than 2 percentage points above the rate of the three best performing countries in terms of price stability, and

5.   Exchange Rate Stability: exchange rates must stay within "normal" fluctuation margins of the European Exchange Rate Mechanism (ERM II) for at least two years without severe tensions.

The stability criterion also provides indication of the appropriate conversion rate that is applied to the country upon its qualification and the currency becomes fixed.[38]

*EU membership roster and future member candidates.* The European Union has made significant progress over the past decade in becoming a unified market. With six beginning members in 1952, the European Union has now grown to a total of 28 members with the accession of Croatia on July 1, 2013. Listed below are the current EU member countries and the date of their entry is in parenthesis.

- Austria (1995)
- Belgium (1952)
- Bulgaria (2007)
- Croatia (2013)
- Cyprus (2004)
- Czech Republic (2004)
- Denmark (1973)
- Estonia ((2004)
- Finland (1995)
- France (1952)
- Germany (1952)
- Greece (1981)
- Hungary (2004)
- Ireland (1973)
- Italy (1952)
- Latvia (2004)
- Lithuania (2004)
- Luxembourg (1952)
- Malta (2004)
- Netherlands (1952)
- Poland (2004)
- Portugal (1986)
- Romania (2007)
- Slovakia (2004)
- Slovenia (2004)
- Spain (1986)
- Sweden (1995)
- United Kingdom(1973)

Candidate nations include, the former Yugoslavia Republic of Macedonia, Turkey, Iceland, Montenegro, and Serbia. Potential candidates include Albania, Bosnia and Herzegovinian, and Kosovo.[39]

## KEY CONCEPTS

- Bretton Woods Agreement
- Economic and Monetary Union (EMU)
- Exchange rate
- Foreign Exchange (FX) Market
- Global financial markets
- Gold Standard
- Interbank markets
- International Monetary Fund (IMF)
- Law of one price
- Monetary systems
- Over-the-counter (OTC) market place
- Purchasing power parity (PPP)
- Securities exchanges
- Smoot-Hawley Tariff Act
- World Bank

# Chapter 5 Exercises: Observational Analysis

*Ponder on the following key concepts and ideas as you read the chapter*

1. The importance of global financial markets in promotion of the exchange of goods and services across national borders. The importance of supply and demand to the price of goods and services.

2. The Foreign Exchange Market functions, terminology, and effects of exchange rates on global business; the importance of stable exchange rates, and the impact of unstable exchange rates.

3. The historical development of the Global monetary system: gold standard, Bretton-Woods agreement, and the establishment of the World Bank, floating exchange rates, and the European monetary system

4. Start a list of books, journals, and scholarly websites that would aid in the understanding of the chapter's main concepts and ideas. Start a journal for your own thoughts and ideas. What outside sources support your conclusions?

# Chapter 5 Exercises: Key Terms Analysis

*Match the answers by writing the correct letter in the space provided*

_____ 1.  International Monetary Fund (IMF)

_____ 2.  Speculation

_____ 3.  FX swap

_____ 4.  Future positions

_____ 5.  Currency board

_____ 6.  Forward Exchange

_____ 7.  Direct quotation

_____ 8.  Indirect quotation

_____ 9.  Variable interest rate loan

_____ 10. Forward discount

_____ 11. Convertible currencies

_____ 12. Revaluation

_____ 13. Law of one price

_____ 14. Floating exchange rate

_____ 15. Spot rates

_____ 16. Arbitrage

_____ 17. Fixed exchange rates

_____ 18. Foreign exchange market

_____ 19. OTC Market

_____ 20. Hedging

A.  Require a margin deposit to be posted & maintained daily

B.  Rate at which currency can be purchased in the future

C.  Upward change in the currency's value

D.  American: value of foreign currency in domestic currency

E.  Government/Central Bank ties the official exchange rate to another country's currency or price of gold

F.  Where the borrower and lender share the interest rate risks

G.  Currencies that can easily be exchanged for other currencies

H.  Currency of one country is exchanged to currency of another country.

I.  Simultaneous purchase and sale of a currency for different delivery dates

J.  Exchange rate of one currency in units of another currency immediately

K.  Similar goods in different countries should remain at the same price after conversion of currencies

L.  Buying a commodity when its price is low and then reselling it after prices rise in order to make a profit.

M.  Traders take risks as they buy/sell currencies based on predicted rise/fall in the price of given currency

N.  Decentralized market of securities not listed on an exchange market

O.  Measures taken to protect from loss that may occur due to exchange rate or currency fluctuation

P.  The difference between a spot rate and a forward rate

Q.  Freely determined by the interaction of supply and demand

R.  Maintain order in the global monetary system

S.  European: value of domestic currency in foreign currency

T.  Monetary authority for a country/operates like a central bank

# Chapter 5 Exercises: Theoretical Analysis

*Analyze the questions and select the answer based on the reading of the chapter material*

1.  On August 15, 1971, President _____ announced that the U.S. would no longer redeem currency for gold.

    a.  Franklin D. Roosevelt

    b.  Bill Clinton

    c.  John F. Kennedy

    d.  Richard Nixon

2.  The OTC Market has gradually evolved into the largest, fastest, and most flexible currency trading market in the world.

    a.  True

    b.  False

3.  The _____ of the world have become highly interdependent because of improvements in _____ and transportation technologies and the lowering of barriers to trade.

    a.  Societies, education

    b.  Economies, communication

    c.  Cultures, living standards

    d.  Nations, religious acceptance

4.  Currency arbitrage means buying a currency in one market at a low price and reselling moments later in another market at a higher price.

    a.  True

    b.  False

5.  Select the two reasons that global financial markets are important to borrowers.

    a.  Expanding the supply of money and expanding lending opportunities

    b.  Expanding lending opportunities and reduce the cost of money

    c.  Reduce the cost of money and expand the supply of money

    d.  Reducing risk and expanding lending opportunities

6.  In the United States, the Federal Reserve Bank is responsible for regulating the growth of the economy, which is accomplished by the increase or decrease of money supply.

    a.  True

    b.  False

7.  Participation is voluntary, but before qualifying to adopt the Euro, a country must participate in the _____as one of the convergence criteria for entry

    a.  ERM

    b.  EMU

    c.  ERM II

    d.  EEC

    e.  ERM I

8. With 11 beginning members in 1952, the European Union has now grown to a total of 28 members.

   a. True

   b. False

9. The Foreign Exchange Market is a physical and virtual institutionalized structure whereby currency of one country is exchanged to currency of another country.

   a. True

   b. False

10. The 1922 Fordney-McCumber Act raised U.S. tariffs to historically high levels.

    a. True

    b. False

11. All of the following are EU Member countries except

    a. Portugal

    b. Peru

    c. Malta

    d. Lithuania

12. The role of the IMF is to supervise the exchange rate practices of member countries and to encourage the free convertibility of any national money into the monies of other countries.

    a. True

    b. False

13. Primary guardians of national currencies and usually responsible for setting monetary policy and exchange rate policy.

    a. Commercial Banks and Investments Banks

    b. Corporations

    c. Central Banks and Governments

    d. Investment Firms

14. The membership requirements for the European Monetary Union (EMU) are based on the 5 convergent criterion: Price Stability, Sound Public Finance, Sustainable Public Finances Commodity, Durability Convergence and Exchange Rate Stability:

    a. True

    b. False

15. Which of the following is not an industrial product exchanged within the global financial market?

    a. Food

    b. Shares of stock

    c. National currencies

    d. Child labor

16. The law of PPP states that similar goods or commodities in different countries should remain at the same price after conversion of currencies according to current exchange rates.

    a.  True

    b.  False

17. Use the FX market to facilitate international business activities

    a.  Commercial Banks and Investments Banks

    b.  Corporations

    c.  Central Banks and Governments

    d.  Investment Firms

18. The most prominent major financial markets are located

    a.  New York City, Tokyo, and London

    b.  Atlanta, Shanghai, London

    c.  New York, Shanghai, Switzerland

    d.  Chicago, Tokyo, London

19. The end result of the global competition is _____ products and _____ for consumers.

    a.  Lower quality, lower prices

    b.  Higher quality, higher prices

    c.  Lower quality, higher prices

    d.  Higher quality, lower prices

20. Two most popular products traded on the security exchange markets are stocks and bonds.

    a.  True

    b.  False

21. In the United States, the _____ is responsible for regulating the growth of the economy

    a.  FX Market

    b.  NYSE

    c.  Federal Reserve

    d.  The President

22. A pegged exchange rate is an exchange rate that is freely determined by the interaction of supply and demand.

    a.  True

    b.  False

23. If a currency price is expected to rise in the future, what is the higher price a buyer pays?

    a.  Forward Exchange

    b.  Forward Discount

    c.  Forward Neutral

    d.  Forward Premium

24. The European Community established its Exchange Rate Mechanism (ERM) in 1979 and formed the initial steps for the creation of a single European currency.

    a.  True

    b.  False

25. Reasons that global financial markets are important to lenders.

    a.  Expand the supply of money and reduce the cost of money

    b.  Reducing risk and reducing the cost of money

    c.  Expanding lending opportunities and reducing risk

    d.  Reduce the cost of money and regulate the supply of money

26. Which of the following is NOT a typical way lenders expand lending opportunities to borrowers?

    a.  Fixed Interest Rate Loans

    b.  Secured Loan

    c.  Up-Front Cash

    d.  Short-Term Loan

27. The majority of transactions on the FX include operations with the Euro, where one party sells or buys dollars using other world currencies.

    a.  True

    b.  False

28. Generally the market makers on the foreign exchange

    a.  Commercial Banks and Investments Banks

    b.  Corporations

    c.  Central Banks and Governments

    d.  Hedge Funds

29. The _____ Market has gradually evolved into the largest, fastest, and most flexible currency trading market in the world

    a.  NYSE

    b.  NASDAQ

    c.  FX

    d.  Derivatives

30. Which if the following is true concerning the IMF?

    a.  The IMF was created to maintain order in the global monetary system

    b.  It assists nations in their development through capital loans to developed nations

    c.  It was one of the results of the Geneva Convention

    d.  The purpose was to achieve economically stable standards of living among its citizens

# Chapter 5 Exercises: Practical Analysis

*Write a short essay in the space provided to each of the following questions.*
*Please use outside references for each answer to support your ideas and thoughts.*

1. Conduct an Internet search on any 3 Fortune 500 company. Describe each company's interaction with the foreign exchange market.

2. To understand the Purchasing Power Parity on an individual level, compare the cost of living in the city that you live with that of Paris, Mexico City, and Beijing. What results did your research provide? Explain your answer.

3. Stable exchange rates are desired by global businesses. What actions can a nation take to destabilize its exchange rate.

4. The global business professional understands the importance of floating exchange rates. Conduct an internet search and explain the current exchange rate policy between the U.S.A. and China and the implications it has on business. Should any changes be made to the current policy?

# Chapter 5 Exercises: Biblical Worldview Application

*Write a short essay in the space provided to each of the following questions.*
*Please use biblical references and research, where applicable, to support your ideas and thoughts.*

1. Conduct an Internet search using the following descriptors: biblical worldview and money. Consider your findings in the light of any topic in this chapter related to money. Compose a short essay on your findings.

2. The global economy is one based heavily on the use of debt and principles of monetary leverage. Discuss the pros and cons of using debt and leverage from the Biblical Worldview.

3. We have studied the IMF and its purpose. Write a short essay proposing adding a Biblical Worldview component to the IMF.

# Regional Economic Integration and Trade Agreements

## CHAPTER OVERVIEW

Regional integration is the process whereby countries remove barriers to trade between themselves, but each country determines its own barriers against nonmembers.

> **Elements That are Addressed in the Process of Integration**
>
> - Alleviating the barriers to trade of goods and services.
> - Reduction of barriers to investment.
> - Easier movement of labor between members.
> - Tax and monetary policies.
> - Administration of the integration agreement.[1]

These agreements are designed to reduce and ultimately remove tariff and non-tariff barriers to the free movement of goods, services, and factors of production between each other. Tariff barriers involve financial methods (e.g., taxes on imports) of protecting national industries from competition by foreign corporations. Non-tariff barriers refer to laws and regulations affecting trade; these include barriers that governments use to ensure accountability and quality.[2] Successful regional economic integration is contingent upon the integration of national economies and multilateral links between firms and provinces of integrating countries.[3] Cooperation from geographically proximate nations forms a group with the goal of abolishing discrimination between economic units belonging to member nations. The end result promotes transactions in various economic, political, and social activities to benefit all citizens of the participating nations. Thus, the intended outcome of regional economic integration is to promote economic prosperity and stability among signatory nations.

Agreements between participating nations are managed and promoted through trading blocs. A regional trading bloc is a group of nations in a geographic region engaged in economic integration.[4] Paradoxically, the intent to form a trading bloc may range from the potential of trade creation to the desire for economic protectionism. As such, trading blocs are a notable feature of the international economy, enabling scope and scale advantages—a result of globalization. Signatory nations and their corporations exploit existing competencies, resulting in increased global competitiveness. Some established regional agreements, such as the European Union, incorporate the highest level of integration. Meanwhile, the Americas, Asia, and Africa have created trading blocs with lesser and varying levels of integration. Currently, most industrialized and less-developed nations are participants of at least one trading bloc. It is estimated that more than 50 percent of world trade is conducted through regional trade agreements. This includes bilateral free trade agreements between countries or groups of countries not in the same region of the world.[5]

A paradox exists in that trading blocs can provide protection from global competitiveness prompted by nations outside of the bloc. The objectives behind the desire to protect the trade interests of participating regions are as follows:

- Establish some form of regional control regarding trade that fulfills the interests of nations within that region
- Establish tariffs that protect intra-regional trade from "outside" forces

- Promote regional security and political concerns or to develop trade in such way as to enhance the security in the region
- Promote South-to-South trade, e.g., between Africa and Asia, and between Latin American countries
- Promote economic and technical cooperation among developing countries[6]

Measures that are frequently deployed to regulate the effects of global competition include the following:

- Import quotas (limiting the amount of imports into the country so that domestic consumers buy products made by their countries in their region)
- Customs delays (establishing bureaucratic formalities that slow down the ability for the imported product from abroad to enter the domestic market
- Subsidies (government financial assistance toward sectors of the home economy so that they have an influx of capital)
- Boycotts and technical barriers
- Bribes and voluntary restraints[7]

While the topic of barriers to trade was discussed in Chapter 3, a review of the barriers is included because they are essential to understanding regional economic integration.

For most of the world, regional trading blocs are committed to officiate and develop trade activities for signatory nations. Trading blocs typically maintain two global, environmental business agendas for participating nations: economic benefit and political benefit. The largest trading blocs include the European Union (EU), North American Free Trade Agreement (NAFTA), El Mercado Común del Sur (MERCOSUR), Common Market of Eastern and Southern Africa (COMESA), and Association of Southeast Asian Nation (ASEAN). These blocs trade natural resources, healthcare, labor, and manufactured resources.

These agreements are designed to reduce and ultimately remove tariff and non-tariff barriers to the free movement of goods, services, and factors of production between each other. A major benefit is improvements in the standards of living for signatory nation citizens. The global business professional understands that these trade blocs develop over time, and generally follow a sequence of evolutionary stages.

## DEVELOPMENTAL STAGES

The core element of regional economic integration is the trading bloc. These blocs serve to help integrate the economies of signatory nations. However, differences exist among the various types and levels of trading blocs. "The result is a bewildering array of regional entities, with different bodies having very different sizes, purposes, aims, depths of integration, legal foundations, and fulfillment of their stated aims."[8] Different agreements are created among different nations. Trading blocs develop in progressive stages; this is determined by the degree of economic integration, varying from the least to the greatest integration. These stages, in order of intensity of integration, are Free Trade Area, Custom Union, Common Market, Economic Union, and Political Union.

NOTES

## Preferential and Free Trade Area

The first stage of economic integration is establishment of preferential or free trade agreements. Preferential Trade Areas allow preferential access to certain products from certain nations via the reduction of tariffs. The reduction does not necessarily remove tariffs entirely. An example is the Africa, Caribbean, and Pacific (ACP) pact. This pact includes nations from Africa, the Caribbean, and the Pacific Rim. The Lomé Convention of 1976 resulted in the agreement to establish a formal cooperation between the then European Community and developing ACP nations—in particular, former British, Dutch, and French colonies. The two goals of the agreement were to accomplish the following:

1.  Allow most ACP agricultural and mineral exports to enter the European Community with preferential access, free of duty. This preferential access included a quota system agreed upon for agricultural and mineral products that were in competition with similar European products.

2.  Provide $3 billion in aid and FDI from European Community to the ACP nations.

The Lomé Convention was replaced by the Cotonou Agreement in 2000, which includes the EU and seventy-seven developing nations. The goals of the Cotonou Agreement are threefold: (1) the reduction and eventual eradication of poverty in signatory island and land-locked nations, (2) sustainable economic development in signatory island and land-locked nations, and (3) the gradual integration of signatory countries into the world economy.

The free trade area is essentially a preferential trade area where tariffs, quotas, and preferences on most (if not all) goods among members are removed, and each member can determine its own trade polices with nonmembers. Free Trade Areas are suitable in cases where economic structures in signatory nations complement one another and trade in products that do not compete with each other. The U.S.-Chile Free Trade Agreement of 2003 is an example of a Free Trade Agreement. Those in support of this agreement believe trade between the U.S. and Chile will increase as a result of the reduction in trade barriers. Those in opposition believe Chile's over-dependence on scarce, natural-resource exports will increase.

## Customs Union

The next stage of regional economic integration is the Customs Union. All barriers of trade among members are removed, and a common external trade policy is adopted. Members have the same rights as in a free trade area, with the exception that they will now all have the same trade policy towards nonmembers. The purposes for establishing a customs union are twofold: to increase economic efficiency and to establish closer political and cultural ties between signatory nations. An example of a Customs Union is Mercosur, whose members include Brazil, Argentina, Uruguay, Paraguay, and Venezuela. Bolivia is an accessing member, and associate members include Chile, Colombia, Ecuador and Peru. Mercosur was established in 1991 with the goal of promoting free trade and the fluid movement of goods, people, and currency among signatory nations.

## Common Market

The next stage of regional economic integration is known as the Common Market. A Common Market includes all of the elements of a Customs Union and freedom of movement of the four factors of production: goods, services, capital, and labor. The Caribbean Community and Common Market (CARICOM) is an example of a Common Market. CARICOM established an administrative arm known as The Secretariat of the Caribbean Community, which includes a Secretary General who serves as the chief executive officer. The mission statement of the Secretariat is to provide dynamic leadership and service in partnership with Community Institutions and groups towards the attainment of a viable, internationally competitive, and sustainable Community, with improved quality of life for all.

## Economic Union

The next stage of regional economic integration is the Economic Union. An Economic Union is an agreement wherein nations remove all barriers to trade and the movement of labor and capital and erect a common trade policy against nonmembers. It requires that member countries harmonize their tax, monetary and fiscal policies, create a common currency, and concede a certain amount of sovereignty to the supranational organization to which they belong.[9] An example of the Economic Union is the European Union (EU).

## Political Union

The final and most advanced form of regional economic integration is the Political Union. The main aspect is the common government among members. An example of the Political Union is The United States of America where there is a central federal government. Individual states have a level of autonomy in their own state and local governments as well as state representation in the legislative branch of the federal government.

---

**Stages of Regional Economic Integration**

- Free Trade Agreement (FTA)—Zero tariffs between member countries and reduced non-tariff barriers;
- Customs Union (CU)—FTA + common external tariff;
- Common Market (CM)—Customs Union + free movement of capital and labor, some policy harmonization;
- Economic Union (EU)—Common Market + common economic policies and institutions.
- Political Union (USA)—Economic Union + unified political government

---

Nations are free to negotiate economic integration agreements as they see fit; however, in practice, formal agreements rarely fall neatly into one of the distinct stages. This can lead to some confusion of terminology and the state of economic integration in some parts of the world. For Example, Canada is part of the North American Free Trade Agreement with the United States and Mexico. NAFTA, however, also includes common market elements as it frees the flow of labor and capital throughout the region.[10]

Regardless of the stage and level of economic integration, arguments can be made regarding the purposes and outcomes of such agreements. Typically, the arguments promote the political and economic impact experienced by the person making the argument. In general, those who have been impacted in a positive manner tend to promote the idea that regional economic integration is a good thing. Likewise, those who have experienced negative outcomes tend to hold the idea that regional economic integration is not a good thing. The astute, global-business professional seeks to understand all aspects of the debate, both positive and negative.

## REGIONAL ECONOMIC INTEGRATION & AGREEMENTS

### *Regional Economic Integration*

Five basic value goals are espoused by national governments: (1) peace, (2) freedom and the absence of random violence, (3) prosperity and economic development, (4) the reduction in the incidence of poverty, and (5) democracy and a clean and healthy environment. Depending on the circumstances and their degree of development, it seems possible that regional economic integration efforts have contributed to the achievement of at least three of the basic value goals: economic prosperity, international peace, and democracy.[11] "According to its proponents, free trade helps nations take advantage of the unprecedented wealth the global economy is producing."[12] Compared to a nonparticipating nation, a participating nation in a trading bloc benefits from the established trade agreement, as a result of greater bargaining power. Consequently, the participation in a trading bloc leads to the minimization of duplication, thin spreading of resources, and wasteful competition. Some nations have benefited from a more efficient transportation system. In addition, trading blocs offer the opportunity for a greater division of labor and specialization in production.

The specialization in production and integration allows for greater prospects for technological advance and innovation. The nations' and citizens' income and wealth will increase from the freedom of transferring goods, services, labor, and capital. A growing nation results in inquiries from foreign investment. Additionally, regional integration further unites political alliances.[13] The political alliances are deepened as a result of incentives from economic growth within their own countries. These solid alliances minimize the threat of intense conflict between participating nations. The political power of these alliances can broaden trade with nonparticipating nations and different trading blocs.

Opponents of Regional Economic Integration have argued that regional economic integration agreements are dangerous because such agreements advance and establish procedures that protect participating nations from the benefits of free trade. In addition, some analysts argue that the concept of regional economic integration is relatively a new idea and the world and economists have limited data to evaluate the future economic and political benefits and limitations.

## Regional Agreements

The purpose of this section is to provide an overview of established regional economic integration; it includes descriptions of agreements, lists of participating members, and major issues concerning the established agreements. The regional agreements discussed in this section include the Americas, Europe, Asia, Middle East Organizations, and African nations.

### The Americas

North America is one of the largest trading blocs (NAFTA) in the world. Currently, all of Latin America, with the exception of Cuba, is governed by elected regimes, even if the depth and stability of democracy in a number of South American countries remains an open question.[14] The Americas present new opportunities for trade, investment, and services for the economic growth for the western hemisphere.

*North American Free Trade Agreement—NAFTA.* In 1989, Mexican President Carlos Salinas invited United States President George Bush to organize a trade agreement that would increase investment and decrease tariffs between the two nations. Furthermore, Canada joined Mexico and the United States in the negotiations. The U.S. and Canada had established a free trade agreement prior to NAFTA, called (CFTA). CFTA allowed trade of agriculture between the two nations. However, CFTA was incorporated within the establishments of NAFTA. The process of the development of NAFTA resulted in several years and was signed by the presidents of Mexico, United States, and Canada in 1992.[15] Eventually, NAFTA was officially in operation on January 1, 1994. It was the first major FTA between a developing country (Mexico) and developed countries (The U.S. and Canada).[16] The country of Chile became a participating nation within NAFTA at the end of 1994.

NAFTA immediately lifted tariffs on the majority of goods produced by the signatory nations. It also calls for the gradual elimination, over a period of 15 years, of most remaining barriers to cross-border investment and to the movement of goods and services among the three countries.[17]

### Important Developments of NAFTA

- The elimination of tariffs as well as import and export quotas,

- The opening of government procurement markets to companies in the other two nations,

- An increase in the opportunity to make investments in each other's country,

- An increase in the ease of travel between countries, and

- The removal of restrictions on agricultural products, auto parts, and energy goods.

The proponents of NAFTA point to the success of millions of jobs created because of the formation of NAFTA. This, however, has sparked a firestorm of debate as to whether or not these jobs have actually been created. The Office of the United States Trade Representative (USTR) has shown that the overall effect of NAFTA has been good for all

NOTES

member nations, especially the United States. During the period of 1993–2005, trade rose from $297 billion USD to $810 billion USD. Employment opportunities rose by about 22.6 million new jobs, a 20 percent increase.[18] Industrial production in the United States rose by 49 percent, far outperforming the increase achieved during the previous twelve-year period of 1982–1993. The USTR reported that the U.S. economy experienced stronger growth during the twelve years since NAFTA'S inception than the twelve years prior.[19]

The benefits of NAFTA are still evident with the U.S. and its NAFTA partners. U.S. goods and services trade with NAFTA totaled $1.6 trillion in 2009 and U.S. goods and services trade with the Western Hemisphere totaled $1.7 trillion in 2011. Whereas exports totaled $817 billion and imports totaled $865 billion.[20] As of 2012, NAFTA included a population of more than 460 million people and a GDP in excess of $17 trillion. An additional indicator of the benefits of NAFTA is that Western Hemisphere Countries FDI in the United States was $271.1 billion in 2008, up 2.8% from 2007.[21] NAFTA appears to be good for the economy.

NAFTA opponents posit that though one-million jobs were created through exports under NAFTA, two-million jobs were displaced as a result of imports through NAFTA. In other words, one-million jobs were displaced, mainly because of products that, prior to NAFTA, would have been created in the United States. Manufacturing jobs formerly held in the United States were lost to overseas operations. Opponents offer the following analogy: if the U.S. exported one-thousand cars, many Americans were employed to manufacture these automobiles. The converse of this is also true: if the U.S. imports the same one-thousand cars from Mexico, then the same workers will have to find employment elsewhere.[22] The evidence for and against NAFTA still needs to be weighed, as both proponents and opponents make formidable arguments for and against NAFTA.

*Southern Common Market—Mercosur.* Mercosur was established in 1991 with the intent of increasing the competitiveness of its five member nations' economies through the use of research on economic development.[23] Full-member nations include Argentina, Brazil, Paraguay (suspended), Uruguay, and Venezuela. Associate member nations include Bolivia (an assessing member), Chile, Columbia, Ecuador, Peru, and Guyana and Surinam. The population of Mercosur nations including the newly inducted Venezuela is more than 280 million and they have a combined GDP (PPP) in excess of 3 trillion.[24] As such, Mercosur ranks as one of the four largest trading blocs and one of the largest economies in the world. Cooperation among trading blocs is of special interest because the EU has established an ongoing relationship with Mercosur and seeks to serve as a catalyst towards Mercosur moving to the next stage of economic development—a common market.

*Andean Common Market—ANCOM.* The Andean Community or Comunidad Andina (CAN) as it is known in its Spanish translation has an estimated 2011 GDP PPP amounting to US $902.86 billion.[25] Current ANCOM membership includes Bolivia, Columbia, Ecuador, and Peru. The associate members of ANCOM are Argentina, Brazil, Paraguay, Uruguay, and Chile. ANCOM was established in 1969 with the Agreement of Cartagena, or Andean Pact, between Bolivia, Peru, Ecuador, and Chile. The goal of the Agreement was to abolish all barriers to trade by the competition of 1980. In addition, a common external tariff would become established at the end of 1980. These establishments were to increase trade among the participating countries and capitalize on joint efforts for combining industrial resources to increase stagnant industries. In addition, a goal of common currency was to be established during the participation of this integration. However, before that period, Venezuela agreed to join in 1973, and Chile withdrew membership in 1976. During the 1980s the trading bloc had diminished and was reestablished as the ANCOM in 1996.

The ANCOM consists of a council, a General Secretariat, and a common external tariff. In 2006, Venezuela resigned its membership from ANCOM in response to the actions of Peru and Columbia establishing free trade agreements with the U.S. Venezuelan President, Hugo Chavez, said the nation's decision to leave ANCOM was irrevocable and "a strategic decision to safeguard Venezuela's national interests," adding that his country could compete with "subsidized U.S. products."[26] Additional issues confronting the Andean Community are as follows:

- In 2006 Chile officially rejoined ANCOM as an associate member.[27] However, Chile and Peru have had a conflict since the nineteenth century of claiming ownership of a seaport on the coastal border of the two countries.

- Signatory nations such as Chile are promoting trade negotiations with Asia. "Chile argues that South American countries need to pool their export efforts to be able to supply the volume of products demanded by China and other Asian countries."[28]

- The establishment of an energy trade agreement between Chile and Bolivia. Chile is in need of energy and Bolivia has an excess stock. In 2006, Chile discarded import duties on most Bolivian imports.[29]

The goal of the ANDEAN community is to establish promotion of economic and social cooperation through a free trade agreement. However, the leaders of the ANDEAN community need to combine efforts to lay aside conflicts and positively establish agreements that will lead to the growth of all the participating economies.

*Caribbean Community and Common Market—CARICOM.* Established with the Treaty of Chaguaramas in 1973, CARICOM's purpose is to promote economic integration and development, with a main focus in less-developed areas of the region. Signatory nations include Antigua and Barbuda, the Bahamas, Barbados, Belize, Dominica, Grenada, Guyana, Haiti, Jamaica, Montserrat, Saint Kitts and Nevis, Saint Lucia, Saint Vincent, and the Grenadines, Suriname, and Trinidad and Tobago.[30] The Cayman Islands, the Turks, and Caicos Islands are associate members. CARICOM manages a common market and formulates policies on health, education, labor, science, technology, tourism, foreign policy, and the environment. Institutions affiliated with CARICOM include the Caribbean Court of Justice, the Caribbean Development Bank, the University of Guyana, and the University of the West Indies. The Caribbean Court of Justice was established by the organization in 2005. This organization acts as a final court of appeals and as a court of original jurisdiction for settling disputes among member countries.[31]

*Central American Common Market—CACM.* CACM was established in 1960 between Guatemala, El Salvador, Honduras, and Nicaragua. Costa Rica joined the organization in 1963. In 1969, the organization collapsed because of the Futbol War between Honduras and El Salvador, but it was reinstated in 1991. This five-day war (also known as the Football War or the Soccer War) was the result of political differences between Hondurans and Salvadorans, including immigration from El Salvador to Honduras. The name derives from the timing of the war, which overlapped with rioting from a series of soccer matches.[32]

CACM removed duties on most products that move between member nations, unified external tariffs, and increased trade within member nations. However, signatory nations have not been able to achieve their wider aims of stronger economic and political unification—one of the key goals of the organization. The problem stems from the organization's failure to settle trade disputes.[33] Efforts were focused on resolving political issues within the organization rather than focusing on economic integration growth. In the early 1990s, the agreement was strengthened by the addition of the Protocol to the General Treaty on Central American Economic Integration: the Guatemala Protocol.[34] The Guatemala Protocol allowed greater commercial exposure and diminished the protectionist nature of the original 1960 CACM agreement.[35]

More recently, signatory nations are working to establish an additional agreement. The new free trade agreement mirrors NAFTA. Countries such as Costa Rica, Dominican Republic, El Salvador, Guatemala, Honduras, and Nicaragua will begin trade activity with the United States—similar to the way Canada and Mexico currently trade with the United States. The new agreement will include arrangements on agriculture, automobile, and manufacturing tariffs, which will be eliminated or reduced over the next twenty years. In addition, market barriers will be eliminated or reduced. Pharmaceutical, textiles, and clothing industries will benefit from the established trade agreements.[36]

*Europe (European Union—EU)*

- Austria (1995)
- Belgium (1952)*
- Bulgaria (2007)
- Croatia (2013)
- Cyprus (2004)*
- Czech Republic (2004)
- Denmark (1973)
- Estonia ((2004)*
- Finland (1995)*
- France (1952)*
- Germany (1952)*
- Greece (1981)*
- Hungary (2004)
- Ireland (1973)*
- Italy (1952)*
- Latvia (2004)*
- Lithuania (2004)
- Luxembourg (1952)*
- Malta (2004)*
- Netherlands (1952)*
- Poland (2004)
- Portugal (1986)*
- Romania (2007)
- Slovakia (2004)*
- Slovenia (2004)*
- Spain (1986)*
- Sweden (1995)
- United Kingdom (1973)

The EU is an economic union of twenty-eight member states which are listed above. Candidate nations include, former Yugoslavia Republic of Macedonia, Turkey, Iceland, Montenegro, and Serbia. Potential candidates include Albania, Bosnia and Herzegovinian, and Kosovo.[37] To become a member state, a prospective country needs to fulfill political and economic preconditions known as the Copenhagen Criteria. This requires a democratic and secular government, an independent judiciary, and corresponding personal freedoms.

The EU aims to enhance political, economic, and social cooperation through a process known as European Integration. Formed in 1992 by the Maastricht Treaty, the EU supersedes the European Common Market that had been in existence since 1951. The organization operates a common single market that incorporates a customs union. Included within the Common Market rules are a common agricultural policy, a common trade policy, and a common fisheries policy. The EU has also adopted a common foreign and security policy and established formal cooperation in areas of police and judicial investigation into criminal matters. People living within the EU hold EU citizenship. They can live and work in any EU country without the requirement for visas or work permits. The Schengen Agreement abolished passport and border controls within the internal-national boundaries of the EU. These measures aim to eliminate barriers to trade, investment, and the movement of labor.

Eighteen of the nations (as denoted by an asterisks in the list above) have formed a single currency area, the Euro Zone, which consists of approximately three-hundred and thirty-two million people. This effectively makes the Euro Zone area a true monetary and economic union. The European Central Bank (ECB) is responsible for monetary policy for the Euro and sets interest rates across the twelve participating members. All EU members are obliged to adopt the Euro as their national currency, with the exception of Great Britain and Denmark, which have been exempted under the terms of the Maastricht Treaty. Prior to acceptance into the Euro Zone, EU members must satisfy strict economic convergence criteria. This includes limits on national inflation and budgetary deficits.

The most important EU institutions include the Council of the European Union, the European Commission, the European Court Justice, The European Central Bank, and the European Parliament. The Union cannot transfer additional powers from state onto itself without member agreement through further international treaties. The European Parliament was established in the 1950s. Elections are held every five years, and all registered EU citizens are allowed to vote. The European Commission is the executive body of the EU. Consisting of twenty-five commissioners and originating from each member state and several thousand supporting civil servants, the European Commission drafts and implements legislation and enforces existing treaties. The Council of Europe contains ministers from the governments of member nations. It passes EU law on the recommendations of the European Commission and the European Parliament. The Council also approves the EU budget and seeks to coordinate the adoption of common economic, defense, and judicial policies across the EU. The European Court of Justice (ECJ) interprets European Law and adjudicates in areas of dispute. The ECJ examines and decides on claims brought by the European Commission against member states for noncompliance with EU laws or directives. Similarly, the ECJ judges claims by member states that the European Commission has exceeded its authority. The ECJ also assists national courts in the interpretation of EU law—its decisions are binding on the national courts.[38]

## Asia

Asia is the world's largest continent, covering 43.6 million square miles. Home to nearly four billion inhabitants, Asia has experienced a population explosion in the last fifty years and now contains over 60 percent of the world's population.[39] Enormous differences in standards of living and life expectancy occur between the most advanced nations, such as Japan and Singapore, and its least advanced nations, such as Afghanistan and Bangladesh. Increasing attention is being paid to the rapidly growing economies of China and India, as they evolve from primarily agricultural dependence into industrial giants with regional superpower status.

South Korea, Hong Kong, Singapore, and Taiwan are known as The Four Tigers, because of high levels of prosperity and standards of living. Recently, however, the economies of the four Asian tiger nations which benefited from American consumption were hit hard by the financial crisis of 2007-2008. By the fourth quarter of 2008, the GDP of all four nations fell by an average annualized rate of around 15 percent. Exports have also fallen by a 50 percent annualized rate. Weak domestic demand has also affected the recovery of these economies as demonstrated by the decrease in 2008 retail sales by 3 percent in Hong Kong, 6 percent in Singapore and 11 percent in Taiwan.[40] Other nations that have developed economically are Thailand, Malaysia, Indonesia, and Vietnam. Japan is the world leader in manufacturing and consumer goods. China's exports are high in the United States, and the country attracts foreign investment. However, China is a political risk for investors because it is divided between communism and capitalism. The major regional economic integration agreements in this region include the Association of Southeast Asia Nations, the Asia Pacific Economic Cooperation, and the South Asian Association for Economic Cooperation.

*Association of Southeast Asian Nations—ASEAN.* ASEAN includes Brunei Darussalam, Cambodia, Indonesia, Lao PDR, Malaysia, Myanmar, Philippines, Singapore, Thailand, and Vietnam. The goal is to attain economic, social, and cultural aims through joint endeavors, collaboration, and assistance. They show mutual respect for the independence, sovereignty, equality, territorial integrity, and national identity of all nations. ASEAN gives every state the right to lead its existence free from external interference. The association's members also undertake to avoid interference in the internal affairs of one another and are committed to the settlement of differences or disputes by peaceful means. ASEAN includes renunciation of the threat or use of force and effective cooperation amongst members. Political and security dialog and cooperation should promote regional peace and stability by enhancing regional resilience.[41]

*Asia Pacific Economic Cooperation—APEC.* APEC's founding member countries include Australia, Canada, Indonesia, Japan, Malaysia, New Zealand, Philippines, Singapore, South Korea, Thailand, and the United States. In 1991 China and Hong Kong became members, followed by Mexico and Papua New Guinea in 1993, Chile in 1994, and Taiwan, Peru, Russia, and Vietnam in 1998. India is seeking APEC membership. Guam is also seeking membership, but is currently represented by the United States. At this time, the majority of nations on the coastline of the Pacific Ocean are organization members.[42]

*South Asian Association for Regional Cooperation (SAARC).* SAARC, the largest agreement in the world (approximately 1.56 billion people), is comprised of the following Southern Asia nations: Afghanistan, Bangladesh, Bhutan, India, Maldives, Nepal, Pakistan, and Sri Lanka. Potential future members include the countries of China, Myanmar, and Russia.[43] Due to political and military tensions between India and Pakistan, SAARC has not been effective in integrating the economies of signatory nations. The ineffectiveness is manifested in a fear that the more integrated South Asia becomes, the greater will be India's dominance over SAARC signatory nations. SAARC currently serves as a mere platform for annual talks and meetings between its members.[44]

### Middle East

The majority of economic growth and stability in the Middle East depends upon the natural resource of oil. After the September 11, 2001 attacks on U.S. soil, the Middle East gained more attention through news reports. The conflict and partnership between the Middle East regions is a concern for nations not located in the region. The natural resource of petroleum influences the worldwide economy. This region of the world is the majority producer of petroleum. Organizations have been established to evaluate the producing of the resource.

*Organization of Arab Petroleum Exporting Countries—OAPEC.* OAPEC was created in 1968 by Kuwait, Saudi Arabia, and Libya. Since 1968, the addition of Algeria, Bahrain, Egypt, Iraq, Qatar, Syria, Tunisia and United Arab Emirates has strengthened the economy of OAPEC. However, Tunisia has disassociated membership from the OAPEC organization. The following excerpt reveals the mission statement of OAPEC:

> OAPEC is a regional inter-governmental organization concerned with the development of the petroleum industry by fostering cooperation among its members. OAPEC contributes to the effective use of the resources of member countries through sponsoring joint ventures. The Organization is guided by the belief in the importance of building an integrated petroleum industry as a cornerstone for future economic integration amongst Arab countries.[45]

The resource of oil is valuable to the majority of industries throughout the World. This organization faces continuous pressure from these industries, as well as political conflict. History has displayed how conflicts can affect the supply and demand of oil resources, resulting in price fluctuation. OAPEC has witnessed war in the 1970s, 1990s, and the current wars in Iraq and Afghanistan. However, they have proactively invited members to discuss these issues. By May 2012, the ninth Arab Energy Conference had been implemented. Issues discussed included the following:

- To establish an Arab institutional framework for oil and energy issues in order to develop a Pan-Arab perspective

- Coordinate relations among Arab institutions concerned with energy and development

- Harmonize energy policies with development planning

- Investigate present and future Arab energy requirements and the means of meeting them

- Identify and assess existing energy resources in the Arab countries

- To coordinate and enhance efforts to develop these resources

- To identify and evaluate the impact of international energy policies on the Arab countries[46]

OAPEC has established successful committees and leaders to regulate and monitor practices within the organization. The accomplishments of OAPEC include the creation of four companies that operate with their board of directors. The Arab Maritime Petroleum Transport Company's (AMPTC) objective is to oversee entire operations related to the marine transportation of hydrocarbons. The Arab Shipbuilding and Repair Yard Company (ASRY) is responsible for repairing, building, and maintaining all types of marine transportation machinery. The Arab Petroleum Investments Corporation (APICORP) assists in financing projects related to the oil industry. The Arab Petroleum Services Company (APSCO) provides oil services by developing specialized subsidiaries of different branches of oil services. OAPEC has implemented effective measures to ensure success in different areas of supplying petroleum to nations. However, progress is continuous in the area of political conflict affiliated with oil demands.

### Gulf Cooperation Council—GCC

Established in 1981, the goal of the Gulf Cooperation Council (GCC) is to create economic wealth and maintain the growth of nations affiliated with the Persian Gulf. Currently, the members include Bahrain, Oman, Kuwait, Saudi Arabia, Qatar, and the United Arab Emirates. The GCC operates as a common market, granting national treatment to all GCC firms and citizens in any other GCC country, as well as removing all barriers to cross country investment and services trade.

### Africa

Africa, the world's second largest continent, covers 11.6 million square miles and has a population of approximately 800 million people. More than 60 percent of Africa's people depend upon agriculture, with farming being mostly of the subsistence variety.[47] Despite extensive natural resources, there are no developed countries in Africa. Many countries have low indicators for education, health, life expectancy, and nutrition. Significant manufacturing capability remains a rarity, the exception being South Africa. Africa suffers from ill-conceived national boundaries that were drawn up by the colonial powers. These boundaries often separate peoples of the same tribe or bring antagonists from different tribes into contact with each other. The result is often internal conflict or regional strife.

A major factor that inhibits success of trade is the 1,000 various languages among 750 million citizens. In addition, African history has demonstrated much political instability, which results in low foreign investment because of high risk. Against this difficult background, progress has been made to integrate regional economic activity for mutual gain. The two most notable trade organizations are the Economic Community of West African Nations and the South African Customs Union.

*Economic Community of West African States—ECOWAS.* ECOWAS was formed in 1975 and included fifteen nations. Through the years, there have been a few changes in its membership. The original fifteen nations were Faso, Ghana, Mali, Sierra Leone, Benin, Burkina, Cote d'Ivoire, Gambia, Guinea, Guinea-Bissau, Liberia, Mauritania, Niger, Nigeria, Senegal, and Togo. One year after the organization was founded, Cape Verde joined to increase membership to sixteen countries. In 2002, Mauritania decided to withdraw from the organization, which left fifteen countries in ECOWAS. The main objective of ECOWAS was to integrate economies and partake in shared development of economic growth.

ECOWAS has faced numerous problems in attempting to unite the region. Contributing factors include a lack of infrastructure, not having diverse economies, the existence of other organizations with the same purpose, and political instability. Member nations have tried to agree on a common currency: the ECO. The thought was that a common currency would introduce and encourage the members to join the global commerce community through free trade. The creation of this currency has been postponed several times, as member countries have been unable to meet the minimum requirements for the creation of the currency. They are still in the process of attempting to meet the minimum criteria.

Another obstacle is hunger. It is very difficult to create and sustain an economy if the individuals cannot obtain food. In 2005, a Common Agricultural Policy (CAP) was approved. The main objective of CAP was to create a sustainable food source for the member countries. In order for them to succeed in uniting ECOWAS countries, they must find a way to overcome starvation in this region.

Another issue is the need to improve the current electrical grid to create a cheaper and more reliable energy sector to produce jobs, stimulate the economy, and increase trade inside and outside of the member nations. In a related issue, a natural gas pipeline is under consideration to provide a natural gas link to Togo, Ghana, and Nigeria.[48] The idea behind these improvements is that the provision of reliable and inexpensive energy will lead to the stimulation of the ECOWAS economies. Currently, only one-third of the citizens in the member countries have access to electricity. Finally, ECOWAS has attempted to make traveling between member nations easier through the implementation of a program that generates certificates instead of passports, so the citizens can travel more freely. The certificates will be administered by a single agency instead of each country. This will reduce costs and confusion and hopefully increase the tourism industry.

*Southern African Customs Union—SACU.* In 1970, an agreement between the nations of Botswana, Lesotho, Namibia, South Africa, and Swaziland was implemented as a customs union. The SACU goals are to maintain the free interchange of goods between signatory nations and provide for a common external tariff and a common excise tariff. All customs and excise collected in the common custom area are paid into South Africa's national Revenue Fund. The Revenue is shared among members according to a revenue-sharing formula as described in the agreement.[49] Since the beginning of the integration, agreements within SACU have improved economic standards. The United States has played a major role in the economic and political growth in SACU. "SACU is the United States' second largest trading partner in Africa behind Nigeria whose exports are almost exclusively petroleum products."[50] However, this trading bloc creates many issues dealing with the needs of each participant involved with the SACU. The SACU and United States consider industry, labor rights, and environmental regulations very important to the prosperity of this region.[51]

*Other International Groups*

Establishments of International Groups are aimed to benefit the economic and social growth of the participating parties. These groups establish committees that govern the production and issues concerning the reason for the agreement. Listed below are two examples of cooperation groups that aim at establishing organization within the petroleum industry and the social and economic benefit of conducting research. These cooperations involve countries from neighbor regions and overseas. The involvement is to benefit the global economy and the economy within the participating nations.

*Organization of the Petroleum Exporting Countries—OPEC.* OPEC was founded in 1960 in Baghdad. The major function is to help member countries coordinate oil production in an effort to stabilize the oil market, while achieving a reasonable return on oil investment. As a result of soaring fuel prices, OPEC has received much attention in the U.S. Consumption of oil and oil products has greatly increased, with the majority of the growth in developing countries. OPEC nations produce 30 million barrels of oil each day. The U.S. Energy Information Administration estimates that world consumption exceeds 90 million barrels per day.[52]

Oil prices are not set by OPEC, but the organization does have an indirect influence on price. By increasing or reducing production, OPEC nations impact price through the theory of supply and demand. Simply put, the more they produce, the cheaper the product. By producing less oil, the cost increases. This theory holds true only if demand remains unchanged or increases. Instability in the oil-producing region, along with political issues with Iran and other nations, has led to the speculation of shortages, which leads to higher prices.

The decisions made by OPEC either directly or indirectly affect the majority of consumer goods being produced, sold, or used. The world has become smaller over time because of the ability to travel. This convenience has also produced opportunities for trade. The transportation used to import and export products requires oil or gasoline, either as a primary fuel or as a lubricant. Therefore, if oil is more expensive to buy, then the cost of the actual product being carried will probably increase. The importing and exporting companies will pass the cost of transportation on to the wholesalers; the wholesalers will pass it on to the retailers; and ultimately, the customer will pay for it.

*Organization for Economic Cooperation and Development—OECD.* The Organization for Economic Cooperation and Development was established in 1960 as an economic counterpart to the North Atlantic Treaty Organization (NATO). Currently, the thirty-four members of OECD include the following:[53]

- Australia
- Austria
- Belgium
- Canada
- Chile
- Czech Republic
- Denmark
- Estonia
- Finland
- France
- Germany
- Greece
- Hungary
- Iceland
- Ireland
- Israel
- Italy
- Japan
- Korea
- Luxembourg
- Mexico
- Netherlands
- New Zealand
- Norway
- Poland
- Portugal
- Slovak Republic
- Slovenia
- Spain
- Sweden
- Switzerland
- Turkey
- United Kingdom
- United States

The objective of the organization is increasing economic welfare through the world by covering issues associated with social work and economic efforts within participating governments and nonparticipating governments. It focuses on areas such as macroeconomics, science and innovation, development, education, and trade. The organization reports statistics dealing with social and economic issues to better educate the governments—such as consensus.[54] For example, a study conducted by OECD reported the reading proficiency of students in the participating countries. The study found that students in highest levels of reading proficiency are Shanghai-China, Korea, and Finland. The countries with the lowest level of reading proficiency are Brazil, Argentina, and Indonesia. Students in Norway, France, the United States, Denmark, and Switzerland are clustered in the middle.[55] The research and development by OECD demonstrates the importance of information to governments to ensure proper programs to educate, monitor, and enrich citizens' lives.

## KEY CONCEPTS

- Andean Common Market (ANCOM)

- Asia Pacific Economic Cooperation (APEC)

- Association of Southeast Asian Nations (ASEAN)

- Caribbean Community and Common Market (CARICOM)

- Central American Common Market (CACM)

- Common Market

- Customs Union

- Economic Community of West African Nations (ECOWAS)

- Economic Union

- European Union (EU)

- Free trade area

- Globalization

- Gulf Co-operation Council (GCC)

- Non-tariff barriers

- North American Free Trade Agreement (NAFTA)

- Organization for Economic Co-operation and Development (OECD)

- Organization of Arab Petroleum Exporting Countries (OAPEC)

- Organization of the Petroleum Exporting Countries (OPEC)

- Regional Economic Integration

- South African Customs Union (SACU)

- South Asian Association for Regional Cooperation (SAARC)

- Southern Common Market (Mercosur)

- Tariff barriers

- Trading blocs

# Chapter 6 Exercises: Observational Analysis

*Ponder on the following key concepts and ideas as you read the chapter*

1.  Regional Economic Integration and the Levels of Integration: Free Trade through Economic Unions. How the stages of integration allow for the free movement of goods and services and impact the political, economical, social, and environmental landscapes of the integrated regions.

2.  The basic goals and aspirations for regional integration and the political and economical arguments: for and against

3.  Regional trade agreements and pacts in the Americas, Europe, Asia, the Middle East, Africa, and other regions. Cartels, including Organization of the Petroleum Exporting Countries (OPEC) and the Organization for Economic Co-operation and Development (OECD)

4.  Start a list of books, journals, and scholarly websites that would aid in the understanding of the chapters main concepts and ideas. Start a journal for your own thoughts and ideas. What outside sources support your conclusions?

# Chapter 6 Exercises: Key Terms Analysis

*Match the answers by writing the correct letter in the space provided*

_____ 1. Preferential Trade Areas

_____ 2. ACP

_____ 3. Mercosur

_____ 4. Trading bloc

_____ 5. NAFTA

_____ 6. Free trade area

_____ 7. ASEAN

_____ 8. Four Tigers

_____ 9. CACM

_____ 10. The Schengen agreement

_____ 11. Regional economic integration

_____ 12. Economic Union

_____ 13. ECJ

_____ 14. Custom Union

_____ 15. Common market

_____ 16. Customs delay

_____ 17. European central bank

_____ 18. Council of Europe

_____ 19. Political union

_____ 20. OPEC

A. Was signed by the presidents of Mexico, United States, and Canada in 1992

B. A regional agreement that includes countries of Brunei Darussalam, Cambodia, Laos, Philippines, and Thailand

C. Most advanced form of regional economic integration

D. Unified external tariffs, removed duties on products, increased trade between Central American countries

E. Mercosur

F. European Union

G. Committed to officiate and develop trade activities for signatory nations

H. Country reduce/remove tariff/non-tariff barriers to trade between members; decide own barriers for non-members

I. Passes EU law on the recommendations of the European Commission and the European Parliament

J. Bureaucratic formalities; slow down imported product from entering the domestic market

K. Africa, Pacific, Caribbean Pact; Lomé Convention

L. Includes all elements of a Customs Union and freedom of movement of the 4 factors of production

M. Abolished passport and border controls within the European Union

N. U.S.–Chile Agreement of 2003

O. Helps member countries coordinate oil production to help stabilize the oil market

P. A Preferential Trade Area that includes Africa, the Pacific, and the Caribbean

Q. Decides on claims brought by the European Commission regarding noncompliance with EU laws

R. South Korea, Hong Kong, Singapore, and Taiwan

S. Is responsible for monetary policy of the Euro

T. Established in 1991 to promote free trade and the fluid movement of goods, people, and currency

# Chapter 6 Exercises: Theoretical Analysis

*Analyze the questions and select the answer based on the reading of the chapter material*

1.  Which of the following is NOT a problem ECOWAS faces?

    a.  Attempting to unite the region

    b.  Hunger

    c.  Updating the current electrical grid to create more reliable energy

    d.  The strict use of passports as the means of travel between the countries

2.  Regional integration is the process whereby countries remove barriers to trade between themselves, but each country determines its own barriers against nonmembers.

    a.  True

    b.  False

3.  Eighteen of the European union nations have formed a single currency area called _____

    a.  The Euro currency zone

    b.  The Eurozone

    c.  The European finance area

    d.  The Economic zone of Europe

4.  Approximately 50 percent of all world trade is conducted through regional trade agreements.

    a.  True

    b.  False

5.  The goals of the The Lomé Convention are threefold: (1) the reduction and eventual eradication of poverty in Signatory Island and land-locked nations, (2) sustainable economic development in Signatory Island and land-locked nations, and (3) the gradual integration of signatory countries into the world economy.

    a.  True

    b.  False

6.  A Common Market includes all of the elements of a Customs Union and freedom of movement of the four factors of production: goods, services, capital, and labor.

    a.  True

    b.  False

7.  Which of the following countries is NOT a founding member of APEC?

    a.  New Zealand

    b.  China

    c.  Singapore

    d.  Indonesia

8.  In 1979, Mexican President Carlos Salinas invited United States President Bill Clinton to organize a trade agreement that would increase investment and decrease tariffs between the U.S. and Mexico.

    a.  True

    b.  False

9. Mercosur was established in 1991 with the intent of increasing the competitiveness of its five member nations' economies through the use of research on economic development. Full-member nations include Argentina, Brazil, Paraguay, Uruguay, and Venezuela.

    a. True

    b. False

10. Trading blocs provide protection from global competitiveness.

    a. True

    b. False

11. ANCOM was established in 1990 with the Agreement of Cartagena, or Andean Pact, between Bolivia, Peru, Ecuador, and Chile.

    a. True

    b. False

12. OPEC was founded in 1960 in Baghdad.

    a. True

    b. False

13. CACM was established in 1960 between

    a. Guatemala, El Salvador, Honduras, and Nicaragua

    b. Guatemala, Puerto Rico, Honduras, and Nicaragua

    c. Guatemala, El Salvador, Honduras, and Costa Rica

    d. Brazil, El Salvador, Honduras, and Nicaragua

14. Which of the following is not a member of OECD?

    a. Greenland

    b. Korea

    c. Israel

    d. Greece

15. A study conducted by the OECD reported the students who had the highest level of reading proficiency include

    a. Finland, Canada, Norway

    b. United States, Denmark, Luxembourg

    c. Shanghai-China, Korea, Finland

    d. Japan, Korea, Finland

16. The participation in a trading bloc leads to the minimization of duplication, thin spreading of resources, and wasteful competition.

    a. True

    b. False

17. Which of the following is the order of the stages of regional economic integration?

    a.  FTA, EU, CM, CU, PU

    b.  EU, CM, FTA, PU, CU

    c.  FTA, CU, CM, EU, PU

    d.  CM, PU, CU, EU, FTA

18. Preferential Trade Areas are suitable in cases where economic structures in signatory nations complement one another and trade in products that do not compete with each other.

    a.  True

    b.  False

19. Which of the following countries is NOT a member of Mercosur?

    a.  Brazil

    b.  Argentina

    c.  Uruguay

    d.  Costa Rica

20. All of the following are important EU institutions except

    a.  Euro Zone

    b.  Council of the European Union

    c.  European Commission

    d.  European Court of Justice

# Chapter 6 Exercises: Practical Analysis

*Write a short essay in the space provided to each of the following questions.*
*Please use outside references for each answer to support your ideas and thoughts.*

1. Regional integration agreements, also known as regional trading blocs, are intended to reduce and ultimately remove tariff and non-tariff barriers to trade in order to enhance the free movement of goods, services, and factors of production between the integrated regions.

   a. Are simply limiting/reducing tariffs and barriers to trade effective in enabling the free flow of goods and services? How are non-tariff barriers to free trade beneficial?

   b. What are some driving forces behind Regional Trade Agreements? Would a government seek a regional trade agreement for security concerns? Could this or any other factor enfeeble the economic reason that would support participation within a regional trade agreement?

2. How are trade agreements useful to trade strategies between nations? In what ways has globalization effected trade development and strategies between nations?

3. Pick any two regional agreements listed within the text and using the World Wide Web answer the following questions in the space provided:

   a. What is the basis and intention for the regional agreement?

   b. What stage does the agreement most resemble? Does it remove tariff and non tariff barriers?

   c. What are the benefits to the participating members?

   d. What are some arguments for and against this particular agreement?

# Chapter 6 Exercises: Biblical Worldview Application

*Write a short essay in the space provided to each of the following questions.*
*Please use biblical references and research, where applicable, to support your ideas and thoughts.*

1. Developmental stages of regional economic integration Include: Free trade area, Customs union, Common Market, Economic Union, and Political Union. Each stage requires a demonstration of trust before moving on to the next. Likewise, global business managers who operates from a Biblical Worldview must engender trust in all associates and agreements overseas. What behavioral characteristics make this possible, and what behavioral characteristics make this impossible?

2. The objective of the OECD is increasing economic welfare through the world by covering issues associated with social work and economic efforts within participating governments and nonparticipating governments. It focuses on areas such as macroeconomics, science and innovation, development, education, and trade. How might Christian ministries be able to partner with OECD efforts in terms of development and education?

3. I Kings chapters 7-10 provide a wealth of insight into the concept of cross-border trade. After reading these chapters, compile a list of the nations King Solomon traded with, as well as the details regarding goods and services traded. Include prices and other details, if available.

# Global Market Entry

NOTES

# CHAPTER OVERVIEW

Numerous variables must be considered in the decision to move domestic operations and products into the global marketplace. These decision variables include the desire to increase sales and profitability and to realize cost savings and profitability as a result of a partial or whole relocation in a foreign nation. Although most firms typically choose to enter into global markets from a proactive stance, some are forced to enter the global market in a reactive stance. Such firms would rather remain domestic, but the market forces them global in order to remain profitable. The figure below depicts additional decision variables to consider for competition in global markets.

| Competing in Global Markets | |
|---|---|
| **Competition on Quality and Price** | Overseas competitors can attack a firm's domestic market by offering higher quality and lower prices. |
| **Competition by Counterattack** | If attacked in their home market by higher quality and lower prices, the domestic firm can counterattack the overseas competitor's home market. |
| **Realization of Additional Profits** | Domestic firms often discover foreign markets to be opportunities to potentially realize higher profits than in the home market |
| **Economies of Scale** | If domestic markets become saturated, the firm may need a larger customer base to maintain economies of scale. |

These factors serve as the basis to drive global expansion when combined with conditions necessary for expansion into global markets. The necessary conditions include (1) expanding markets, (2) gaining access to resources, (3) cutting costs, and (4) capitalizing on special features of location.

# EXPANDING INTO GLOBAL MARKETS

*Conditions Necessary for Expansion into Global Markets*

The investigation of opportunities for global expansion requires the careful consideration of various business-environment conditions. Organizations should identify their strengths and weaknesses and understand how these may apply overseas. Organizations should identify the unique resources and capabilities that may be offered to them. These considerations could determine whether or not a firm's products or services in the home market extends internationally and will meet foreign demand. Organizations should research the demographics of the potential market in which they are hoping to enter to see if there is a viable market for their product. Although population growth is a great reference to start with, it is not always the key indicator of a strong potential market. The percentage increase and decrease of a population and the average life expectancy in a global market serve as indicators of the global-market potential. Usually, the most attractive markets are in nations that seem to be growing in population and increasing in economic resources.

Organizations should consider the new risks and increases in business complexity typically associated with global expansion. Depending on the makeup of the firm, some may need to expand elements of their supply chain as well as manage an increased number of foreign relationships. Foreign markets may require adaptations to certain existing products, thus requiring the organization to manage multiple products and market strategies simultaneously. This can be a very difficult challenge for small firms that lack the strategic internal resources that are available to larger firms to meet the legal, financial, and trading requirements of that specific foreign nation in which business expansion is desired. The challenge for multinational corporations would be to develop a portfolio of products and marketing programs that will result in effectively reaching the global needs and wants of its market. The challenge for smaller firms would be to identify new markets, develop a marketing niche within them, and fill the gaps left by the larger MNCs, with respect to competition.

A business may decide to expand by entering global markets. However, entering global markets is not necessarily an easy task or a right decision for the business. Certain conditions are necessary for successful global expansion, and a number of risks must be considered. If these potential risks are understood, taken into account, and properly planned for, then the firm can focus on primary conditions, such as the firm's managerial commitment and the motivations behind global market entry. The following figure depicts the kinds of risks that should be considered.

| Market Expansion Risk Variables | |
|---|---|
| National Customer Preferences | This occurs when the firm may not understand foreign customer preferences and fail to offer "globalized" products and services. |
| National Business Culture | This occurs when the firm does not know how to effectively deal with foreign nationals, which directly impacts the ability to understand their business culture. |
| National Regulations | This occurs when the firm incurs unanticipated costs as the result of underestimating foreign regulations. |
| National Political Risks | This occurs when governments change commercial laws, devalue currency, or undergo political revolution and expropriate foreign property. |
| Lack of Global Experience | This occurs when the firm lacks managers with international experience. |

### Managerial Commitment

The decision to expand into global markets is an enormous undertaking for all areas of the organization, not just corporate executives. Successful international expansion requires total commitment from management across the organization. The planning and execution stages of global expansion typically require long hours, overseas travel, and a team attitude. Additionally, the globalization team may need to consider the cost of adding needed personnel, initial expansion expenses, and strategies for overcoming potential employee resistance to the change. Corporations will have to utilize their complete management team—from marketing to facilities—to ensure that no detail is left out. The figure below provides a series of vital questions for firms to consider when determining the commitment of their management employees.

Many corporations find that managerial commitment is not a problem. In fact, there may be much enthusiasm about the prospects of growth and professional development. However, it is important to understand that transferring current managers to run new foreign operations might not be the best strategy to pursue. Benefits accrue to firms that hire a global manager who has a proven track record and the strengths needed to lead the international expansion.

Successful global managers tend to possess experiential knowledge specific to many cultures rather than in-depth experience in a few. They may speak only one language fluently; but, what they do have is an understanding of how to appraise and adjust to the requirements of doing business in a culture different from their own. Global managers are needed because cultures themselves are becoming less distinct.[1] Senior management must effectively communicate the importance of these benefits to other managers and gain their support. Regardless, the commitment of the firm's management team is essential to the successful growth of international operations.

> **Managerial Commitment Questions**
> - How committed is top management to going global?
> - How quickly does management expect its international operations to pay off?
> - What in-house, international experience does the firm have (international sales experience, language skills, etc.)?
> - How much senior management time should be allocated to the company's global efforts?
> - What organizational structure is required to ensure success abroad?

*Motivation*

Different motivating factors serve as drivers for organizations to enter the global market. Some examples of motivating factors include:[2]
- Avail the firm of international market opportunities
- Current markets have been saturated
- Reduce strategic risk
- Reduce the volatility of the income stream
- Increase net earnings
- Seek new economies of scale and scope
- Reduce costs through getting access to lower cost factors of production
- Support overseas trade barriers
- Establish new competitive advantages

Market entry motivation can be classified into two separate areas: (1) proactive and (2) reactive.

Proactive reasons are based on the firm's internal situation and are firm initiated, while reactive reasons are based on the firm's behavior with respect to the environment and adaptation to changes from outside the firm. Firms with proactive motivations go international because they want to, while reactive firms go international because they must.[3]

*Proactive.* Possibly the greatest proactive motivation for global expansion is the prospect of increased profits. The firm might see an opportunity in a foreign market that could reap greater profit margins than in their domestic market. A firm might also proactively expand internationally to give itself a strategic advantage over its competitors. The proactive motivation for smaller firms tends to relate to an exclusive product or some type of competitive or strategic technological advancement. "Firms with more than twenty-five employees export also to achieve economies of scale and to avoid losing out on foreign opportunities."[4]

Other motivators for international expansion could be that enterprises have obtained special information about promising customers or market opportunities abroad or are motivated by incentives of some sort, such as tax benefits granted by foreign governments. Since the major underlying motivation is the quest for increased profit, the need is for increased output to benefit from economies of scale and the consequent drive to expand business beyond the national boundaries.[5]

> **Major Proactive Motivations for International Expansion**
> - Quest for profit
> - Competitive advantage
> - Market opportunities
> - Economies of scale
> - Tax benefits[6]

*Reactive.* In contrast, some firms make the decision to enter global markets based on reactive motivations. In this case, the firm is reacting to external environmental factors and are forced to expand internationally. These situations occur when there is saturation in the domestic market and the firm must expand in order to survive financially. The firm could also be looking for ways to reduce costs, and foreign expansion could offer the firm cheaper production costs. The firm could even be reacting to tremendous pressures from competition or the political environment.

The following factors are reactive motivations for firms to expand into the global economy:[7]

- Competitive pressure
- Excess capacity
- Overproduction
- Saturated or declining home market

Regardless, the reactive firm expands as a response to other forces, and not because of its own desire to globalize.

# MARKET ENTRY CONSIDERATIONS AND FACTORS

*Basic Entry Considerations and Questions*

As a number of organizations research, examine, identify, and evaluate potential entry opportunities into international markets, businesses must carefully consider the potential benefits, advantages, challenges, and risks involved in the efforts of competing within an international market. Some domestic organizations have achieved long-term success, while others have experienced failure when competing in local, regional, and national markets. As previously mentioned, the decision to expand into a global market can be intimidating. The process of international expansion may be time consuming and difficult, but it is a process that could reap great rewards for the organization. A few basic steps are essential when considering global expansion:

- Begin the global expansion campaign by preparing an international business plan to evaluate organizational needs and goals
- Conduct foreign market research and identify international markets
- Evaluate and select methods of distributing products overseas
- Learn how to set prices, negotiate deals, and navigate the legal morass of exporting. Cultural, social, legal, and economic differences make exporting a challenge for business owners who have only operated in the U.S
- Secure government and private sources of financing
- Package and label products to comply with legal requirements of the target nation's market[8]

Although these steps may seem simple, much time and effort must go into the implementation of each step to create an effective, successful, global expansion plan of action. A more comprehensive plan includes, but is not limited to the following:

- Secure company-wide commitment
- Define the business plan for accessing global markets
- Determine how much is available to invest in the international expansion
- Plan at least a two-year lead time for world market penetration
- Build a website and implement the international plan sensibly
- Pick a product or service to take overseas
- Conduct market research to identify prime target markets
- Search out the data needed to predict how the product will sell in a specific geographic location
- Prepare the product for export
- Find cross-border customers
- Establish a direct or indirect method of export
- Hire a good lawyer, a savvy banker, a knowledgeable accountant, and a seasoned logistic specialist[9]

In addition to these considerations, three questions are especially important to international expansion: location, timing, and scale.

*Location—Which Markets to Enter?*

New entrants desiring to expand and compete in foreign markets must place considerable focus on identifying potential global markets that will prove to be favorable towards the firm's profitability, performance, and financial goals. The global strategic planning process is complex and entails more factors, variables, challenges, and risks than domestic strategic planning. In formulating a global strategic entry plan, firms should research, assess, and analyze the external environments that exist in the foreign markets being considered. The global strategic planning process is an important systematic assessment and analysis approach that should be utilized by new entrants attempting to determine the direction and stability of global market considerations. Clearly, new entrants must be able to assess the direction and stability of trade practices, financial markets, social, economic, technological, environmental, political, and legal external market influences existing within potential international markets.

One of the most important questions to answer when entering the global market is that of location. Managers should ask what or which markets can the organization enter and be successful? The figure below depicts the business attractiveness of a location, divided among location-specific categories.

| Business Attractiveness - Location | |
| --- | --- |
| Market Existence | A market must exist for the product or service. There is no need to attempt penetrating the market if the market does not exist. The product/service must be one that foreign consumers can use, are attracted to, and can afford . |
| National Attributes | The country must have attractive attributes desired by the firm. In some cases, the firm may desire to locate a local office within the foreign nation. |
| Geography and Socio-Economic Attributes | This includes the attractiveness of the geography of region, the socioeconomics of the population, proximity to required resources, labor costs, costs of living, and quality of life variables. |
| Openness to Global Trade | These variables include the legal system, political structure, and the business customs unique to that nation. Governments that create and promote free trade zones or other means encourage trade with other nations are deemed more attractive than locations that do not. |

*Timing—When is The Best Time To Enter These Markets?*

The question of timing is another important aspect. Entering the market at the right time, or the wrong time can have tremendous effects on the success or failure of the expansion. Firms must take into account the needs of the foreign market, the current economic trends, political environment, and other important factors when timing their global expansion strategy. Sometimes a move toward globalization can be timed perfectly by evaluating key indicators. Another consideration in timing a global strategy is to find the right partner. Going into business with the wrong partner can ruin the expansion efforts before they even get started. Organizations must ensure that they do not plan hurriedly or rush into foreign markets to jump on an opportunity for quick cash: "Some entrepreneurs who expanded too quickly into export markets now are struggling to survive, and some have soured on globalization completely. It takes at least three years for a company to penetrate a foreign market."[10] Organizations are well advised to exercise due diligence in terms of planning and wait until the timing is right before expanding into the global market.

### Scale—Large Scale or Small Scale?

The question of the scale of expansion is a complex one that varies from organization to organization. Advances in technology, particularly in regards to the World Wide Web, allow all sizes of organizations to compete in the global economy. The global marketplace is no longer defined by corporate juggernauts but is composed of an array of organizations from large corporations to small businesses. No longer are organizations forced to set up operations on foreign soil, although many do. Small businesses can take advantage of foreign distribution companies that will take companies' products and place them in overseas markets. Small businesses can also turn to e-commerce to sell to foreign markets. Through the Internet, Business to Customer (B2C) and Business to Business (B2B) transactions can be made easily and instantaneously, without the need for brick and mortar operations. However, one must understand that combining foreign exporting and web technology does include additional costs to the firm.

### Key Factors That Influence the Entry Mode Selection

Firms entering new foreign markets choose from a variety of different forms of entry: licensing and franchising, exporting (directly or through independent channels), and foreign direct investment (FDI) (joint ventures, acquisitions, mergers, and wholly owned, new ventures). Entry modes vary the degree of control the firm has over invested tangible and intangible resources and the transactions costs associated with that resource commitment.[11] The key factors that influence the entry mode selection are (1) international experience of the firm, (2) size of the market, (3) production and shipping costs, and (4) political, legal, cultural, and labor environments.

### International Experience of the Firm

A primary characteristic of the globalization of markets is the advent of the global consumer. The expectation of standardized goods and services with a corresponding level of consistency in service, quality, and performance across nations and regions signifies the trend towards global commerce. The convergence of international and domestic pricing also indicates the era of the global consumer.[12] However, technology appears to be the engine of customer globalization, fueled by increased personal contact. The result is a new level of segmentation of customer requirements, which transgresses traditional political and cultural boundaries. Companies must look at the world in terms of a worldwide marketplace with segments based on commonalities of preferences.[13] Market orientation is a significant contributor to the positional advantage of the company and is related to the long-term, overall firm performance. Therefore, global organizations should possess the capability of acquiring, interpreting, and integrating intelligence in order to identify past, present, and potential commonalities to help determine global trends in customer prefrence.[14] The firm should also be able to monitor the environmental changes (regulatory, economic, and sociopolitical) and estimate their impact on the commonalities present in the customer base. The successful development of a global, customer–knowledge management process will make a positive impact on the success of the company.

In a global industry, the competitive position in one country is dependent on the position present in other countries. Moreover, organizations pursuing a global strategy are facing both global and local competition. Consequently, companies have to coordinate their competitive moves on a global basis on a competitive battlefield, constituting the entire world. In addition, companies often use competitors as sources for benchmarking and best-practice transfer.[15] A key capability for firms is the competitive market knowledge process, the amount, timeliness, and accuracy of competitor intelligence constraining the ability to respond to competitive moves globally. Like customer knowledge competence, competitor knowledge competence is characterized as the knack to acquire, interpret, and integrate information regarding the global competitive environment. The competitor knowledge process is one of the global market knowledge competencies required to succeed in the global marketplace. The ability to acquire knowledge regarding global competitors may result in a significant positive impact on the performance of the company.[16]

### Size of the Market

Market potential is an important variable in determining which market a firm will enter. In attractive markets, long-term profitability for a firm is expected to be provided through these investment modes.[17] A firm may sometimes choose investment modes, even if scale economies are not very large. Investment modes provide a great chance for a firm to enter, even if the economies are not significant. A company may choose investment modes since they give the greatest chance for a firm to institute a long-term market presence.

Uncertainty over current economic, political, and government policies plays a part in the investment risk in home countries. They are critical for the profitability and survival of a company's operation in the country of choice.[18] Problems can arise when changes in a country's governmental policies take place in relation to earnings, and in extreme cases, expropriation of assets. Researchers have suggested that limiting policies of foreign governments are likely to hinder inward investments.[19] While a company would be better off by not going into a country with changing policies, non-investment options might favor the firm if it does choose to enter. Market factors in target countries consist of general business environment and competitive structure of local companies.[20]

The size of the target market is an important factor when deciding on the entry mode. Small markets support entry modes that have low break-even sales volumes, like indirect or agent exporting, licensing, and some contractual arrangements. However, markets with high sales potential are possible for entry modes with substantial break-even sales volumes. Entry modes for high break-even sales volumes are subsidiary exporting and equity investment in local production.

### Production and Shipping Costs

A country's local production costs play an essential role in determining the profitability of the investment in production. Low production cost in a country encourages local production, the country's high cost goes against local manufacturing. A firm's production costs are related to energy, labor, raw materials, and other productive agents. Also, the quality and cost of an economic infrastructure has an evident bearing on the entry-mode decision. Other applicable factors include raw materials availability and experienced labor. If the raw materials or the labor is high, it is possible that the cost would be driven up. In the host country, factors might exist that could inhibit the firm's ability to transfer resources. More accurately, the host country firms often have the inability to receive and absorb its resources.[21] Certain benefits are usually achieved when a firm uses exporting strategies, such as accessing the international market more quickly. Direct market accession offers a firm low risk, gives them a simple way to initiate the process of entering a global market, and helps the firm meet demands and challenges.[22]

Exporting also has its disadvantages, such as the high cost of transportation and the potential of tariffs being placed on incoming goods. In addition, the exporter has less of a handle on the distribution of its products in the chosen country of entry, and the distributor usually gets part of the profits—either in the form of pay or adding extra to the price. The exporting mode of entry is usually used by small businesses that have a limited number of resources. If the firm thinks that it is not able to grasp a production-related advantage in the country of choice, it may choose indirect exporting if the possibility exists to generate a competitive advantage on the marketing side.

A number of firms use exporting as entry into the international market. Exporting can be a strategic alternative that helps maintain the efforts and resources, while giving the firm a chance to exploit international opportunities.[23] Exporting can become an international learning experience. Many industrial firms choose to export for their first international entry mode.[24] However, some companies succeed globally while operating primarily as exporters.[25]

*Environments—Political, Legal, Cultural, Labor, etc.*

A host of external environmental factors influence a firm's choice of direction, action, and ultimately, its organizational structure and internal processes.[26] External environmental factors can affect the entry of new entrants in another country, whether they are economic, social, political, cultural, or legal.

- Economic factors concern the nature and direction of the economy in which a firm operates. Because consumption patterns are affected by the relative affluence of various market segments, each firm must consider economic trends in the segments that affect its industry.

- Developed from cultural, ecological, demographic, religious, educational, and ethnic conditioning, the social factors that affect a firm involve the beliefs, values, attitudes, opinions, and lifestyles of persons in the firm's external environment. As social attitudes change, the demand for various types of clothing, books, and leisure activities change as well.

- The direction and stability of political factors are a major consideration for managers in formulating company strategy. Political factors define the legal and regulatory parameters within which firms must operate. Political constraints are placed on firms through fair-trade decisions, antitrust laws, tax programs, minimum wage, legislation, pollution and pricing policies, administrative jawboning, and many other actions aimed at protecting employees, consumers, the general public, and the environment. Since such laws and regulations are most commonly restrictive, they tend to reduce the potential profits of firms.

- To avoid obsolescence and promote innovation, a firm must be aware of technological changes that might influence the industry. Creative technological adaptations can suggest possibilities for new products, improvement in existing products, or in manufacturing and marketing techniques.[27]

Each of these variables or factors can present major challenges and risks to entrants. However, for those organizations devoted to the development and implementation of their formulated global strategic plans, whose members act responsively to address operational or consumer issues, they can eventually experience profitability and achieve their performance and financial objectives. International business managers should carefully examine, assess, and evaluate a country's organizational, social, cultural, political, judicial, market, economic, technological, and industry trends to determine whether entry into an international market is financially feasible, unfavorable, or risky.

Environmental turbulence has a significant effect on the market–knowledge-competence–performance relationship. Environmental turbulence has two dimensions: technological turbulence and market dynamism. Technological turbulence is the extent to which production/service technology in a principal market has changed over the last years.[28] Technological changes provide a firm huge opportunity in industries that are subject to high technological turbulence. In these industries, the organizations will enjoy abnormal returns from alternative opportunities, rather than those created by their market knowledge competencies. The technological turbulence will inhibit the global–market-knowledge–performance relationship. On the other hand, market dynamism is related to the rate of change of customer preferences, market segments, and demand patterns.[29] Organizations have to adapt more rapidly to the customers' changing demands in such an industry. In a dynamic global market, companies need to develop stronger knowledge competencies in the global market and focus on the global customer knowledge process and on the global responsiveness in order to succeed. Therefore, environmental turbulence is expected to have a significant role on the market, knowledge, competence, development, and utilization of the global company.

Another moderator that has been incorporated into the previous market orientation and learning frameworks is the competitive intensity present within an industry. When strong global competition is scarce, the global firm should perform well, even though it does not develop global-market-knowledge competencies or global responsiveness. This occurs because customers do not possess alternatives. However, firms with intense global competition will be forced to quickly respond on a global scale, be able to acquire, interpret, and integrate the market knowledge, and coordinate the efforts on a global basis, in order to create higher value for their customers.

Another type of uncertainty that influences transaction costs is created by the target market environment. Environmental uncertainties are risks associated with doing business in a foreign country. The firm must feel reasonably secure in its ability to enforce contracts and manage other types of political and legal risks. If a company wants to increase control, it must commit additional resources, which could mean that the company exposes itself to other environmental risks.

Firms are better off selecting non-equity, low-investment entry modes in countries that have high environmental uncertainty. This strategy "not only avoids resource commitment, but frees entrants to change partners or renegotiate contract terms and working arrangements relatively easily as circumstances develop and change."[30] A company can keep itself flexible by following a low-resource commitment plan which allows the firm to switch partners or exit the market altogether if the need arises.

# MODES OF BUSINESS ENTRY

Businesses that look to expand internationally understand that other markets have to be included into the fold of its operations. These other markets could be investments in other markets outside of the company's main focus, or possibly, a company taking its product and introducing it into another area. Two types of entry modes are available into a market: low intensity or high intensity. The main difference between the two depends on how much risk and/or control an entering business is willing to take.

Low-intensity entry refers to no investment into the new market, which is optimal for businesses that may not have enough financial capital to initiate operations in a new market. However, a business can also align itself with an organization already established in the new market. Exporting and importing are great examples of low-risk (and also low control) entry modes into a new market. With no investment, a company cannot have a great amount of control, because there is no investment to be gained or lost. High-intensity entry involves making significant amounts of investment, not just financial but also with marketing, distribution, and possibly in executives.[31] Because of greater investment, businesses would have a greater amount of control over the new market entity; therefore, they would be able to influence operations in order to maximize growth potential. The key consideration is managerial control.

In the following sections, different modes of global-market entry will be discussed. These modes vary from low control to high control and also low risk to high risk. The entry modes include exporting and importing, licensing and franchising, management contracts, turnkey projects, joint ventures, and wholly owned subsidiaries.

## Exporting and Importing

Businesses seeking to expand internationally can engage in the practices of exporting and importing. Exporting is the sending of goods abroad for trade or sale. Importing is the bringing in of goods from abroad to trade or sale—which may be the best option to gain a foothold. Exporting and importing generally requires a minimal initial investment and may allow a business to develop key relationships with export/import firms (intermediaries) that will aid in ensuring success into the new market. However, businesses must ensure that the necessary market and customer demand analyses demonstrate that exporting would be profitable, both financially and strategically. Multinational corporations (MNC) value the importance of exporting and importing. In the United States over 45 percent of exports and over 52 percent of imports occur among MNCs.[32] Firms seeking to export and import products and services to or from a foreign country may employ the services of intermediaries and facilitators.

## The Importance and Use of Intermediaries

Export intermediaries are utilized to provide expertise to inexperienced exporters as they enter overseas markets. They are also contracted to assist the experienced exporter in entering markets in unfamiliar countries. Intermediaries are organizations that act as a facilitator for a potential supplier and consumer. These firms can facilitate the transfer of goods and services from a company to the consumer in a new market. Ordinarily, a business decides to use an intermediary when there is a value-added benefit. For example, the intermediary might have an extensive list of potential connections in the foreign market that would assist the business in its entry. By taking on the responsibilities of marketing, intermediaries also ensure that the manufacturer's products get maximum exposure in the foreign market.

The utilization of intermediaries was originally bolstered by the Export Trading Company Act of 1982 (OECTA). OECTA created new U.S. trade incentives by promoting the export of United States goods and services and encouraging the formation of export trading companies and export management companies.[33] Furthermore, OECTA empowered United States banks to make equity investments in commercial ventures that qualify as export trading companies. Two types of intermediaries, export management and export trading companies, demonstrate how a business can enter into a new market with minimal investment costs.

*Export management companies.* A company that may not have the time and/or resources to establish an export department might consider employing the services of an export management company (EMC). EMCs are independent businesses that liaison between the parent company (manufacturer) and the customer (another business, nation, or people). One of the most important advantages in using an EMC is that it can handle all aspects of exporting a company's product into the new market(s). An EMC would have contacts and knowledge of the designated market to make exporting successful.[34] Typically, an EMC will work with a manufacturer by either performing duties as an agent or a distributor. The EMC acts as an agent by facilitating the order fulfillment process between the exporter and foreign customer. As a distributor, the EMC actually buys the manufacturer's products and then sells them to the customer. An EMC functions in foreign markets just as a sales representative or exclusive wholesaler functions for a manufacturer in the United States. An EMC usually has a formal agreement with manufacturers. The primary disadvantage of using an EMC is that "a manufacturer may lose control over foreign sales. Most manufacturers are properly concerned that their product and company image be well maintained in foreign markets."[35]

*Export trading companies.* An export trading company transacts commercial and financial activities to facilitate exports by unaffiliated persons. These activities include distribution, shipping, warehousing, and finance. Such transactions are increasingly conducted online. An export trading company usually takes title to the goods.[36] Therefore, the terms export trading company and export management company are often used interchangeably. A special kind of export trading company is a group organized and operated by producers. These export trading companies can be organized along multiple- or single-industry lines and can also represent producers of competing products.

The advantages of utilizing intermediaries are summarized as follows:
- Intermediaries are responsible for managing all of the technical and legal issues associated with the export activities.
- Intermediaries are responsible for generating the local business clientele and maintaining the business relationship. Intermediaries usually have a network of foreign agents and distributors and can generate sales at a more rapid pace.
- Intermediaries are responsible for the distribution of the product within the host country.
- Intermediaries can be helpful in determining the credit status and worthiness of potential clientele.
- Intermediaries can determine the competitive balance within the selected host country

NOTES

- Intermediaries can be helpful in training corporate staff to eventually become expert exporters in that particular market.

The disadvantages of utilizing intermediaries are summarized as follows:

- Intermediaries are independent commercial entities and are primarily interested in reaping the most profits for their business; therefore, these companies might not be providing a plan for future growth of the contracting company within the foreign marketplace.
- Intermediaries have limited financial resources and will usually rely on the contracting company to provide immediate financial support to finance and distribute the product and or service.
- Utilizing an intermediary will usually result in the contracting company having less control of its product, distribution, and customers in the host market. This may result in smaller profit margin for the contracting company, as the intermediary is paid prior to distribution of any profits.
- Utilization of intermediaries requires a multifaceted legal relationship between the contracting company, the intermediary, and the clientele.

Finally, choosing which intermediary to use can be assisted by asking the following questions:

- What is the historical and financial history of the intermediary company?
- Does the intermediary have the proper resources to ensure the success of your export operation?
- Does the intermediary have the facilities to support your export operation and future goals?
- How long have they been in the business as an intermediary, including specifically in this foreign market?
- What is the intermediary's banking reputation in the foreign market?
- What is the reputation of the intermediary's financial officers within the business community?

*Facilitators*

As an organization embarks on entering a new market, whether domestic or international, problems will arise that may need amelioration. For example, one should consider a firm that wants to determine the mode of global market entry that meets the criteria of being both cost efficient and ensuring the highest instance of success. The firm may employ the services of a facilitator to assist in making this determination. A facilitator is an individual whose job is to help manage a process of information exchange. "While an expert's role is to offer advice, particularly about the content of a discussion, the facilitator's role is to help with how the discussion is proceeding."[37] Facilitators are often considered "coaches" or outside consultants brought in to help steer the firm in the right exporting direction. While this may be the end result, a facilitator's role is not to motivate employees but to make an action. Facilitators aid employees in determining what may be the best methods of making the action. Facilitators can benefit organizations in both the private and public sectors.

*Private sector.* The primary private sector facilitator for intermediaries, outside of export management and trading companies, are commercial banks. Commercial banks are in the business of being profitable and will assist businesses in international ventures and finance as part and parcel of their business mission. Many commercial banks employ international business experts who are knowledgeable in all areas of export finance. This includes, but not limited to, foreign currency exchange, correspondent relationships, funds transfer, collection of foreign debts and invoices, and foreign finance laws. Additionally, most large commercial banks either maintain local banking branches globally or have foreign representation to assist their customers within the borders of the host country. Proper intermediaries may be located via the National Association of Export Companies, one of several associations that contains a directory of export management and export trade companies, which can be utilized by United States small businesses and corporations.

*Public sector.* The primary public sector facilitators for intermediaries are located at both state and federal government levels. At the state level, state export assistance agencies engage in counseling sessions and sponsor conferences and trade events to educate and assist local exporters on numerous topics, including export documentation, licensing, franchising, export trading companies, market-entry in-country research, and trade policy initiatives. The International Trade Division of the Virginia Economic Development Partnership is a leading example of a public sector facilitator (http://www.exportvirginia.org). The International Trade Division provides resources, programs, and services on a global basis for the benefit of promoting economic development for those firms who employ Virginia citizens.

The United States Department of Commerce Export Centers and the United States Department of Commerce Commercial Service provide facilitating services and programs at the federal level. These facilitators have a network of approximately 1,750 trade exporters in over eighty nations to assist a global business in generating export sales and services. Export assistance centers of The United States Department of Commerce may be accessed via several Internet websites, including http://www.ita.doc.gov. Numerous other U.S. government facilitators exist, including the following:

- The United States Department of Agriculture (USDA)—The USDA acts as the primary starting point for United States companies interested in exporting agricultural products to foreign markets. The USDA, via its Foreign Agricultural Services branch, can provide United States corporations assistance in accessing foreign agricultural markets and/or accessing United States foreign agricultural programs.

- United States Small Business Administration (SBA)—Small businesses are extremely active in the foreign export market. As one of the primary government facilitators for small businesses, the SBA agency will provide corporate services, which include financing, trade counseling, and commodity brokerage. The SBA will also provide prospective businessmen with "face to face" services at one of their approximately 73 regional offices located within the United States.

- Export Trade counseling—one of the primary methods utilized by the United States Small Business Administration in both educating and empowering small businesses within the global marketplace. This counseling is usually developed in part and parcel of larger conferences or workshops for small businesses. The counseling includes information on licensing procedures, favored nation status, trade policy initiatives, and utilization of legal counsel.

- Export Legal Assistance Network—a nationwide directory of attorneys with experience in international trade which will usually provide an initial consultation without cost to the client.

NOTES

*Licensing and Franchising*

Licensing and Franchising are other foreign market entry modalities. These modes can be considered indirect forms of the exporting process. Instead of exporting goods or services, a company exports technology. Technology, in this sense, is defined as the means to accomplish the goals and objectives of the organization. This includes all business function and human resource capabilities of the firm.

A license is an agreement that allows one party to use a property right in exchange for payment to the other party. The party giving the license is the licensor, while the party that gets to use the right is the licensee. A licensor does not have to invest into the foreign market because the licensee (more than likely) is established in the market. A licensee purchases the license and then afterwards pays a set fee, based on revenue, to the licensor. Similar to an alliance, the license is limited to a set period of time. Licensing enables a firm to penetrate markets that might not otherwise have been accessible because of foreign policy or laws. China serves as an example of a country that does not allow foreign countries implicit access to its market. Rather, it compels interested firms to form alliances or joint ventures in order to enable domestic firms to gain technological advancements or other resources. Through licensing, a foreign business can circumvent this policy and still obtain financial profits.

Franchising is an alternative to licensing that also does not necessitate an initial investment into a foreign market. In this case, a company sells its name, business strategies, and standard operating procedures to another party for a fee. Fees typically include an initial fee for the franchise and then a percentage of annual revenues. The franchisor usually continues to support the operation of the franchisee's business by providing advertising, accounting, training, related services, and in many instances, products needed by the franchisee.[38] The United States has the greatest number of franchisors, followed by Africa and Asia. The number of franchise establishments in the U.S. in 2012 was 746,828 and was expected to grow by 1.4 percent to 757, 055 in 2013. In 2012 the franchise sector had a Gross Domestic Production of $454 billion and was projected to be $472 billion in 2013, an increase by 4.1 percent.[39]

A number of benefits may accrue from the use of franchising and licensing. Franchising is considered attractive to firms in that it allows entry into the international marketplace without completely needing to "reinvent the wheel" (redevelop the firm in another nation). Franchising provides an effective avenue to internationalize the business. The franchisee, or licensee, attains revenues from an established product and/or brand. Licensing allows a firm to enter a foreign market without incurring significant investment costs.

Licensing and franchising also have several drawbacks. The risks associated with licensing intellectual property and the specific portions of the contract are left to interpretation. Furthermore, after factoring in the discrepancies in international laws, it is difficult to ensure the licensee will not use the intellectual property to its advantage, after the contract has expired. Piracy can occur anywhere that licensing is used as a mode of entry and is most prevalent in countries where antipiracy laws are neither recognized nor encouraged.[40]

### Management Contracts

Management contracts "represent situations where a company with experience in specific business areas or industrial sectors makes personnel available to perform general or specialized management functions for another company."[41] The duration of most management contracts is between three and five years, with renewal terms varying within individual contracts. Developing countries utilize management contracts for two primary purposes:

1.  In commercial fields where technical expertise is required to manage the day-to-day operations of a corporation or government entity.

2.  Within corporate circumstances where in-depth institutional knowledge or skill is a prerequisite for proper facility management to manage a facility or entity.

A management contract not only meets the current needs of the host country, but should also be used to develop and train host managers who will eventually manage the facility after the expiration of the contract. Management contracts offer the following advantages:

*   The management contractor does not utilize many of its assets to meet the contract demands.
*   The host nation provides the funds for any infrastructure associated with the project management.
*   The contractor helps to develop a local workforce in the host company, which is eventually trained to manage these fields.

The disadvantages of management contracts include the following:

*   The corporation's personnel within the host country are subject to any risks, personal and financial, associated with that country.
*   The development of host company managers eventually creates a direct competitor, not only within the country but also in other global markets.

### Turnkey Projects

Turnkey projects are another mode of foreign market entry. In a Turnkey project "one client company contracts another company to build and deliver a ready to operate industrial plant or infrastructure facility, such as a power plant, a highway or a port. In such cases, the client can be a government agency."[42] Turnkey projects are common when developing with infrastructure projects or other complex subcontracting:

> Turnkey projects have become quite common in recent decades, and it has become a successful mode of business operation, particularly in developing countries. Foreign banks and donors often make recommendations to developing countries on turnkey deliveries to minimize risks involved. An advantage of the turnkey project is that a single party will coordinate all the interfaces with its sub-contractors and will have all liabilities and guarantees. It also relieves the purchaser in a developing country of the responsibility of managing and coordinating the various technical and managerial aspects in a situation where there are often inadequate technical and managerial capabilities.[43]

The advantages of Turnkey projects include the following:

*   Turnkey projects are helpful in the creation of the infrastructure in developing countries.

- Turnkey projects usually help to develop the contractors' capacities for subcontracting and developing managers.
- During a Turnkey project, the contractor assumes all of the responsibility of the overall project, which usually helps the client avoid any construction delays or prospective price gouging.

The disadvantages of Turnkey projects include the following:
- The Turnkey project, usually developed via bidding, can become highly political with high tendencies for bribery and illegal kickbacks.
- The Turnkey project not only creates a direct competitor to the contractor, but also builds a facility that the host contractor has designed and tested.

### *Joint Ventures*

Joint ventures are another modality of market entry and are used as alternative-business strategic alliances for corporations in the global marketplace. A strategic alliance is a voluntary arrangement between companies involving exchange sharing, co-development of products, technologies, or services. Joint ventures are a "special type of alliance in which a new firm is created and owned by the alliance partners."[44] In other words, joint ventures usually involve an alliance where two or more companies contribute assets, which results in the formation of a new legal entity.

Organizations considering the use of the joint venture strategy must carefully consider the legal aspects of engaging in such a partnership. Legal counsel should be aware of the host nation's laws concerning, but not limited to, the following:
- The percentage of ownership allowed by foreign countries
- Limitations concerning the ownership of minority shares within the host country; technology and licensing agreements
- Local and United States antitrust laws[45]

When entering into a joint venture alliance, it is prudent to retain legal counsel in the U.S. and in the host foreign country, in order to be prepared for the various legal ramifications outlined above. U.S. firms should also request a business review letter from representatives of the Department of Justice when there are significant antitrust issues.

Finally, joint venture alliances are predicated on economic, social, and cultural issues. Whenever a firm enters a relationship with a foreign entity, it must be aware of the customs of the foreign partner, from both a marketing level and in developing human resource protocols.

The advantages of joint ventures include the following:
- The joint venture alliances help lessen and/or defend from the risks associated with the foreign market.
- The alliances allow a novice corporation immediate presence within a foreign country and ease the initiation process into the marketplace.
- The joint venture lessens the overhead costs of a solo operation within a foreign country.
- A joint venture allows the U.S. partner the ability to obtain foreign technology, foreign brands, and foreign managerial techniques.
- The joint venture alliances provide a tactical shield for the U.S. company because the "face" of the company is usually the foreign partner.[46]

Some of the disadvantages of the joint ventures include the following:

- The loss of managerial control in the foreign country predicated on legal ramification, minority interests, or the makeup of the entity.
- Sometimes an international manager in the alliance cannot master the sociocultural elements of the host country including, but not limited to, values, norms and beliefs, and inferior product quality.
- The U.S. company may be restricted from full ownership interests and be required to establish the alliance to enter the target market.[47]

### *Wholly Owned Subsidiaries*

Wholly owned subsidiaries are the final entry modality to be discussed in this chapter. Wholly owned subsidiaries are market entry structures:

Where total control of the subsidiary business is a strong requisite, either for reasons such as the protection of intellectual property, because of a deeply rooted corporate culture, or because control by the headquarters is critical to the success of international marketplace activities.[48]

This market strategy is utilized when a corporate entity needs complete control over every detail of the structure within the host country. Total liability for any risks associated with the structure comes with complete control.

There are two advantages for firms deploying this entry modality: First, the parent company has complete control over every aspect of the business in the foreign market, including customer base, warehousing, distribution, accounts receivable, accounting practice, customer base, etc. Second, the wholly owned subsidiary is relatively free to establish additional subsidiary and contracting relationships with other partners in the host country. The two disadvantages of wholly owned subsidiaries include the full responsibility for all monetary aspects of the company resting with the parent company of the wholly owned subsidiary, making the alliance extremely expensive. Second, the wholly owned subsidiary is liable for all aspects of the operation in the host country.

Establishment of a wholly owned subsidiary in a foreign country is a high-risk challenge for even the largest of multinational corporations. A company may control all the operations of its subsidiary, but it also bears all the costs and associated struggles to establish a share in the new market. Additionally, the strategy may lead to more efficient operations since all decisions will be made from one parent company. Taking these factors into account, a company willing to take the risks associated with this mode of market entry could find itself in a favorable position in the new market.

## KEY CONCEPTS

- Why domestic firms expand into global markets
- Conditions necessary for expansion into global market:
  - Managerial commitment
  - Motivations
- Basic entry questions:
  - Location—which markets to enter?
  - Timing—when is the best time to enter these markets?
  - Scale—large scale or small scale?
- Key factors that influence the entry mode selection:
  - International experience of the firm
  - Size of the market
  - Production and shipping costs
  - Environments—political, legal, cultural, labor, etc.

- Entry modes (include description, advantages, and disadvantages)
  - Exporting and importing
  - The importance and use of intermediaries
- Export management companies
- Export trading companies
- Facilitators
  - Private sector
  - Public sector
- Licensing and franchising
- Management contracts
- Turnkey projects
- Joint ventures
- Wholly owned subsidiaries

# Chapter 7 Exercises: Observational Analysis

*Ponder on the following key concepts and ideas as you read the chapter*

1. Why firms decide to expand globally. Conditions necessary for expansion into global markets and the managerial commitment and motivations required for successful entry and expansion into global markets and the need to conduct a SWOT analysis before global market expansion.

2. Forming and understanding basic entry questions: which markets to enter? When is the best time to enter these markets? Should the entry be large scale or small scale?

3. Understanding the specific key factors that influence the entry mode selection: international experience of the firm, size of the market, production and shipping costs, and political, legal, cultural, and labor environments.

4. Start a list of books, journals, and scholarly websites that would aid in the understanding of the chapter's main concepts and ideas. Start a journal for your own thoughts and ideas. What outside sources support your conclusions?

# Chapter 7 Exercises: Key Terms Analysis

*Match the answers by writing the correct letter in the space provided*

_____ 1. National regulations

_____ 2. Proactive

_____ 3. Expanding into the global marketplace

_____ 4. Market orientation

_____ 5. Competitor knowledge competence

_____ 6. License

_____ 7. Political constraints

_____ 8. Global managers

_____ 9. Successful international expansion

_____ 10. Reactive

_____ 11. Strategic alliance

_____ 12. Low-intensity entry

_____ 13. Market Dynamism

_____ 14. Intermediaries

_____ 15. Small Business Administration (SBA)

_____ 16. Turnkey projects

_____ 17. Wholly owned subsidiaries

_____ 18. Public sector facilitator

_____ 19. Joint Venture

_____ 20. High intensity entry

A.  Allows one party to use a property right in exchange for payment to the other party

B.  Competitive pressure, excess capacity, overproduction, declining home market

C.  Tend to possess experiential/knowledge to many cultures

D.  There is no investment into the new market

E.  Common when developing with infrastructure projects or other complex subcontracting

F.  When a firm incurs unanticipated costs from underestimating foreign regulations

G.  Provide corporate services including financing, trade counseling, commodity brokerage for small business

H.  Voluntary arrangement between companies

I.  The rate of change of the customer preferences, market segments, and demand patterns

J.  Antitrust laws, tax programs, minimum wage, legislation, pollution and pricing policies

K.  New firm created, owned by the alliance partners

L.  Quest for profit, competitive advantage, market opportunities, economies of scale, tax benefits

M.  United States Department of Commerce

N.  Knack to acquire, interpret, and integrate information regarding the global competitive environment

O.  Corporate entity needs complete control over every detail of the structure in the host country

P.  Financial, marketing, distribution, and possibly executive investment

Q.  Gaining access to resources , cutting cost, capitalizing on special feature location, expanding markets

R.  Commitment from management across the organization

S.  Act as facilitator for a potential supplier and consumer

T.  Contributor to the positional advantage of the company and long-term, overall firm performance

# Chapter 7 Exercises: Theoretical Analysis

*Analyze the questions and select the answer based on the reading of the chapter material*

1. Most firms typically choose to enter into global markets from a proactive stance, but some are forced to enter the global market in a reactive stance.

    a. True

    b. False

2. Which of the following is NOT an area of competition for business in a global market?

    a. Quality and price

    b. Counterattacks

    c. Economies of Scope

    d. Realization of additional profits

3. Population growth is a great reference, and is always the key indicator of a strong potential market.

    a. True

    b. False

4. Successful global managers have an understanding of how to appraise and adjust to the requirements of doing business in a culture different from their own.

    a. True

    b. False

5. The necessary conditions for expansion into global markets include all of the following except:

    a. Expanding markets

    b. Obtaining government authorization

    c. Cutting costs

    d. Capitalizing on special features of location

6. The global strategic planning process is complex but does not entail as many factors, variables, challenges, and risks as domestic strategic planning.

    a. True

    b. False

7. Organizations must ensure that they do not plan hurriedly or rush into foreign markets to jump on an opportunity for quick cash.

    a. True

    b. False

8. The three aspects which are especially important to international expansion are location, timing, and scope.

    a. True

    b. False

9. What are the two types of entry modes available into a market? (Circle the correct answer)

   a. Low intensity: No investment into the new market; high intensity: Significant amounts of investment in the market

   b. Exporting: sending of goods abroad; importing: bringing of goods from abroad

   c. Low intensity: significant amounts of investment in the market; high intensity: no investment into the new market

   d. Exporting: bringing of goods from abroad; importing: sending of goods abroad

10. A major Proactive motivation factor includes:

    a. Competitive pressure

    b. Excess capacity

    c. Overproduction

    d. Economies of scale

11. The expectation of standardized goods and services with a corresponding level of consistency in service, quality, and performance across nations and regions signifies the trend towards global commerce.

    a. True

    b. False

12. One of the most important questions to answer when entering the global market is that of

    a. Current market share

    b. Labor restrictions

    c. Location

    d. None of the above

13. Direct market accession offers a firm low risk, gives them a simple way to initiate the process of entering a global market, and helps the firm meet demands and challenges.

    a. True

    b. False

14. Businesses must carefully consider the benefits, advantages, challenges, and risks involved to compete within an international market.

    a. True

    b. False

15. The key factors that influence the entry mode selection are

    a. International experience of the firm

    b. Size of the market

    c. Production and labor costs

    d. A and B only

    e. None of the above

16. In most cases, exporting and importing requires a maximum initial investment and may allow a business to develop key relationships with export/import firms (intermediaries) that will aid in ensuring success into the new market.

    a.  True

    b.  False

17. _____ is a significant contributor to the positional advantage of the company and is related to the long-term, overall firm performance.

    a.  Facility location

    b.  Market segmentation

    c.  Market orientation

    d.  Managerial experience

18. External environmental factors that can affect the entry of new entrants in another country can be

    a.  Economic, social, political

    b.  Cultural, legal, religious

    c.  Economical, legal, technological

    d.  None of the above

19. Which is not a vital consideration for determining managerial commitment to expanding globally?

    a.  Commitment of top management to go global

    b.  Managements timeframe/timeliness for the international operations to pay off

    c.  The international experience the firm possesses internally

    d.   Low-level management's time allocation on the company's global efforts

    e.  The organizational structure required for success

20. Joint ventures usually involve an alliance where two or more companies contribute assets, which results in the formation of a new legal entity.

    a.  True

    b.  False

21. _____ are utilized to provide expertise to inexperienced exporters as they enter overseas markets.

    a.  Facilitators

    b.  Brokers

    c.  Export intermediaries

    d.  Export Management Companies

22. A franchise is an agreement that allows one party to use a property right in exchange for payment to the other party.

    a.  True

    b.  False

23. _____ represent situations where a company with experience in specific business areas or industrial sectors makes personnel available to perform general or specialized management functions for another company.

    a. Joint venture

    b. License

    c. Turnkey projects

    d. Managerial contracts

24. The greatest reactive motivation for global expansion is the prospect of global sales.

    a. True

    b. False

25. What market strategy is utilized when a corporate entity needs complete control over every detail of the structure within the host country?

    a. Turnkey project

    b. Wholly Owned Subsidiaries

    c. Managerial contract

    b. Joint venture

# Chapter 7 Exercises: Practical Analysis

*Write a short essay in the space provided to each of the following questions.*

*Please use outside references for each answer to support your ideas and thoughts.*

1. Before a firm considers global expansion, they should conduct a SWOT analysis (Strengths, Weaknesses, Opportunities, and Threats) and determine the risk factors involved in global expansion. Using the World Wide Web, find a company that is still domestic and provide the following information:

    a. What strengths do they possess for global expansion; what strengths would the company need to acquire for the global expansion?

    b. What are some weaknesses the company may possess?

    c. What are opportunities for going global; what are opportunities for staying domestic?

d. What are some threats the company will encounter; what are some threats they should consider? (Consider outside competition and market forces).

e. What are some internal/external risk factors that the firm should consider before global expansion?

f. Given the analysis, is it feasible or realistic for the firm to expand globally?

2. For a firm to succeed in the international market, they must have a clear understanding of the vision, mission, objectives, and strategies of their domestic company, as well as their global operation and ability to strategically assess and understand the various risk factors. Using the World Wide Web, find a company (or the company used in question (1) that is still domestic and provide the following information:

a. Write a vision and a mission statement for the firm's global expansion operation

b. Give 5–7 short-term (6mos–1 yr.) and long-term (>1yr) objectives the firm should have.

c. What specific strategies should the firm use in order to accomplish the objective

d. What are the financial costs associated with accomplishing the firm's objectives?

# Chapter 7 Exercises: Biblical Worldview Application

*Write a short essay in the space provided to each of the following questions.*
*Please use biblical references and research, where applicable, to support your ideas and thoughts.*

1. Visit *Gap Missions* ministry at their website: www.gapmissions.org and answer the following:
   (1) Provide a brief overview about the organization. (2) Identify and briefly describe the different global mission ministries and projects they are involved with and support. (3) Is their focus in one or multiple countries? (4) What type of mode(s) of entry as described in the chapter do they most closely engage and resemble?

2. Visit *Allow the Children* ministry at their website: www.allowthechildren.org and answer the 4 aspects as listed in number 1 above.

3. Visit *Global Partners in Peace and Development* ministry at their website: www.gpartners.org and answer the 4 aspects as listed in number 1 above.

# Managing Global Operations

NOTES

## CHAPTER OVERVIEW

In the fundamental sense, global business involves the buying, selling, and trading of goods and services across national borders. While many managerial aspects directly impact the profitability of a business, it is the management of business operations that determines a company's total growth potential and earning capabilities. Management involves the process of developing decisions and taking actions to direct and control the activities of employees toward the attainment of organizational goals.[1] Operations management specifically involves the management of the process and production activities that produce the goods or services. Operations managers are concerned with every aspect of the production process, including key areas such as research and development, acquisition and distribution, inventory management, technology, transportation, manufacturing, and customer service.[2] The overall success of the business is dependent upon the efficiency and effectiveness of every function within the production process.

The continuous and rapid expansion of world markets is a mitigating factor for the globalized perspective of operations management. Taking a business to the global marketplace necessitates the development of a global operations strategy, which requires three strategic capabilities:

- Global-scale efficiency and competitiveness
- National-level responsiveness and flexibility
- Cross-market capacity to leverage on a worldwide basis[3]

Based on the extent to which these capabilities exist within the firm, operations managers are involved in the ongoing processes of strategic issues, such as planning, production, logistics, and supply chain management to maximize the business output potential. The key components in successful operations management are efficiency and effectiveness. Global organizations differ from domestic in that operations must not only efficiently move products from multiple locations but also from multiple continents.

## PLANNING ISSUES

When planning an effective global business strategy, a company should consider the fundamental issues that drive production level output. These issues include, but are not limited to, the capacity of the operation, the location of the organization's facilities, the varying processes by which the products are produced, the internal layout of the facility workspace, the decision process for determining whether various components should be manufactured or purchased, and the process by which both raw material and fixed assets are selected and ultimately acquired.

### *Capacity*

Capacity, in terms of production-oriented firms, refers to the total amount of products that can be produced by the entire operation in a given amount of time. In service-oriented firms, capacity is measured in terms of the total number of customers that can be served in a given amount of time. In either case, capacity is the metric used to measure the ability to meet customer needs. Organizations first estimate demand levels in relation to the overall capacity of their facilities and then make adjustments to meet the projected demand levels.

One should note that the capacity of a multistep production process is limited to the total output of the slowest process—also known as the operational bottleneck. Organizations identify elements of the production process that are creating constraints or bottlenecks in the overall flow of the production system. The Theory of Constraints (TOC) suggests that the greater gain will come from identifying which part of the process is a constraint to the whole, rather than focusing on increased output from an entire process. Once the constraints are identified, the organization should focus improvement energy solely in that area.[4] Thus, overall production levels will increase as a result of implementing ways to increase performance output at the source of the constraint. Another method related to improving production capacity requires the firm to focus only on key capabilities or the specific processes that an organization performs better than other organizations. This may require that some processes be outsourced to other agencies, which in turn frees up needed resources that can be dedicated to other key capabilities.

**Capacity Issues**

- Facilities location
- Location economies
- Organizational structure

*Facilities Location*

Decisions must be made to determine the optimal location in which to conduct operations. The final decision concerning which nation or region in which to operate must be based on comprehensive business research. A key determinant in the facility location decision is the proximity the site has to the organization's largest customer base and suppliers.

A company's physical settings, support services, and environmental conditions must be used effectively to add value to business objectives, strategies, and processes. This becomes increasingly important in the global business environment, as firms move towards greater flexibility to integrate new business ideas and emerging technologies in their facilities location planning strategies.[5]

Additionally, cost variables associated with a site selection must be considered in the facilities location decision: distribution channel costs, energy costs, tax costs, labor costs, raw materials costs, and so forth. Thus, facility location is one of the most important and most difficult decisions that must be made.

Many organizations are drawn overseas by the lure of diminished labor costs. Typically, facility costs are second only to labor costs, but there may be hidden facility costs associated with moving operations overseas. While lower labor costs may be attractive, other considerations may make relocation unworthy of the investment, such as the following:

- Transportation costs
- Duties on components versus those on finished goods
- Need for proximity to the market
- Foreign-exchange risk
- Economies of scale in the production process
- Technological requirements[6]

One way to reduce the risk of incurring these costs is to engage in the business arrangement known as a joint venture, where two separate entities enter into a contractual agreement to do business together. Each party provides some part of the production process, and the profits are shared between the two organizations.[7] This joint venture works especially well for organizations wanting to do business in a foreign country. A domestic firm will partner with an organization that is native to the host country, which provides assistance in dealing with the cultural and language barriers that are often present when foreign companies seek to do business overseas.[8] A caveat for those considering a joint venture is that while the joint venture may help alleviate some of the risk associated with doing business overseas, certain unavoidable problems may be encountered. For example, many third world nations that would provide the lowest labor costs have huge infrastructure shortcomings. Another shortcoming is that the political climate around the world is increasingly volatile. Terrorism is not a topic that would have raised many concerns a few decades ago, but today it is a deep concern when determining the most appropriate and profitable facility location.

### Location Economies

Another key component in the decision-making process concerns the resources available within the community where the facility will be located. Companies must consider the resources available to their employees in foreign cities. In some countries, social services may be available from the local government. In other countries, the services are lacking or nonexistent. Some corporations have used their influence to improve the local services as "a way of ensuring social cohesion and a stable community, facilitating the recruitment of employees, and the safe passage of goods and people to and from company operations."[9]

### Centralization vs. Decentralization

An important component of strategic planning is organizational structure planning. Strategy defines the goal or purpose of the organization, while structure defines how personnel will collectively implement the strategy.[10] One ongoing debate among strategic planners concerns deploying a centralized structure versus a decentralized structure. The difference between the two is the locus of decisions: are decisions controlled primarily by the home office (centralized) or are they allowed to be controlled in the foreign location (decentralized)? The debate has grown to include the argument of whether or not there should be any structure at all.

The bureaucratic hierarchy is the most common centralized organizational structure. This organizational structure has a clear chain of command and allows for a firm control over every aspect of the organization. Decision making is a top-down process in this form of structure. While this structure was highly successful during the twentieth century, it h as grown increasingly ineffective in the twenty-first century global business model.

Organizational structures may change over time, cycling from a centralized structure to a decentralized structure and back to a centralized structure. The continual change is a result of the strengths and weaknesses of each model. A centralized structure provides control, stability, and the potential for highly effective coordination of all the organizational processes. However, it does not allow for innovative thinking, nor does it engender employee initiative for problem solving. The decentralized model, on the other hand, allows decision making authority to occur where the decisions are to be made, promoting innovation, initiative, and teamwork. When problems arise, decisions can be made immediately so production can go on. The problem with a decentralized model is the inevitability that divisional communication will break down, causing coordination efforts to become difficult and complicated.

*Process*

Typical processes within an organization include procurement (purchasing), distribution channels, and the following areas requiring management:

- Product and service: the management of an individual good or service such as creation, production, and marketing

- Quality: customer satisfaction and Total Quality Management

- Inventory: utilizing methods such as Just-In-Time, providing products and services in an efficient manner

- Facilities: buildings, computer systems, furnishings, equipment, signage, etc.

- Configuration: various versions of products manufactured and distributed by a company (example: computer software)

- Logistics and transportation: the flow of goods or materials from suppliers throughout the organization and then to the customer

- Human Resources: employee matters, benefits, retirement packages, safety issues, training, motivation, etc.

Thus, the process of global operations management requires making a number of interrelated decisions regarding several issues, as depicted in the figure below.

> **Process Issues**
> - Standardization vs. Adaptation
> - Facility location
> - The design and layout of a production facility
> - The make or buy decision
> - The selection and acquisition of raw materials
> - The selection and acquisition of fixed assets

*Standardization vs. Adaptation*

Companies considering the possibility of expanding beyond the borders of their home countries must determine whether or not production processes and procedures will be consistent across facility locations. This standardization maintains the various aspects of the production process and ensures product uniformity. Additional cost savings accrue because machinery, training, and processes can be kept uniform across standardized production facilities. In the event of a natural disaster or economic downturn, the company can stop production at a facility in one nation while boosting production in a location that is more conducive to profitability.

Adaptation may be necessary for products that require adjustments in order to meet local market demand. For example, a company in the food industry might use a different set of suppliers that produce similar products with some subtle differences to make the item more valuable to the consumers in the local economies. Organizations s that focused primarily on standardized products are realizing the potential to produce customized products due to expanding global markets and reduction of trade restrictions. The strategy

NOTES

of mass customization requires the firm to tailor mass production products to meet the expectations of the customer. Mass customization allows a producer to adapt its products to a particular group of consumers. Demand for different features or options may be based on climate, culture, or personal preference.

### Facilities Layout

Once the overseas location has been selected, the design for the space to be built or modifications for a leased space is considered. Factors to be considered in the layout design include utilizing the space for the handling of materials, safety, shipping and receiving, employee movement and communication, and the possibility for future expansion. Different types of businesses adhere to different standards when determining layout design. A service-orientated business or an office would require a pleasing atmosphere for the customer or client. A manufacturing business would design a workspace that could withstand the daily effects of industrial work.

Two basic manufacturing layout designs are typically used: process or product. Process layout groups similar machines together. A company that manufactures packaged baked goods would utilize the process layout. The bakery would group all the mixers in one section and the ovens in another section of the facility. Product layout groups machines according to their roles in the production process. An assembly line would be an example of product layout. Retail locations choose between three basic layout designs: grid pattern, free-flow pattern, and self-service. The grid pattern allows for premium merchandise exposure and simplifies cleaning and security issues. The free-flow pattern provides customers ease of movement and is visually appealing. The self-service layout gives customers direct access to merchandise throughout the store. A grocery store is an example of grid pattern layout. Convenience stores follow the self-service layout. Department stores usually choose the free-flow pattern. Determining the best possible layout for each business will enhance productivity and consumer purchasing.

### Make or Buy Decisions

Most all products available today in the global marketplace involve input from at least one outside source. Many firms lack the required expertise and resources to supply all needed components in the production process. Thus, the need to either make or buy subcomponent parts for products is essential to business operations. Software applications are readily available to assist in the financial determination profitability of make or buy decisions. Regardless, the make or buy decision requires the firm to determine the most cost-effective approach to the production process. Factors that play into this decision include the quality, cost, and delivery timelines of a product or component.[11] The decision to buy or outsource components used in the production process from an external organization must allow for greater benefit to the organization, rather than the component being produced within the organization. Benefits might include decreased inventory and acquisition costs or shorter lead times. Those products that do not provide these benefits to the organization should be produced internally.

### Selection and Acquisition of Raw Materials

Raw materials are inventory items that are used in the manufacturer's conversion process to produce components, subassemblies, or finished products.[12] The selection and acquisition of raw materials varies greatly among the business industry. Proper selection and purchase of raw materials impacts the overall quality and value of a product. Companies planning expansion overseas must conduct substantial research on the availability of the raw materials in that location. The transportation cost of materials not readily available in that region must be determined. This determination is considered in the decision as to whether or not the added transportation cost warrants that site selection. Firms involved in the refinement or distribution of raw materials are especially at-risk. The access to needed raw materials is important and substantial in the planning phase of global expansion.

The operational process of raw material selection is important to the firm's value chain. The value chain is generally considered to consist of the acquisition of raw materials, finished goods manufacturing, and distribution channels.[13] A company should examine its product and the desired characteristics and work backwards to the research and development involved in identifying and selecting the raw materials necessary to make the product. In global markets, companies selecting raw materials must consider local demand, regulatory controls, distribution channels, competition, and shelf life. Quality is also an issue. Firms must examine the quality control procedures of their suppliers to determine whether or not locally supplied raw materials meet the required standards necessary to ensure the integrity of the product. Random sampling and statistical sampling can help an organization monitor and maintain the quality of its materials.

Operations managers understand that success of the value chain depends greatly upon developing successful communication and relationships with suppliers. For example, Japanese firms develop relationships with their suppliers by investing in their organizations. The eventual goal is to place a representative in a board position within the supplier's organization. This type of relationship is considered an interlocking directorate, which has three main benefits. The first advantage is that a company can successfully play a part in the supplier's planning process. Second, this allows the organization the opportunity to more effectively coordinate the output of raw materials to meet the needs of the manufacturing operation. Third, this approach provides for the establishment of raw material design teams that consist of representatives from a company and its suppliers. These teams can custom design the necessary raw materials needed in order to meet the company's production and quality standards. The ultimate outcome is one that saves the organization from substantial costs that can result from the use of generic or substandard raw materials.[14]

Global outsourcing and KANBAN clusters are additional means to enhance the effectiveness of the value chain—in terms of establishing processes and procedures for acquiring raw materials. Global outsourcing is effectively used by corporations to acquire raw materials from the most cost effective sources in the world. Short term contracts are established in order to ensure that future technological advances and new suppliers are not overlooked. Though the actual materials may be inexpensive, the costs associated with shipping the materials from a location on the other side of the globe may be significant. One important concept to keep in mind is that the further away the supplier, the more the shipping costs will impact the raw material acquisition decision.[15]

The KANBAN cluster, developed by Japanese companies, holds the distance between the supplier and the manufacturing hub as a key focus in the acquisition of raw materials. Continuity is an important aspect of this approach. Companies that use this method often mandate that their suppliers have a facility within a certain distance of the manufacturing facility. Any large corporation in Japan may have a network of suppliers located in the region of its production facilities. This network allows a company to experience many of the benefits considered part of Just-In-Time inventory systems. The need for large inventories of raw materials is avoided and manufacturing companies can eliminate the need for long order lead times because of the geographical proximity of suppliers. The outcome results in a reduced set of costs for inventory, shipping, and warehousing.[16]

### Selection and Acquisition of Fixed Assets

Fixed assets is an accounting term that describes tangible property used in the operation of a business, such as buildings, machinery, fixtures, furniture, and equipment. These assets do not include items normally consumed in the course of business operation or production.[17] Fixed assets provide the additional benefit of tax breaks, resulting from depreciation—though real estate values generally appreciate over time. Firms investigating international expansion opportunities must determine how to achieve the right mix of fixed assets. The decision seeks to answer critical questions as to how to gain the necessary facilities and assets in a host nation. Should the firm acquire an existing company or facility? Should it build and/or purchase a new facility? Should it merge with another company to acquire its assets? Each question should be considered in terms of the advantages and disadvantages of the particular course of action. The advantages to purchasing an existing facility are manifold:

- A foreign firm can avoid many of the typical start-up problems and costs associated with building a new facility. This can provide a company with instant cash flow.
- A firm may also find that financing is somewhat easier to obtain due to the access to local capital.
- The company may also be able to avoid the exchange restrictions or controls through the exchange of stock rather than a newly purchased facility.
- In unique cases, a foreign company may also be able to purchase the facilities of a bankrupt or struggling company and avoid the expenses involved in purchasing real estate and building a new facility.[18]

On the other hand, not all circumstances permit the purchase of an existing operation. A Greenfield Investment, a foreign direct investment through the establishment of new facilities, may be more practical depending on the host nation environment. Unlike the case of an acquisition, a Greenfield Investment requires only product adaptation rather than both product and process adaptation. Product adaptation allows the firm to tailor its products to meet regional demand considerations. One possible drawback of a Greenfield Investment is the high marketing costs associated with the establishment of a new organizational element.[19]

| **Advantages and Disadvantages for Greenfield Investments** | |
|---|---|
| **Advantages** | New links to the global market. |
| | New production and job market expansion. |
| | Influx of knowledge and technology. |
| | |
| **Disadvantages** | MNC's tend to crowd out locally owned operations. |
| | The majority of profits are distributed back to the MNC's host country. |
| | MNC's tendency to dwindle natural resources and raw materials. |

Mergers and acquisitions (M&A), the most commonly used form of FDI to acquire fixed assets, are the transfer of existing assets from local to foreign firms. M & A's have advantages and disadvantages as well. The figure below depicts the advantages and disadvantages.

**Advantages and Disadvantages for M&A**

| | |
|---|---|
| **Advantages** | Potential tax savings |
| | Acquisition of established resources |
| | Synergy—the reduction of duplicated offices, such as human resources |
| **Disadvantages** | M & A's can become targets for hostile takeovers. |
| | M & A's are known to damage employee loyalty and morale. |
| | M & A managerial focus is drawn away from productivity to merger management. |

## PRODUCTION ISSUES

Productivity is the ratio of output as it relates to input—the conversion of inputs or resources into outputs of merchandise or services. Organizations have many different elements to consider when setting up international operations. Continuous improvement, delivery systems, inventory, logistics, and supply chain management are key areas to be examined by an organization's management team. The decisions made in regard to these areas will ultimately determine the success or failure of a firm's international initiatives.

*Continuous Improvement*

Continuous improvement, sometimes referred to as Kaizen, is a management technique that historically involves several incremental improvements to a process rather than a single overpowering improvement or change. The term Kaizen, a Japanese term, is derived from the characters (equivalent to letters) kai, meaning change, and zen, meaning good. Thus, Kaizen literally means improvement. The Japanese culture promotes the continuous search for ways to enhance every facet associated with the transformation process—converting inputs into outputs. Kaizen involves both management and labor in finding and eliminating waste in machinery, labor, materials, and production methods.[20]

Although many describe continuous improvement as merely a philosophy rather than a specific technique or method, it has certainly influenced all aspects of business. Continuous improvement is frequently associated with other management and production techniques, such as Total Quality Management (TQM), ISO 9000, and Just-In-Time systems.

*TQM*

Total Quality Management, utilized from the executive levels of the firm to the line workers, is a tool used in the managing of the total production process to generate an exceptional product or service. While numerous definitions exist, most operations managers would agree with the following:

> TQM is a people-focused management system that aims at continual increase in customer satisfaction at continually lower real cost. TQM is a total system approach (not a separate area or program) and an integral part of high-level strategy; it works horizontally across functions and departments, involves all employees, top to bottom, and extends backward and forward to include the supply chain and the customer chain. TQM stresses learning and adaptation to continual change as keys to organizational success. The foundation of total quality is philosophical: the scientific method. TQM includes systems, methods, and tools. The systems permit change; the philosophy stays the same. TQM is anchored in values that stress the dignity of the individual and the power of community action.[21]

*Customer focus.* The philosophy of TQM is to meet and exceed the customer's expectations each and every time with minimal rework. Though each organization's TQM approach will differ, management processes that use data to detect and correct poor performance trends are essential. These processes should provide the organization with the ability to grow and continuously elevate the firm's overall performance, rather than one element of the organization.[22]

*Participation and teamwork.* It has long been held that people are an organization's greatest capital. TQM further supports this concept. Because employees and managers both play a large role in total quality, the entire workforce must be involved in the pursuit of the type of quality that results in customer satisfaction. Quality efforts begin and end with upper management. A mission, vision, and associated set of goals and values should be established by an organization's management team. Managers must disseminate this information to the organization's employees in a way that supports and enhances employee morale and performance. Managers must also remove various barriers that limit or prevent quality improvement. The best approach to removing these barriers is to provide workers with an environment of support and trust that encourages and rewards employees for taking on risks and correcting their own mistakes, rather than hiding them from management.[23]

| **Three Major Principles of Total Quality** |
| --- |
| • Customer Focus |
| • Participation and Teamwork |
| • Continuous Improvement and Learning |

TQM requires a more people-friendly approach that includes the team mentality. Teamwork stresses the importance of customer-supplier relationships and total workforce involvement, which span various functional areas. Cross-functional teams are horizontal in nature and include experts in each technical area within an organizational unit. These teams further cooperate to share information and determine best practices rather than competing for accolades. This type of environment promotes the health of the entire firm rather than a few elements.

Processes and process improvement remain the focus in an organization that practices TQM. Each and every employee of an organization should be involved in TQM planning and strategy development. Though it is often difficult for managers to hear negative reactions to current and proposed processes, it is still vital for an organization to understand that opportunities can be realized by including employees in the implementation of TQM. This involvement is essential to the success of the proposed changes.[24]

*Continuous improvement and learning.* Firms that deploy successful TQM initiatives believe in the importance of focusing all efforts on improving systems and processes. The firm understands that it must constantly audit and advance its capabilities. Continuous efforts to improve organizational performance will lead to the achievement of meeting or exceeding both internal and external customer requirements.

## ISO 9000

Similar in theory and philosophy to TQM, ISO 9000 (also known as the ISO 9000 family or ISO 9000 suite) is a set of guidelines for quality management and quality standards, developed by the International Organization for Standardization in Geneva, Switzerland. The most recent revision to the ISO 9000 series is ISO 9001 (officially known as ISO 9001:2008), which provides a framework for a systematic approach to managing an organization's processes so that their service is consistent and meets client expectation. It also ensures the organization meets applicable laws and regulations. A next version of the standard is expected to be published in December 2015, if the ISO members vote favorably in March 2015.

ISO is, in actuality, a codification or assurance of quality—ISO is an internationally recognized certification system or process. In order for a firm to become ISO certified, it must first prove that it is strictly adhering to ISO standard operating procedures, which involve the inspection of production processes, maintaining equipment, training workers, testing products, and dealing with customer complaints. The benefits of an international certification are numerous to businesses, customers, governments, trade officials, developing countries, and consumers alike. The International Organization for Standardization lists the specific benefits:

- For businesses, the widespread adoption of International Standards means that suppliers can base the development of their products and services on specifications that have wide acceptance in their sectors. This, in turn, means that businesses using International Standards are increasingly free to compete in many more markets around the world.
- For customers, the worldwide compatibility of technology, which is achieved when products and services are based on International Standards, brings them an increasingly wide choice of offers, and they benefit from the effects of competition among suppliers.
- For governments, International Standards provide the technological and scientific bases underpinning health, safety, and environmental legislation.
- For trade officials negotiating the emergence of regional and global markets, International Standards create a level playing field for all competitors in those markets. The existence of divergent national or regional standards can create technical barriers to trade, even when there is political agreement to do away with restrictive import quotas and the like. International Standards are the technical means by which political trade agreements can be put into practice.
- For developing countries, International Standards that represent an international consensus on the state of the art constitute an important source of technological know-how. By defining the characteristics that products and services will be

expected to meet on export markets, International Standards give developing countries a basis for making the right decisions when investing their scarce resources and thus avoid squandering them.

- For consumers, conformity of products and services to International Standards provides assurance about their quality, safety, and reliability. For everyone, International Standards can contribute to the quality of life in general by ensuring that the transport, machinery, and tools we use are safe.
- For the planet, International Standards on air, water, soil quality, and emissions of gases and radiation can contribute to efforts to preserve the environment.[25]

### Just-in-Time Systems (JIT)

Just-in-time production or systems is a comprehensive set of doctrines and systems founded on the philosophy that businesses should hold slight or zero inventory outside what is necessary for immediate production or distribution. The goal of this management system is eliminating waste, making best use of cost efficiency, and creating and sustaining competitive advantage. The intention behind just in time systems is to concentrate on eradicating waste and reducing warehouse inventories; however, the high degree of coordination required to efficiently function within such a system only underscores many of the pre-existing issues, such as bottlenecks, inventory loss or spoilage, and unreliable suppliers.[26] Internet-based collaborative work tools—such as paperless pricing, ordering, restocking, shipping, and product delivery—enable any business to implement just-in-time systems. In fact, "all this facilitates just in time deliveries of parts and components and matching the production of parts and components to assembly plant requirements and production schedules, cutting out unnecessary activities and producing savings for both suppliers and manufacturers."[27]

Also known as the Toyota Production System, JIT was initially developed after WWII when the Japanese car industry was lagging far behind its U.S. competitors. The outlook for survival was calling for drastic and immediate changes. At that time, the average U.S. worker was nine times more efficient than his Japanese counterpart. Japanese industry based JIT improvements on the already existing concepts found in the U.S. factories. They recognized the importance of inventory control and based development on the elimination of waste through just-in-time and automation. Automation refers to mechanized production, where human attention is needed only when a problem occurs. Further, a number of observable production-oriented wastes were identified:

- Product defects
- Process waste
- Overproduction
- Inventory
- Waiting time
- Movement of the product through the process
- Transportation[28]

Though it may seem like JIT should be standard operating process for all global businesses, certain problems can accrue. For instance, a depleted inventory stockpile could mean disaster for suppliers who operate in a manner that requires the storage of back up products. It could mean additional problems if the supplier is required to meet emergency demands, or if the customer base is not prepared for supply delays.[30] Additionally, environmental impacts are associated with JIT. More frequent movement of inputs and outputs may cause roads to become congested with delivery trucks, resulting in increased levels of air pollution. Moreover, many companies that decide to switch to JIT fail to address the issue of empty warehouses and trucks once used for storing inventories. These unused assets are the company's property and are an additional form of waste. Finally, JIT often fails when the relationships between suppliers and customers are not strong enough to guarantee the quality and timing needed for the system to work.[31]

> **Benefits of JIT**
>
> - Better quality products
> - Quality, the responsibility of every worker, not just quality control inspectors
> - Reduced scrap and rework
> - Reduced cycle times
> - Lower setup times
> - Smoother production flow
> - Less inventory of raw materials, work-in-progress and finished goods
> - Cost savings
> - Higher productivity
> - Higher worker participation
> - More skilled workforce, able and willing to switch roles
> - Reduced space requirements
> - Improved relationships with suppliers[29]

*Inventory*

Because of the nature of their product or service, not all international firms and businesses are able to operate within the confines of a JIT system. Nonetheless, these businesses must remain vigilant in their pursuit of accurate and timely inventory control. An unnecessarily large inventory will retain money and resources which ought to be utilized in other aspects of the business. Additionally, unsold or underutilized inventory costs businesses in other ways, such as the expense incurred for storage, vulnerability to theft, and the fact that many states tax inventory separately.

The signs that a global business is experiencing inventory problems include the following:

- Inventories are mounting quicker than sales

- Back orders are numerous

- Customers complain that products or services are unavailable

- Production is interrupted because of a lack of materials

- Inventory turnover rates are slower than expected[32]

Although the above list is abbreviated and certainly not all encompassing, it is a logical starting point to identify inventory issues.

Three main categories of inventory control emerge:

1.  Inventory planning and ordering: This is approached through material requirement planning (MRP) and through the Kanban ordering system to maintain a smooth flow of inventories throughout the production process.

2.  Inventory optimizations systems: Calculations are made to maintain sufficient inventories for predetermined supply chain system needs.

3.  Physical inventory control: This includes all the actions needed to check the physical state of inventories throughout the process.[33]

The ABC Classification System is used to categorize inventory items and is also known as stock keeping units (SKU's). Though companies may use slightly different approaches for this classification, the basic principle lies in dividing the inventories into three categories, according to associated values. An example of category A would be where 20 percent of the company's inventory accounts for 80 percent of the profit. Category C would then represent 40 percent of SKU's with a 5 percent value, and B category would include all the items in between. This categorization system allows managers to focus on the most important items when forecasting, controlling, and scheduling inventories.[34] Once this step is approached, three types of costs must be examined. Specifically, ordering, carrying, and stockout costs must be analyzed and considered in order to implement the most suitable inventory control model.[35]

## GLOBAL LOGISTICS AND SUPPLY CHAIN MANAGEMENT

*Global Logistics (Materials Management and Physical Distribution)*

Logistics increasingly focuses on the global functions of materials management and physical distribution. The term logistics refers to the movement of finished products, semifinished products, components, and materials between various locations. Global logistics is a little more complex because it includes a wide range of locations, plants, warehouses, vendors, and customers that need to be managed across great distances, time zones, and cultures. The figure below depicts the key issues of global logistics.

### Key Issues of Global Logistics

- Movement of product
- Movement of information
- Time/service
- Cost
- Integration[36]

In principle, logistics is a fast evolving and changing field of management, attributed to the fast growth and evolution of new technologies, services, and markets. The main decisions in logistics remain unchanged and have to be addressed on both national and international levels. These decisions are made primarily on three different levels:

1.  The strategic planning level

2.  The network level

3.  The operations level[37]

Strategic planning level decisions are the highest level of logistics decisions. The main strategic planning issues include performance objectives, the degree of vertical integration, outsourcing within the supply chain, what will be measured, and how to accomplish the measurement. These decisions are based on the existing mission and strategies of the organization. Additional considerations include customer expectations, competition, availability of financial resources, and the current logistics system.

Furthermore, related strategic level decisions exist beyond logistics that must be addressed to secure success. Such decisions include the organization's economic objectives and strategy, geographic scope of production, distribution, and marketing, along with marketing and information management objectives and strategy.[38] Though the design and development of a new product takes twelve to eighteen months to complete, on average, other factors of the supply chain network change more rapidly. Thus, it is crucial for a company to reevaluate strategic level decisions at least once a year. Some do not hesitate to do so, even if it means looking at various aspects on a monthly basis.[39]

Network level decisions include the Physical Facility Network and Communication/Information Network decisions. Based on the strategic level decisions, this set of decisions starts with determining the network strategy first. Such considerations include the degree of centralization/decentralization, degree of hierarchy, and number of echelons. After these areas are examined, the physical facilities come to the attention of the organization's management team. The type, number, location of activities, and services provided by each facility are analyzed. Finally, the communication and information network must be designed for effective flow of information along the supply chain. Therefore, the decisions must be made on the amount and type of information flow, use of information technology for transfer, processing, and storage of information.[40] It is important to remember that cost savings do not only result from looking for the cheapest method but also from looking for the most efficient method.

Operations level decisions are decisions that are rather short term and less sophisticated than the other sets of decisions. Despite this reality, these decisions are no less important. Such decisions are divided into the following categories:

- Demand Forecasting: This particular step is very important because it tells the company whether the suggested plans will be profitable. Drawing from historical data, competition analysis and market research, cost, and time restraints, a company chooses one of three main forecasting models: judgmental, intrinsic, or extrinsic.[41]

- Inventory Management: This step in logistics is very important and must be approached from the forecasted demand as well as the nature of the products. The inventory method and safety stock allowance are part of this decision. "Inventory growth may be both a cause and effect of a poorly aligned supply chain." Despite the popularity of the JIT inventory system, higher inventory, and thus warehousing costs, can offset the even higher freight costs and help improve customer service.[42]

- Production: These decisions include the movement of the inputs through the production process. Once the product design and development is planned, decisions on facility location and layout, capital equipment, work design, material, inventory, and quality management must be made in order to ensure a smooth production process.[43]

NOTES

- Procurement and Supply Management: Decisions in this area include such considerations as where to purchase and what to purchase. Specifically, a company must decide how much raw material it needs. An organization must also look at the number or amount of parts, components, products, supplies, and other items needed for production. Selecting suppliers is very crucial for success because they are an important part of an organization's cost savings. The right supplier can assure timeliness and good quality. These aspects can reduce costs and are critical to a successful organization. No matter how reliable a company's suppliers are, a good quality control system must also be established.

- Transportation: Selecting a means of transportation must be based on the product's characteristics, delivery dates, and cost. The selected type of transportation can greatly affect the quality of the products. As a result of this, the cost should not be the driving factor in the decision-making process. The latest approach to transportation strategy involves the use of the internet. Software and other resources are available to assist organizations in developing an appropriate set of transportation strategies that maximize operational efficiency, cost savings, and process standardization. These tools also assist in decreasing communication time and allowing for improved information sharing.[44]

- Product Packaging: Packaging should be selected based on considerations such as the type of product and desired cost savings. The environmental impact of a product's packaging must also be considered. One popular option of environmentally friendly or "green" packaging is the use of "returnables." These are reusable containers that can be repeatedly used for refill by the supplier and in the transportation of materials. Logically speaking, this type of packaging does not work for every type of product or organization. There are a number of factors that must be considered in this area. Such considerations include the life and characteristics of the product, frequency of shipments, and quantity of shipments.[45]

- Material Handling: An appropriate means of handling material from the loading and unloading processes through the storage and production processes is selected based on the nature of the material and bundled according to the inventory and production scheduling.

- Warehousing: Decisions relating to the type, location, and layout of warehouses are critical components in global operations management. In a case of outsourcing, a company should have a thorough knowledge of the warehousing capacities in order to avoid pitfalls, such as paying higher costs for warehousing services and doubled handling charges.[46]

- Order Processing: Orders should be handled through the communication and information processing network. These networks are established to assist in guaranteeing time, cost, and quality efficiency. Other factors, such as specific customer requests, need to be considered as well.

### Supply Chain Management

Supply chain management (SCM) is a major concern for managers in two significant ways. First, if properly managed, the organization may recognize a competitive advantage, ensure long-term success, and be able to make rapid and confident decisions.[47] Second, a wrong decision in the SCM design could "result in a rapid loss of expertise and competitive stature by reducing a company's leverage and splitting supplier relationships across multiple sites, businesses, and geographies."[48] The need for a dynamic SCM system is significant, as the results of a survey of global management executives has proven. Over 95 percent of those surveyed rated efficient supply chain management as "critical" to their long-term success.[49]

An efficient supply chain management system must be built on five fundamental principles:

1. Constraint management—recognize and minimize the impact of constraints.

2. Concurrent versus serial planning—plan across supply chain (synchronization).

3. Global insight—grasp the global impact of local changes.

4. Advance warning—when local changes occur, immediately notify stakeholders in terms of sales, downtime, inventory, etc.

5. Built-in business optimization—the ability to recommend operational solutions to changing business scenarios.

Each of these five fundamental principles will contribute to the overall goal of an intelligent SCM system: "to achieve maximum customer responsiveness at the least possible cost."[50] The availability of tools, such as forecasting, distribution and inventory planning, and e-commerce allow many organizational processes to be integrated across supply chains.[51] Even with these modern advances in SCM, suppliers can still effect 60 to 70 percent of an organization's cost structure, ensuring that these major concerns will remain relevant.[52]

A variety of factors can contribute to the overall success of an organization's supply chain. One factor is how efficiently the organization is able to take a customer request and turn it into a desirable service or product. Another factor is the ability to adapt to market shifts or changes in customer demand. Also, the size difference between outsourcing partners can enable or hinder an organization's ability. Finally, the level of integration between suppliers will have an influence on the effectiveness of the supply chain. Proper management of these factors may have a significant impact, as operation managers ensure that all parties work together, share information, and operate in a way that guarantees the lowest costs and the highest levels of availability throughout the chain.

Third party logistics suppliers (3PLs) play a significant role in supply chain management. In the past, 3PLs were limited to noncritical processes within an organization, such as storage, transportation, or documentation. Very few 3PLs actually had a substantial role in the overall performance or success of the supplying company. The 3PL was more or less viewed as an outside source for providing the incidentals, rather than a strategic business partner. Today, that role has changed as the result of ongoing globalization and the need for companies to manage increasingly complex supply chains. 3PLs can contribute to nearly all aspects of an organization, including purchasing, finance, marketing, and operations. The continuing integration of supplier and 3PL is having an impact in the international business community.

**NOTES**

## KEY CONCEPTS

- Adaptation
- Buy decisions
- Capacity
- Centralization
- Continuous Improvement
- Decentralization
- Facilities layout
- Facilities location
- Fixed assets
- Global logistics
- Inventory
- ISO 9000
- Just-in-time systems
- Location economies
- Make decisions
- Operations Management
- Outsourcing
- Process
- Raw materials
- Standardizations
- Supply Chain Management
- TQM

# Chapter 8 Exercises: Observational Analysis

*Ponder on the following key concepts and ideas as you read the chapter*

1. Capacity considerations: facilities location and processes, facilities layout, make or buy decisions, selections and acquisitions of raw materials, and election and acquisition of fixed assets

2. Production Issues: continuous improvement with regard to TQM and ISO 9000, Just-in-Time Systems, and inventory.

3. Global Logistics: materials management, physical distribution, and supply chain management

4. Start a list of books, journals, and scholarly websites that would aid in the understanding of the chapter's main concepts and ideas. Start a journal for your own thoughts and ideas. What outside sources support your conclusions?

# Chapter 8 Exercises: Key Terms Analysis

*Match the answers by writing the correct letter in the space provided*

_____ 1. ISO 9000

_____ 2. Decentralized organizational structure

_____ 3. Configuration

_____ 4. Supply chain management

_____ 5. Operations level decision

_____ 6. Network level decision

_____ 7. Just-in-time productions or systems

_____ 8. Product layout

_____ 9. The value chain

_____ 10. Productivity

_____ 11. Total quality management (TQM)

_____ 12. Global outsourcing/KANBAN clusters

_____ 13. Principles of total quality

_____ 14. Locus of decisions

_____ 15. Cross functional teams

_____ 16. Operational bottleneck

_____ 17. Capacity

_____ 18. Theory of constraints

_____ 19. 3PLs

_____ 20. MRP

A. Means to enhance the effectiveness of the value chain

B. Various versions of products manufactured and distributed by a company

C. Degree of centralization/decentralization, hierarchy, and number of echelons

D. The acquisition of raw materials, finished goods manufacturing, and distribution channels

E. Greater gain comes from identifying which parts of the process is a constraint to the whole

F. Tool used in managing of the total production process to generate an exceptional product or service

G. Demand forecasting, inventory management, production, procurement, transportation, warehousing

H. The slowest process in a multistep production process that limits total output

I. Customer Focus, Participation and Teamwork, Continuous Improvement and Learning

J. Business should hold slight or zero inventory outside what is necessary for immediate production/distribution

K. Decisions controlled by home office or in foreign location

L. Allows decision making authority to occur where the decisions are to be made

M. Total amount of products that can be produced by the entire operation in a given amount of time

N. Include experts in each technical area within an organization are at horizontal in nature

O. Manage noncritical process within an organization and can contribute to nearly all aspects of an organization

P. Constraint management, concurrent planning, global insight, advance warning, built-in business optimization

Q. Ratio of output as it relates to input

R. Groups machines according to their roles in the production process

S. Comprises the inventory planning and ordering category of inventory control

T. Set of guidelines for quality management and standards

# Chapter 8 Exercises: Theoretical Analysis

*Analyze the questions and select the answer based on the reading of the chapter material*

1. Which of the following is a strategic capability to necessitate the development of a global operations strategy?

    a. Global-scale efficiency and competitiveness

    b. National-level responsiveness and flexibility

    c. Cross-market capacity to leverage on a worldwide basis

    d. All of the above

2. The key components in successful operations management are efficiency and effectiveness.

    a. True

    b. False

3. All of the following are capacity issues except

    a. Facilities location

    b. Location economies

    c. Organizational structure

    d. Production requirements

4. Typical processes within an organization include which of the following areas requiring management:

    a. Inventory, Human Resources, product pricing

    b. Logistics and transportation, procurement, quality

    c. Quality, product and service, configuration

    d. Financial resources, human resources, facilities

5. Capacity, in terms of production-oriented firms, refers to the total amount of products that can be produced by the entire operation in a given amount of time.

    a. True

    b. False

6. The Theory of Constraints (TOC) suggests that the greater gain will come from identifying which part of the process is a constraint to the whole, rather than focusing on increased output from an entire process.

    a. True

    b. False

7. A disadvantage of M & A is:

    a. Damage employee loyalty and morale

    b. Tendency to dwindle natural resources and raw materials

    c. They tend to crowd out locally owned operations

    d. They can become targets for reverse takeovers

8. Kaizen, utilized from the executive levels of the firm to the line workers, is a tool used in the managing of the total production process to generate an exceptional product or service.

    a. True

    b. False

9. _____ is the ratio of output as it relates to input—the conversion of inputs or resources into outputs of merchandise or services

    a. Optimal production output

    b. Optimal capacity level

    c. Productivity

    d. None of the above

10. Just-in-time production or systems is a comprehensive set of doctrines and systems founded on the philosophy that businesses should hold a large  inventory above what is necessary for immediate production or distribution.

    a. True

    b. False

11. The ABC Classification System is used to categorize inventory items and is also known as stock keeping units (SKUs)

    a. True

    b. False

12. The term logistics refers to the movement of finished products, semi-finished products, components, and materials between various locations.

    a. True

    b. False

13. Continuous improvement, sometimes referred to as _____, is a management technique that historically involves several incremental improvements to a process rather than a single overpowering improvement or change

    a. TQM

    b. Six Sigma

    c. Kaizen

    d. JIT

14. Strategic planning level decisions are the highest level of logistics decisions.

    a. True

    b. False

15. Which of the following is NOT a type of observable production-oriented waste?

    a. Product defects

    b. Process waste

    c. Inventory

    d. Underproduction

16. It is important to remember that cost savings do not only result from looking for the cheapest method but also from looking for the most efficient method.

    a. True

    b. False

17. All of the following are key issues of global logistics except

    a. Movement of product

    b. Movement of information

    c. Time/service

    d. Cost

    e. Obtaining scarce resources

18. The availability of tools, such as forecasting, distribution and inventory planning, and e-commerce allow many organizational processes to be integrated across supply chains.

    a. True

    b. False

19. _____ issues include performance objectives, the degree of vertical integration, outsourcing within the supply chain, what will be measured, and how to accomplish the measurement.

    a. The strategic planning level

    b. The network level

    c. The operations level

    d. The organizational level

20. What are the three types of demand forecasting models?

    a. Judgmental, intrinsic, extrinsic

    b. Intrinsic, extrinsic, historical

    c. Extrinsic, judgmental, progressive

    d. External, internal, historical

# Chapter 8 Exercises: Practical Analysis

*Write a short essay in the space provided to each of the following questions.*
*Please use outside references for each answer to support your ideas and thoughts.*

1.  In what ways are global operations management similar; in what ways are they different?

2.  Describe some products that are sold internationally that require standardization; describe some products that are sold internationally, requiring adaptation.

3. Suppose an exporting/importing company is considering ISO 9000 certification; what is the process that a company would need to take to become ISO 9000 certified?

4. Conduct Internet research on 3rd party logistic suppliers; identify a few firms and describe their services.

# Chapter 8 Exercises: Biblical Worldview Application

*Write a short essay in the space provided to each of the following questions.*
*Please use biblical references and research, where applicable, to support your ideas and thoughts.*

Read Luke 6:27-31, also known as the "Golden Rule." Now consider the 3 major principles of total quality: Customer Focus, Participation and Teamwork, and Continuous Improvement and Learning. Write a short essay that explains possible ways In which a global operations manager could connect the Golden Rule concepts to the 3 major principles of total quality

Read Exodus 12 and 13, also known as "The Great Exodus." Now consider the key Issues of global logistics: Movement of product, Movement of information, Time/service, Cost, and Integration. Write a short essay that explains possible ways which a global operations manager could connect The Exodus concepts to the key issues of global logistics.

What distinctives should a Christian business espouse when considering outsourcing manufacturing and product development? How could a Christian business use outsourcing to help support poor nations and economies, global missions, and evangelism? Write a brief essay answering both questions.

# Supplemental
# Material

*This supplemental material was written and provided by Dr. Anita Satterlee.*

NOTES

# WORKING AND TRAVELING ABROAD

Organizations are focusing attention and resources, such as energy, capital, and time to devel managers for overseas business assignments. The rationale behind deploying these resources to create the managerial global perspective essential for success in global markets. This glob perspective empowers managers with business knowledge, basic skills, and a keen sensitivity of t cultures of other countries in which they may be assigned. Thus, managers must be equipped wi a global mindset and skills needed to thrive in cultures completely different from their own.

This supplemental material is divided into two inter-related sections. The first section de with working overseas as an expatriate including (1) motivations to accept an expatriate assignmer (2) expatriate selection procedures and success indicators, (3) adjusting to cultural change, ( compensation and taxation issues for expatriates, and (5) personal security in the Age of Terroris

# WORKING OVERSEAS

Those who work overseas are sometimes referred to as expatriates or ex-pat for short. The ter expatriate, derived from the Latin *ex*, meaning out of, and the Greek *patria*, meaning country, used to describe a people temporarily or permanently residing in a nation other than their own where they hold citizenship. Most would not consider managers who travel overseas for busine meetings and negotiations expatriates.

*Expatriate Trends in Business*

*Overview*

The trends in using expatriates as a strategic tool have altered in recent years due to seve underlying factors, most notably the increased financial restrictions on companies to cut co wherever possible. This includes cutting costs associated with expatriates. The recent econom downturn has caused many companies to consider alternate means of infiltrating internatior markets that either exclude or reduce their investment in expatriates. According to a rece expatriate talent market survey conducted by Sibson Consulting in 2009, some of the mc prominent expatriate trends include reducing the number and/or the length of internatior business assignments, hiring and training more local talent which bypasses the need for expats, ar implementing new human resources compensation strategies for expats to further reduce costs.[1]

In the survey conducted by Sibson Consulting, over 100 top executives in companies we given questionnaires to find current trending patterns in the use of expatriates. The results the survey indicated that about 47 percent of companies are not making any changes to the si of their expatriate workforce. About 37 percent of companies have decreased or plan to decrea their expatriate workforce and a meager 18 percent of companies are planning on increasing th expatriate workforce. It was indicated that of the companies who employ expatriates do so or global scale rather than in any particular region.

The companies who decided to increase the expatriate workforce did so as a strategic busin move and were not deterred by the current trends in the economic environment. Of the compan who made little to no change in their expatriate workforce, the use of expatriates neither harm nor helped the company's business strategy regardless of the economic trends. The companies w reported a planned decrease in the use of expatriates did so because of the high compensation co which far outweighed any strategic benefit expatriates could provide.

As mentioned previously, using local talent to replace expatriates is the primary way compan are reducing costs. Closely following this strategy is the shortening of expat assignments a developing internal talent. Adjusting expatriate compensation is also a focus for companies, and the survey indicated that the majority of the companies interviewed had no plans to change expatriate compensation, while approximately 26 percent decided to decrease, and a mere 7 percent decided to increase expat compensation. As the economy improves, 51 percent of companies interviewed stated that they planned on increasing expatriate compensation while 47 percent indicated that they planned on making no change.

## By Function

As the global market place has changed so has the need for the type of expatriate based on job functionality. Operations were and are the highest job function for which expatriates are utilized. While this has consistently remained a trend in the use of expatriates, there has been an increase in hiring expatriates in the fields of finance, sales, and marketing. As the need for different job functionalities in expatriates has shifted, the need for specific skills among expatriates has also shifted. The ability to speak a local language is the most dramatic shift in desired skillset. There is also a rise in the need for expatriates to have cultural awareness and cultural sensitivity. While there is an increased focus on these skills, having a firm knowledge of business and the industry is still the leading desired skill that employers are looking for when hiring or employing expatriates.

## Expatriate Compensation

Companies typically compensate U.S. expatriates well, because all overseas benefits usually are based on the U.S. salaries. U.S. expatriates can expect to receive a "foreign service" or mobility premium beyond their regular pay. Additionally, expatriates receive higher percent premiums for serving in a location that may be dangerous, lacks U.S. amenities, or has many hardships. Other parts of a typical expatriate compensation package include a cost-of-living adjustment, free housing or housing allowance, a car or car allowance, tax assistance, educational allowances for children, and other benefits. Typical expatriate compensation packages include allowances, such as tax assistance, housing and utilities, assistance with goods and services, educational allowances, car allowance, home travel provisions, paid emergency leave and vacation, completion bonus, relocation bonus, health care benefits, home sale assistance, and expenses for spouse and dependents.[2]

## Tax Considerations

U.S. citizens working overseas have an obligation to pay their U.S. taxes. American expatriates may experience lower tax bills as the first eighty thousand dollars in income is tax exempt; but, any remainder is taxable. The exemption also includes the first eighty thousand dollars of a spouse's income. Expatriate citizens must file an income tax return each year of overseas duty. In addition to salary, other items are taxable, including stipends for housing and education expenses for accompanying children. Compensation for housing is exempt from taxation, if paid by the employer. An expatriate may also be obligated to pay taxes to the foreign government; therefore, an expatriate should become thoroughly familiar with any tax rules that might apply to his or her individual situation to ensure that applicable taxes due to either country are paid on time. These details should be thoroughly covered with one's employer before taking an assignment overseas.[3]

NOTES

## Motivations to Accept an Expatriate Assignment

Motivations for accepting an expatriate assignment can be examined from the perspective of the employer and the employee. Organizations investigate every possible advantage, including expatriation, when it comes to establishing and operating businesses in a foreign environment. Successful organizations invest the necessary resources in the professional development of managers who agree to live abroad in cultures that may be very different than their own. The two most prevalent motivations are control over global operations and career development. Control over global operations is the organizational motivation for expatriate assignment development. Expatriatism promotes consistency in operations across the company as the expatriate manager maintains close professional relationships with the home office. Employees are more comfortable when they know that predictable decisions and management practices are in place. Career development increases motivation for providing key employees with an expatriate assignment. Career development motivations can be quite diverse, as the following proves:

• Expatriate assignments offer the opportunity to manage an overseas operation in order to gain experience in management autonomy and self-sufficiency.

• Employees may accept the expatriate assignment to enhance personal growth, expanding their value to the organization by seeking a challenging role with greater responsibility and decision-making authority.

• Many hold the common belief that an international assignment will enhance one's future career. The employee might be motivated to gain exposure to managers or executives at higher levels in the company, which can enhance career progression within the organization.

• Employees may seek expatriate assignments to gain higher levels of compensation. Many organizations will offer premium compensation packages in order to make these types of assignments more appealing—particularly in the less desirable countries.

• The promise of exciting adventures also prompts individuals to seek the excitement and challenge of foreign assignments. The thrill of international adventure, seeking to discover all of the various cultural treasures, which are normally only envisioned or imagined by many, inspires some individuals to seek expatriate status Other reasons for accepting an expatriate assignment include opportunity to travel, interest in a different culture and work, and getting back to one's roots.[4]

## Selection Procedures and Success Indicators

The screening and selection of candidates for expatriate assignments is one of the more critical decisions for the organization. The recruiting and selection of a successful candidate can first be attributed to headquarter leadership practices. For example, leadership may decide that only employees who have completed at least one foreign assignment will be considered in the management succession planning process.[5] Leadership must consider local culture and labor practices in determining candidates for expatriation assignments. Candidates who are intimately familiar with the local culture and labor practices of the host country are less likely to be surprised or intimidated by communication barriers, local customs, or any other environmental factors. Hence, the adjustment for the expatriate is relatively seamless and positive, and results occur much more quickly and efficiently. Expatriates who have a host country background have a tendency to be more successful than those who do not. "Expatriates with an in-depth knowledge of host environments, including shared mental models with locals, are better placed to make wise selection decisions."[6]

Organizational leadership may consider the cross-cultural capabilities of potential expatriate candidates in addition to technical proficiency and managerial experiences. Decision makers may review the potential expatriate's relational abilities with a diverse workforce. Some firms develop more formalized criteria for selection, including an emphasis on cultural sensitivity, a selection board composed of expatriates, previous international experience, hiring foreign born employees who can serve as expatriates at a future date, and screening candidate's spouses and families.[7] Organizations consider expatriate involvement in the selection process appropriate, even encouraging it. The expatriate should fully understand the assignment outcomes and expectations. In this manner, a company clearly and concisely gives an overview of the company requirements and expectations to the expatriate in order to prevent any misunderstandings. If a company has a clear picture of what the expatriate expects career-wise, then it will be easier to meet those expectations or tell the expatriate beforehand that it will not be possible.[8] Regardless of the process, senior management must be involved in the overall expatriate candidate selection decision—just as their involvement, commitment, and direction are key to the successful implementation of any meaningful expatriation process.[9]

Five key steps play a significant role in expatriate success: conducting an expatriate audit, conducting a cultural diversity audit, refining expatriation selection, providing cross-cultural training, and providing repatriation assistance:[10]

1. An expatriate audit requires decision-makers to review current expatriate practices in order to identify expatriate failure rates and address the causes of costly expatriate failure. Auditors also evaluate success stories to determine the causes of success as well. Therefore, organizations can improve upon the success rates of future expatriate assignments.

2. A cultural diversity audit identifies the organization's diversity capabilities for managing in culturally complex environments. Companies can utilize this information for assistance in selecting expatriates.

3. The expatriate is selected.

4. The expatriate becomes engaged in cross-cultural training, designed to reduce expatriate and foreign venture failure. Cross-cultural training is not a fail-safe solution; but, it does help the expatriate adjust to the foreign environment.

5. The final step includes repatriation assistance, whereby the organization allows the repatriate to reap the rewards of the completed foreign assignment. Some organizations fall short in this area by failing to utilize or reward the valuable cross-cultural skills and knowledge that an expatriate brings home. Some companies fail to reward repatriates with assignments at home that enhance career aspirations. In other cases, repatriates have discovered that companies assign them to positions inferior to the one previously vacated, causing the individual to seek employment elsewhere.

NOTES

## *Adjusting to Cultural Change*

Successful expatriate placement depends upon how well these individuals react to the new culture. Culture and norms of host countries are often much different than the expatriate's home country, and much of what comprises culture cannot be taught in the classroom. This can be a source of great stress on an expatriate and family. Expatriates may experience a stress-induced reaction known as "culture shock" when confronted with the reality of their new work and home environment. Key factors that can affect expatriate culture shock include the following:

- The training the expatriate receives.

- The demographic characteristics of the expatriate.

- The dispositional and personality characteristics of the expatriate.

- The level of organizational support provided to the expatriate.

- The level of technical competence of the expatriate.[11]

Managers tend to be very upbeat and excited at the beginning of their overseas assignment. This can change gradually as they begin to encounter frustration and stress from communication barriers and other cultural differences with the local population. Undoubtedly, there will be many stressful experiences in store for the expatriate as a result of cultural differences, but many problems arise among fellow expatriates. Although not widely recognized by management back home, subcultures exist within overseas expatriate circles. Sometimes these differences can cause more stress than the difficulties arising from dealing with locals on a daily basis.

## *Communication Barriers and Training*

Although expatriates use the English language extensively, companies highly value expatriates who are fluent in multiple languages. Foreign language skills training is very important for the expatriate manager; paradoxically, many of today's multinational corporations consider training in this area a weakness. Business etiquette training is another important aspect of doing business overseas. Knowledge of the practices of a particular region can prove invaluable when negotiating business arrangements. For example, some cultures frown upon beginning a business conversation by talking about business. Business managers in such cultures desire to first establish a social relationship prior to developing a business relationship. Trust is a very important relational characteristic in foreign cultures; so, Westerners should be prepared to invest a considerable amount of time into forging a foundation of trust before trying to force negotiations prematurely[12] Often, the social aspects of a business relationship are just as important to foreigners as the business aspects.

It is vital for companies to have a firm pre-training program in place for expatriates. Studies have shown that the number one reason expatriates have failed in overseas assignments is directly related to their inability to adapt to another culture.[13] Companies who have a solid pre-training program in place for their expatriate employees have seen a higher success rate than the companies who do not.

*Non-verbal Communication*

As discussed in Chapter 2, non-verbal communication is another type of "language" that varies greatly from culture to culture—and its use may be conscious or unconscious. Knowledge of non-verbal communication common to a particular country or culture is helpful in establishing relationships and one's own credibility as a person who respects and appreciates the foreign culture. The main classes of non-verbal communication that are of interest to the expatriate are chronemics, kinesics, paralinguistics, proxemics, and haptics, which often occur together, with or without verbal expression.

*Chronemics*

Chronemics is the use of time to convey a message, including punctuality, the amount of time spent with another person, and the amount of time a person is kept waiting. Two classifications of chronemic culture include monochronic and polychronic. In a monochronic culture, individuals promptly keep appointments, meetings start on time, people do not tolerate interruptions easily, and business relationships focus strictly on the task at hand. In polychronic cultures, it is acceptable to keep someone waiting past an appointed meeting time as a normal part of doing business, and business relationships are closer and more personal.

*Kinesics*

Kinesics describes the physical messages communicated by gestures, such as facial expressions, body movement, posture, and gait. While some of these messages are universal in nature, such as sad or angry facial expressions, culturally significant kinesics can be an important way of communicating respect for another person and his or her culture. For example, bowing in Japanese culture conveys respect—even for enemies—when greeting, thanking, or saying goodbye to others. Knowledge of appropriate times and situations to bow to a Japanese person can convey the expatriate's willingness to learn and appreciate Japanese culture. In Arab countries, the gesture of placing one's hand over one's heart when conveying a greeting is a gesture of respect for people of that culture. When a foreigner offers such a gesture in addition to a verbal greeting, the Arabs appreciate the gesture even more.

*Paralinguistics*

Paralinguistics, or the vocal cues other than words, include volume, rate of speech, pitch, and pauses and silences used in speaking. These vocal cues require some knowledge of the local language, which requires additional training in a foreign language. Though English is a second language in many countries of the world, knowledge of the local language carries advantages that cannot be gained through the use of English alone, especially in countries where English is not widely spoken. Since citizens of the expatriate's host country conduct their own business, often in their own language, knowledge of paralinguistics unique to the local culture can be useful in everyday business transactions, especially negotiations in which some or all of the talking may be done in the local language.

### Proxemics and Haptics

Proxemics consists of the spatial cues, such as interpersonal distance, territoriality, and other spatial relationships. Haptics refers to contact cues, such as the frequency, intensity, and type of touch. In Arab nations, men commonly step in close to each other to conduct normal personal or business conversations, and men will hold hands with other men with whom they are close friends. Arabs consider being physically close to or touching women disrespectful and offensive, if done by men outside the immediate or extended family. This type of behavior should be avoided, including shaking a woman's hand—even if done by a non-Arab. Knowledge of these types of cultural conventions is important to maintaining proper decorum in a foreign country so as not to offend or insult one's hosts.

### Personal Security and Terrorism

Personal security is often a reflection of the socio-political situation in each country. Countries that are less stable socially or politically are often less secure for foreigners—who make good targets for kidnappers and other criminals. Expatriates should carefully consider the risks of criminal exposure and personal safety in the country to which they will be assigned. These considerations should include where in the country to live and whether or not to take family along for the duration of the assignment. If required, some companies provide security for their employees, and this should be clearly identified prior to moving to the new location. For example, in Iraq and other politically unstable nations, companies hire their own security personnel or private security firms to provide bodyguards for employees and security for its facilities. Even in more stable countries, companies provide bodyguards to protect their more important or senior employees.

In recent years, Westerners (U.S. citizens in particular) have been the target of international terrorists and their organizations, consisting of multiple, independent cells in various countries around the world. Unfortunately, in this environment, an organization cannot guarantee the personal security of expatriate citizens because their status as American citizens makes them a target. While the statistical risk of an individual American citizen being directly affected by a terrorist attack abroad is very low, the possibility still exists and responsible consideration of this possibility is important before making any decision to go overseas.

Information is available from the United States Department of State regarding terrorism, in the form of travel warnings, issued periodically as the situation warrants by conditions in various countries and distributed to citizens overseas by the embassy in each country. These general steps help decrease vulnerability:

- Keep a low profile. Your dress, conduct, and mannerisms should not attract attention. Make an effort to blend into the local environment. Avoid publicity and do not go out in large groups. Stay away from civil disturbances and demonstrations.
- Be unpredictable. Vary your route to and from work and the time you leave and return home. Do not exercise at the same time and place each day, never alone, on deserted streets, or on country roads. Let people close to you know where you are going, what you will be doing, and when you should be back.
- Be Alert. Watch for anything suspicious or out of place. Do not give personal information over the telephone. If you think you are being followed, go to a pre-selected secure area. Immediately report the incident to your company security officer and local law enforcement agencies. In overseas areas without such above agencies, report the incident to the U.S. Embassy.[14]

The expatriate must know the environment in which he or she will be living and working and know what appropriate actions to take in advance in response to a possible threat. Any actions taken should be planned in advance with company security personnel, including escape routes, emergency contact numbers, and any other appropriate security information.

## CULTURAL NORMS AND BUSINESS CUSTOMS

Cultures and norms vary widely across the globe. One's attitude towards time is very important and significantly affects international business. A U.S. expatriate relocating overseas will undoubtedly have to adapt to the host country's attitude toward time. In the U.S., most consider making someone wait for a business appointment past the scheduled meeting time insulting behavior. In other cultures, such as Latin America or the Middle East, waiting could mean just the opposite. Latin American or Middle Eastern executives may be taking care of the minor details of business so that they can attend to their important visitor without interruption. Whether U.S. expatriates should follow the local or U.S. custom depends. In Spain, a general rule is to never be punctual, as Spaniards consider punctuality being early. Middle Easterners know the punctuality tendencies of U.S. firms well; if an American is late, they consider him or her rude. However, the Middle Easterner can be late and not be looked upon as impolite because he or she is following the local custom.

When considering what countries or regions to conduct business in, it is always helpful to know what the business and cultural expectations are regarding relationships and communication techniques. Consider the following brief synopsis provided of each country from different regions of the world as an overview of what to expect when traveling and conducting business abroad.[15] The facts and generalizations listed here are basic personal and professional working habits that can help solidify relationships or ruin them. The wise business manager will have a firm understanding of the cultural do's and don'ts associated with the companies they are doing business with in different countries.

### *Australia*

In general, Australians are very down to earth and always mindful of not giving the impression of being presumptuous or arrogant. Australians value authenticity, sincerity, and loathe pretentiousness. Consequently, Australians prefer people who are modest, humble, self- deprecating and with a sense of humour. They do not draw attention to their academic or other achievements and tend to distrust people who do. They often downplay their own success, which may make them appear not to be achievement-oriented

#### *Business Do's and Don'ts*

When conducting business in Australia or with Australian natives, it is important to be mindful of the following Australian business practices:

*Relationships & Communication*

- Australians are very matter of fact when it comes to business
- Don't need long-standing personal relationships before doing business with people
- Australians are very direct in the way they communicate so do not take offence

- There is often an element of humour, often self-deprecating, in their speech
- Aussies often use colourful language that would be unthinkable in other countries.

### Business Meeting Etiquette

- Appointments are necessary and relatively easy to schedule.
- They should be made with as much lead time as possible.
- Punctuality is important in business situations. It is better to arrive a few minutes early than to keep someone waiting.
- Meetings are generally relaxed; however, they are serious events.
- If an Australian takes exception to something that you say, they will tell you so.
- If you make a presentation, avoid hype, making exaggerated claims, or bells and whistles.
- Present your business case with facts and figures. Emotions and feelings are not important in the Australian business climate.

### Negotiating and Decision Making

- Australians do not mince words or waste time making decisions.
- They are direct and expect the same communication style in return.
- Negotiations proceed quickly. Bargaining is not customary.
- They will expect your initial proposal to have only a small margin for negotiation. If possible, ignore manipulation during business transactions.
- They do not like high-pressure techniques
- Decision-making is concentrated at the top of the company, although decisions are made after consultation with subordinates, which can make decision making slow and protracted.

### What to wear

- Business dress is mostly conservative and professional in the larger cities.
- In Brisbane or other tropical areas, depending on the job function and company culture, men may wear shirts, ties and Bermuda shorts.

### Business Cards

- Business cards are exchanged at the initial introduction without formal ritual. Occasionally business cards are not offered which simply means the other person did not have one.

## Argentina

Argentineans have a very expressive communication style and are very open about their feelings and ideas. They can be quite blunt and direct but can be quite diplomatic in their conversations if the need arises.

### Relationships & Communication

- Argentines are generally warm and welcoming and passionate peoples.
- They are very expressive with their bodies and will often leave very little room between themselves and the person they are conversing with.
- Argentina is a relationship-driven culture, so it is important to build networks and use them.
- If a favour is done for you, you will eventually be called upon to re-pay it.

- Name-dropping and nepotism do not have the negative connotations as it has in the West and can be used to your advantage.
- Argentines like to do business with people they know and trust and once a relationship is established, they will remain loyal to the person rather than a company.
- They prefer face-to-face meetings rather than by telephone or in writing, which are seen as impersonal.
- Looking good in the eyes of others is important to Argentines.
- It is best to avoid confrontation because Argentines do not like publicly admitting they are incorrect and can become quite passionate about it.
- It is a good idea to repeat details, as you understand them to confirm that you and your business colleagues are in agreement.

### Business Meeting Etiquette
- Appointments are necessary and should be made 1 to 2 weeks in advance, preferably by e-mail or telephone.
- Avoid January and February, which are their vacation times; the middle weeks of July, which is when many go skiing; and during the two weeks before and after Christmas.

### Business Negotiations
- Argentines expect to deal with people of similar status.
- Hierarchy is important in Argentine business culture where decisions are made at the top of the company. Business moves slowly because it is extremely bureaucratic.
- Decisions are not made in meetings and often require several layers of approval.

### What to Wear
- Business attire is formal and conservative, yet stylish with men wearing dark color business suits and women wearing stylish business attire.
- It is important to dress well if you want to make a good impression.

### Business Cards
- Business cards are given without formal ritual and should have at least one side translated into Spanish.

### Canada

In general, most Canadians have a strong allegiance to their province or region. There are some broad differences between regions, which can generally be summed up as follows:

- For businesses, the widespread adoption of International Standards means that suppliers can base the development of their products and services on specifications that have wide acceptance in their sectors. This, in turn, means that businesses using International Standards are increasingly free to compete in many more markets around the world.
- Atlantic Provinces (Nova Scotia, New Brunswick, Prince Edward Island and Newfoundland): The people are somewhat reserved and provincial, to the point that they are seen as old-fashioned.

- Ontario: This is the business hub and the people tend to be business-like and conservative.
- Western Canada (Alberta, Manitoba and Saskatchewan): The people are open, friendly and relaxed.
- British Colombia: The people are less conventional. This province is often viewed as the Canada of the future.
- Quebec: The French region, has a distinct cultural identity. The people are extremely rationalistic/independent.
- North: The people have a strong pioneer spirit.

### Meeting and Greeting

- For businesses, the widespread adoption of International Standards means that suppliers can base the development of their products and services on specifications that have wide acceptance in their sectors. This, in turn, means that businesses using International Standards are increasingly free to compete in many more markets around the world.
- Canadian businesspeople often begin relationships in a reserved manner but is relaxed after people get to know one another
- Canadians appreciate politeness
- Hand shaking is expected upon arriving and departing from informal and formal meetings. Eye contact is expected when shaking hands.
- Titles and surnames are usually not used.
- Academic titles are important in Quebec and are used with the honorific Monsieur or Madame.
- Business cards are exchanged after the initial introduction.
- In Quebec, have one side of your business card translated into French. Hand the card so the French side faces the recipient.

### Communication Styles

It is difficult to specify any national trait in terms of communication in Canada due to its regionalism and cultural diversity. However, there are some basic communication styles that are fairly standard across the country. For example, businesspeople are generally polite, easy-going and somewhat informal. Canadians like their space and prefer to be at an arm's length when speaking to someone.

Canadians are reticent to discuss their personal lives with business associates. They expect people to speak in a straightforward manner and to be able to back up their claims with examples. They do not make exaggerated claims and are suspicious of something that sounds too good to be true

### Business meetings

Canadians begin meetings with little to know small talk although one should expect to spend a few minutes exchanging pleasantries and the like. In Quebec there may be more time spent on relationship-building. Business meetings are generally well-organized and adhere to time schedules and tend to be informal and relaxed in manner.

*China*

## The Importance of "Face"

The concept of 'face' roughly translates as 'honour', 'good reputation' or 'respect' and can be broken down into four general categories:.

1. *Diu-mian-zi*: this is when one's actions or deeds have been exposed to people.

2. *Gei-mian-zi*: involves the giving of face to others through showing respect.

3. *Liu-mian-zi:* this is developed by avoiding mistakes and showing wisdom in action.

4. *Jiang-mian-zi*: this is when face is increased through others, i.e. someone complementing you to an associate.

## Relationships & Communication

- The Chinese build trust in business partners over time and relationships start out professional and distanced. They view individuals are representatives of their companies and expect formal introductions prior to the start of any business relationship.
- It is a good practice to send materials (written in Chinese) that describe your company, its history, and literature about your products and services prior meeting.
- Be very patient as relationship building and decisions take a considerable amount of time and are bound up with enormous bureaucracy.
- Rank is extremely important in business relationships and you must keep rank differences in mind when communicating.
- The Chinese prefer face-to-face meetings rather than written or telephonic communication.
- Business decisions are conducted in business settings.

## Business Meeting Etiquette

- Appointments are necessary and, if possible, should be made between one-to-two months in advance, preferably in writing.
- You should arrive at meetings on time or slightly early because arriving late is viewed as an insult.
- Send an agenda before the meeting so your Chinese colleagues have the chance to meet with any technical experts prior to the meeting.
- Mobile phones ring frequently and conversations tend to be boisterous. It is best to not ask the Chinese to turn off their mobile phones as this causes you both to lose face.
- Seating at a meeting is arranged in descending order of rank. Senior people generally sit opposite senior people from the other side.
- Visual aids are useful in large meetings and should only be done with black type on white background. Colors should be avoided because different colours have different meanings.
- Presentations should be detailed and factual and focus on long-term benefits.

NOTES

## Business Negotiation

- Only senior members of the negotiating team will speak and business negotiations occur at a slow pace.
- Chinese are non-confrontational and will often say "yes" even if they are not in agreement as to the topic.
- Do not use high-pressure tactics and losing your temper will cause you to lose face and ruin any relationship
- Business is hierarchical and decisions do not get made quickly. The Chinese are very through and weigh the benefits and drawbacks of decisions at length. Additionally the Chinese are shrewd negotiators which should be considered when bargaining and negotiating business conditions.

## What to Wear

- Business attire is conservative and unpretentious.
- Women should wear flat shoes or shoes with very low heels.
- Bright colours should be avoided.

## Business Cards

- Business cards are exchanged after the initial introduction and have great importance in Chinese culture.
- Business card should include your title and both English and Chinese translations
- Hold the card in both hands when offering it with the Chinese side facing the recipient.
- Examine a business card before putting it on the table next to you or in a business card case. It is also important to not write on someone's card unless directed.

### France

## Relationships - Public vs. Private

- The French are generally private people and have different rules of behavior for people within their social circle and those who are not and are the most themselves around close friends and family.

## Meeting Etiquette

- The handshake is a common form of greeting for both men and women. Though good friends may greet each other by lightly kissing on the cheeks.
- First names are reserved for family and close friends.

## Relationships & Communication

- Mutual trust and respect is required to get things done and creating a wide network of close personal business alliances is very important.
- If you do not speak French, an apology for not knowing their language may aid in developing a relationship.
- When doing business, the French can be extremely direct and are not afraid of asking probing questions.
- Written communication is formal in a business setting.

*Business Meetings Etiquette*
- Appointments are necessary and should be made at least 2 weeks in advance.
- Avoid scheduling meetings during July or August, as this is a common vacation period.
- Telephone immediately if you are going to be late to a meeting.
- Meetings are to discuss issues and are often not used to make decisions.

*Business Negotiation*
- French business emphasizes courtesy and formality which includes waiting to be told where to sit and maintaining eye contact while speaking.
- Avoid confrontational behaviour or high-pressure tactics when conducting business dealings.
- The French will carefully analyse every detail of a proposal as such, decisions are not made quickly.
- Business is hierarchical and business discussions may be heated and intense.
- High-pressure sales tactics should be avoided. The French are more receptive to a low-key, logical presentation that explains the advantages of a proposal in full.
- When an agreement is reached, the French may insist it be in a formal and precisely worded contract.

*Dress Etiquette*
- Business dress is understated and stylish and of good quality.
- Men should wear dark-coloured, conservative business suits for the initial meeting. Women should wear either business suits or elegant dresses in soft colors.

*Business Cards*
- Business cards are exchanged after the initial introductions without formal ritual.
- Have the other side of your business card translated into French.
- Include any advanced academic degrees on your business card.

*Germany*

*A Planning Culture*
- Germans can be considered the masters of planning and are famous for strict adherence to structure, rules, and regulations. Rules and regulations allow people to know what is expected and plan their life accordingly
- This is a culture that prizes forward thinking and knowing what they will be doing at a specific time on a specific day.
- Once the proper way to perform a task is discovered, there is no need to think of doing it any other way.
- Germans believe that maintaining clear lines of demarcation between people, places, and things is the surest way to lead a structured and ordered life, again, playing on the security gained by careful planning.
- Work and personal lives are rigidly divided.
- If you must remain after normal closing, it indicates that you did not plan your day properly.

NOTES

*Meeting Etiquette*
- Greetings are formal in nature.
- A quick, firm handshake is the traditional greeting.
- Titles are very important and denote respect. Use a person's title and their surname until invited to use their first name. You should say Herr or Frau and the person's title and their surname.

*Relationships & Communications*
- Germans do not need a personal relationship in order to do business and do not have an open-door policy in business.
- They will be interested in your academic credentials and the amount of time your company has been in business.
- Germans display great deference to people in authority, so it is imperative that they understand your level relative to their own.
- Germans will be direct to the point of bluntness.
- Expect a great deal of written communication, both to back up decisions and to maintain a record of decisions and discussions.

*Business Meeting Etiquette*
- Appointments are mandatory and should be made 1 to 2 weeks in advance.
- If you write to schedule an appointment, the letter should be written in German.
- Punctuality is taken extremely seriously and it is viewed as extremely rude to cancel a meeting at the last minute and it could jeopardize your business relationship.
- Meetings adhere to strict agendas, including starting and ending times.
- Maintain direct eye contact while speaking.
- Although English may be spoken, it is a good idea to hire an interpreter so as to avoid any misunderstandings.
- At the end of a meeting, some Germans signal their approval by rapping their knuckles on the table top.
- The eldest or highest ranking person enters the room first during business meetings.
- Men enter before women, if their age and status are roughly equivalent.

*Business Negotiation*
- Do not sit until invited and told where to sit.
- Germany is heavily regulated and extremely bureaucratic.
- Germans prefer to get down to business and only engage in the briefest of small talk.
- Contracts are strictly followed.
- Germans are detail- oriented and want to understand every innuendo before coming to an agreement.
- German organizational structure is very hierarchical and decision-making is held at the top of the company.
- Final decisions are translated into rigorous, comprehensive action steps that you can expect will be carried out to the letter.
- Once a decision is made, it will not be changed and manipulation is not tolerated or respected.

*Dress Etiquette*

- Business dress is understated, formal and conservative and which means not wearing ostentatious jewelry or accessories
- Men should wear dark coloured, conservative business suits.

## India

*Indian Society & Culture Hierarchy*

- The role of hierarchies in relationships is evident across all aspects of life, including business. The influences of Hinduism and the tradition of the caste system have created a culture that emphasizes established hierarchical relationships.
- Indians are always conscious of social order and their status relative to other people regardless of the relationship.

*The Role of the Family*

- People typically define themselves by the groups to which they belong rather than by their status as individuals.
- The extended family creates a myriad of interrelationships, rules, and structures. Along with these mutual obligations comes a deep-rooted trust among relatives.

*The use of "no"*

- Much like in Asian cultures, Indians do not like to express 'no,' be it verbally or non-verbally.
- Other cultures should not view this behavior as dishonest because an Indian would be considered terribly rude if he did not attempt to give a person what had been asked.

*Relationships & Communication*

- Indians prefer to do business with those they know, and both business and personal relationships are built upon mutual trust and respect.
- Indians prefer to have long-standing personal relationships prior to doing business.
- It may be a good idea to go through a third party introduction. This gives you immediate credibility.

*Business Meeting Etiquette*

- The best time for a business meeting is late morning or early afternoon. Reconfirm your meeting the week before and call again that morning, since it is common for meetings to be cancelled at the last minute. Because of this tendency, it is wise to keep schedules flexible so that they can be adjusted for last minute rescheduling of meetings.
- Arrive at formal meetings on time.
- Meetings will start with a great deal of personal and relational dialogue.
- It is wise to follow up a meeting with an overview of what was discussed and the next steps.

## Business Negotiating

- Indians are non-confrontational and it is rare for them to overtly disagree, with decisions being determined by the person with the most authority.
- Decision making is a slow process.
- Most Indians expect concessions in both price and terms. It is acceptable to expect concessions in return for those you grant.
- Never appear overly legalistic during negotiations.
- Successful negotiations are often celebrated by a meal.

## Dress Etiquette

- Business attire is conservative and men should wear dark coloured conservative business suits. Women should dress conservatively in suits or dresses.
- The weather can play a crucial role in determining clothing.

## Titles

- Indians revere titles such as Professor, Doctor and Engineer.
- Status is determined by age, university degree, caste and profession.

## Business Cards

- Business cards are exchanged after the initial handshake and greeting and do not need to be translated into Hindi.
- It is important to use the right hand to give and receive business cards.

### South Africa

## South African Society & Culture

South Africa is one of the most multicultural countries in the world that consist of many different cultural and ethnic groups in urban areas that make up the population. South Africa has a unique population mix of the indigenous black peoples of South Africa colonialism and white Europeans, Indians, Indo-Malays, Chinese and many more that have been brought in by immigration. Consequently, it is difficult to generalise South African etiquettes and culture.

## The Family in South Africa

- In traditional African society, the tribal unit is the most important community and would be the equivalent of an individual nation.
- For South Africans, the tribe provides both emotional and financial security in much the same way the nuclear family would.

## The Rural/Urban Dichotomy

- There are huge differences between the values of the rural and urban dwellers in South Africa. The majority of the whites living in rural areas are Afrikaner farmers who are descended from the Calvinists.
- City dwellers live life in a more modern context, which greatly affects their worldview.

## Relationships & Communication

- South Africans are transactional and do not need to establish long-standing personal relationships before conducting business because they are use to a more authoritative leadership style.
- Networking and relationship building are crucial for long-term business success.
- There are major differences in communication styles depending upon the individual's cultural heritage which can include multiple regional and even local language dialects.
- For the most part, South Africans want to avoid confrontations if possible as a way to maintain good business relationships with business partners.
- South Africans prefer face-to-face meetings to more impersonal communication techniques.

## Business Meeting Etiquette

- Appointments are necessary and should be made as far in advance as possible.
- It is often difficult to schedule meetings from mid-December to mid-January or the two weeks surrounding Easter because these are considered prime vacation times.
- After a meeting, send a letter summarizing what was decided and the next steps.

## Business Negotiations

- It is imperative to develop mutual trust before conducting business negotiations in South Africa.
- It is important to note that women have yet to attain senior level positions. Gender inequality is still very active in South Africa and women do not experience the same level of respect, authority, or consideration as that of men.
- It is considered very rude to interrupt a South African while they are speaking.
- When negotiating, South Africans strive for consensus and win-win situations conducted with very little haggling.
- Delivery dates should be included in all contracts as deadlines are often viewed as fluid rather than firm commitments.
- Decision-making may be concentrated at the top of the company and decisions are often made after consultation with subordinates which significantly slows down the decision making process.

## Dress Etiquette

- Business attire is becoming more informal in many companies.
- Like most other countries, men should wear dark colored conservative business suits and women should wear elegant business suits or dresses.

NOTES

*United Kingdom*

The United Kingdom includes the four countries of: England, Scotland, Wales, and Northern Ireland. It is important not only to be aware of these geographical distinctions; but also, the strong sense of identity and nationalism felt by the populations of these four nations. To some degree, each of these nations has their own business culture. However, the majority of them share similarities and are often grouped together.

*A Multicultural Society*

Britain has become increasingly diverse as it has accommodated large immigrant populations, particularly from its former colonies such as India, Pakistan and the West Indies. The mixture of ethnic groups and cultures make it difficult to define what it means to be distinctly "British" which is often a topic of great debate.

*Stiff Upper Lip*

The British have been historically known for their stiff upper and their 'grin and bear' attitude in the face of adversity or embarrassment lives on today. Also, to be considered is the reserved and private nature of British nationals. They expect others to respect their privacy which includes not asking too many personal questions.

*Greetings*
- A firm handshake is the appropriate greeting method.
- Most people use the courtesy titles or Mr, Mrs or Miss and their surname.
- Business cards are exchanged at the initial introduction without formal ritual and may not be given much consideration.

*Communication Style*

The British have an interesting mix of communication styles encompassing both indirect and direct communication. When communicating with people they see as equal to themselves in rank or class, the British are direct, but modest. If communicating with someone they know well, their style may be more informal, although they will still be reserved.

Written communication follows strict rules of protocol. Written communication is always addressed using the person's title and their surname. Consequently, first names are rarely used in formal/business communication.

*Building Relationships*

The British are known for their formality. They sometimes prefer to work with people and companies they know or who are known to their associates. Networking and relationship building are often key to long-term business success with many British companies. Most British look for long-term relationships with business partners.

*Business Meetings*

It would be wise to share an agenda to the British colleagues in sufficient time for them to review it and recommend any changes. In most cases, the people you are meeting will be on time. Scots are extremely punctual. In British business meetings, the protocol for the meeting will often be determined by the composition of people attending:

- For example, if everyone is at the same level, there is generally a free flow of ideas and opinions.
- If there is a senior ranking person in the room, that person will do most of the speaking.
- In general, meetings will be formal and always have a clearly defined purpose, which may include an agenda.
- The British rely on facts, rather than emotions, to make decisions
- Punctuality is important in business situations

## BUSINESS TRAVEL ABROAD

Business travel abroad is becoming a vital part of international trade and business. Before business transactions occur in a foreign country, leaders recommended that company officials visit the countries to study their markets first. The United States prefers business transactions in person rather than conducting business over some other form of communication. Traveling abroad to cultivate new relationships with other companies in other countries will prove to be an important aspect of international business dealings. Companies must consider certain pre-travel requirements and other affects that come with international travel prior to conducting business in person overseas.

As more companies move into a globalized society and technology rapidly changes the way people communicate, many individuals are taking advantage of the personalized communication tools available to them via mobile communications devices. One of the most used tools is "apps", short for mobile applications, which can be downloaded directly onto mobile devices. There are thousands of apps that can be downloaded and can fall within a plethora of categories. Some of the most helpful apps for the international traveler and businessman are[16]:

**Converse:** Have a conversation with speakers of other languages with Converse app. Converse translates between English, French, German, Spanish, Portuguese, Italian and Dutch

**Wikitude:** Award-winning augmented reality app Wikitude helps you explore as you travel. Take pictures of new sights and scenes. Wikitude will inform you about your surroundings.

**WhatsApp:** Text any smartphone user with WhatsApp, the app that lets you send texts, photos, videos and audio files with your contacts. WhatsApp is also great for group texting among different smartphones.

**AllSubway**: This iOS app is a pocket guide to the world's subway maps. Featuring more than 160 maps, you'll find guides to public transit systems in Europe, North America, South America, Africa, Asia and Australia.

**Photosynth**: Available for Windows Phone and iPhone, this panorama creation app lets you shoot geo-located, interactive images. You can share your Photosynth with other users when you have an Internet connection.

**Skype WiFi:** Skype Wi-Fi lets you use your Skype credit to connect in airports, hotels, coffee shops, and thousands of other locations across the world.

**Google Goggles:** This free AR app for Android will help you identify everything from paintings in museums to ingredients in food.

**TripIt:** This one-shop-stop travel app organizes everything from your business schedule to your hotel reservation to your flight confirmation numbers.

**XE Currency:** Use this app to find the best local currency exchange rates. If you often overspend while you're abroad because you find conversions confusing, this iOS app will help you keep your budget.

### *Planning an Itinerary*

Preparation is the key to effective business travel abroad. A travel itinerary is created in order to aide in the preparation of a business trip. The itinerary enables the traveler to make the best use of their time, while staying organized. Oftentimes, the use of a travel agent expedites the planning process. Travel agents are able to find the best travel rates for air, hotel, and vehicle rental. Their knowledge can be very helpful regarding proper documentation for travel to specific countries. The itinerary, if properly organized, can allow the traveler to be effective yet not overworked. Since international travel is expensive, careful planning is crucial. A well-organized trip will allow up to three appointments evenly spaced throughout the day to ensure the business traveler is adequately rested and not overly stressed. Companies must confirm appointments before departure. The following travel tips should be kept in mind while planning a trip:

- Travel plans should reflect goals and priorities.
- Obtaining names of possible contacts, arranging appointments, and checking transportation schedules should be accomplished before the trip begins.
- Confirm the normal workdays and business hours in the countries being visited.
- The U.S. businessperson should be aware that travel from one country to another might be restricted.

### *Proper Documentation*

An essential aspect of traveling abroad is obtaining the proper documentation. While foreign countries may individually vary on their documentation requirements, a traveler must have certain basic documents. Passports, visas, and ATA carnets are documents that are needed for overseas traveling.

#### *Passports*

The first and most basic form of travel documentation is a passport. A passport is an internationally recognized travel document that verifies the identity and nationality of the bearer. Passports may be obtained from any passport acceptance facility. Only the U.S. Department of State has the authority to grant, issue, or verify United States passports. Applicants must present the agency with proof of U.S. citizenship, a valid form of photo identification–such as a driver's license or military identification tag and two identical passport photographs. Photography shops and drug stores are common places were applicants can have their passport photographs taken. Additionally, some post offices and U.S. district courts will accept passport applications as well. The passport applicant may apply by mail or in person, although certain requirements pertain to each. In most cases, a passport will be issued within six weeks of the agency receiving the application. If an emergency arises where a passport must be expedited within fourteen days of travel, the applicant can schedule an appointment at one of the thirteen regional passport agencies. There is an additional charge to expedite the process, and sometimes the agency will require customers to show proof of departure for urgent travel needs.[17]

## Visas

A visa is an official authorization appended to a passport, permitting entry into and travel within a particular country or region. The visa is a formal document that is issued by a country giving permission to an individual requesting entrance to the country during a certain period of time to fulfill a specific purpose. Most countries require a valid visa for those traveling to a foreign country. In order to obtain a visa, one must go to the foreign country's embassy or consulate located in the United States. One should notify the consulate that the travel is for business, because some countries require visas for business travel but not tourist travel.

Many foreigners who desire to do business in the United States might encounter some difficulty in obtaining a visa. The U.S. offers over twenty types of non-immigrant, temporary stay visas to foreigners seeking entrance into the country. Non-citizens who wish to do business in the U.S. need to obtain a B-1 visitor visa. This visa allows international business people to come into the U.S. and consult with business associates, attend a scientific, educational, professional or business convention, settle an estate, negotiate a contract, and participate in a short-term training.

Concerning U.S. citizens who desire to travel overseas, the Bureau of Consular Affairs offers these steps to remember in applying for a visa:

1. Review visa status and find out if a U.S. visa or a renewal is needed.

2. Review the visa wait-times information for interview appointments and visa processing at each embassy and consular section worldwide. Visit the embassy or consular section website to apply for visa and find out how to schedule an interview appointment, pay fees, and other instructions.

3. Plan on an interview at the embassy or consulate. Usually, a fingerprint scan is required.[18]

## ATA Carnets

ATA (Admission Temporaire) Carnet is a standardized international customs document used to obtain duty-free temporary admission of certain goods into the countries that are signatories to the ATA Convention. Basically, a company wanting to take certain goods into a country, such as product samples, would need to obtain a carnet. A carnet is usually valid for up to a year. The U.S. Council for International Business issues a carnet for the entrance of commercial samples, tools of the trade, advertising material, cinematographic, medical, and/or other professional equipment. The ATA Convention approves these carnets. A fee is incurred by the company, based on the value of the goods being imported. If the imported goods are not re-exported, then the company is charged the cost of the duties and taxes. Before embarking on travel, the carnet holder must issue a bond or bank guaranty of 40 percent of the good's value to ensure that everything is done properly and that the fees will be covered.[19]

### Extra Copies of Documents

Traveling can be unpredictable and oftentimes things can be lost or stolen along the way. Travelers should have two copies of their passport identification page. In case the passport is stolen or lost, the extra copies will be helpful. The traveler should carry one of the copies and give the second copy to someone back home, such as a family member or friend. While an individual should not publicize all of his or her travel plans, the traveler should leave at least a copy of the traveler's itinerary with a family member or friend, in case of emergency.

### Current Documentation

Over the course of time, passports, visas, and other documents might become outdated. As mentioned earlier, travelers can renew passports by mail if they fall under certain criteria. The passport may be renewed by mail if the most recent passport has not been damaged and is able to be submitted, if the passport was received within the past fifteen years, if the passport holder was over the age of sixteen when it was issued, and if the legal name is still the same, Sometimes a visa may be mistakenly called an "expired visa" when actually the visa's status has changed. One should know when the visa status changes so that the traveler can plan well in advance to get it updated.

### Assistance from U.S. Embassies and Consulates

U.S. embassies and consulates are a key element to successful overseas business travel. The embassies and consulates serve several different purposes, including issuing visas to foreigners and providing assistance to U.S. citizens abroad. Over 160 U.S. embassies are located in capital cities of the world. Of those 160 U.S. embassies, 60 are U.S. consulates general—regional offices of embassies. They seek to provide as much help as possible to traveling U.S. citizens. Oftentimes, consular officers have to assist in emergency situations. If a passport is lost while in another country, the consul can issue a replacement, usually within twenty-four hours. They also aid in needed medical assistance, loss of financial resources, death of a U.S citizen abroad, and disaster/evacuation.[20]

A consular can help in many situations but is not able to act in a role other than its own. If another country arrests a consular's citizen, the consular officer cannot protect them against the laws of that country. Legally, that U.S. citizen is under the control of that country's authority. Before embarking on a trip, business travelers should contact the local Export Assistance Center to discuss their needs and any services that they might be able to receive from an embassy.[21] Travelers should contact the U.S. embassy in the foreign country two weeks prior to leaving to inform them of their business travel plans.

### Medical Concerns

Whenever traveling to a foreign country, diseases, allergies, and water contamination become valid concerns. Many other countries do not have the same health standards as the United States. Business travelers must remember to keep all required and recommended vaccinations up-to-date and to be knowledgeable of any known allergies and diseases that tend to be prevalent in that particular country. A person must do research before going to a country to find all possible contamination's that have been reported for the area to which he or she is traveling. Major medical concerns include vaccinations, food allergies, and water contamination.

## Vaccinations

Different vaccinations are needed for travel to different countries. Most physicians will know the different vaccinations that an individual may need for individual countries or sections of the world. However, anyone traveling should take the initiative to learn what precautions to take when entering a particular foreign country. Due to the fact that most vaccinations take time to become effective and require more than one dose over many days or weeks, an individual should see their local doctor four to six weeks prior to leaving the country.[22]

## Food Allergies

Food allergies and contaminated foods are also specific concerns for anyone traveling abroad. Many countries in the world partake in food that is rarely or never eaten in the United States. For example, Latin or Caribbean nations use many different spices, unique to those regions, in the preparation of the food. Furthermore, some countries may prepare foods such as certain domesticated animals or iguana. Many people in the United States believe they do not have food allergies and therefore eat what they want when they travel; but, can become very sick if the proper precautions are not taken. The best way to prevent an adverse reaction is to know what is being served, and if at all possible, eat only foods that are common and known to be non-allergenic. When this becomes impossible, one should do research before entering a country and try to find a doctor who can do a test for food allergies.

## Water Contamination

Probably the largest concern for anyone traveling abroad is the safety of the drinking water. No human being can live for very long without water, so an individual must have access to purified drinking water if the country's tap water is unhealthy. Water is not necessarily the healthiest liquid to drink in foreign countries. One reason for this is that some nations do not use sanitary waste disposal methods and will allow sewage to drain into the same pipes as water. In cases where purified water or bottled water is not available, be prepared to conduct water purification procedures, such as boiling the contaminated water, bringing portable water purifiers, or adding chemicals, such as iodine to disinfect the water.

## Disease and Disaster

The final two medical concerns when traveling are the possibilities of disease and disaster. Reports of outbreaks of diseases have been cited for years across many nations, both under-developed and developed. The same can be said for natural disasters. Once overseas business travel has begun, preparation for dealing with an outbreak or disaster is very difficult. Business travelers should develop contingency plans, based on the research conducted prior to traveling. For example, consider the case of SARS (Severe Acute

Respiratory Syndrome), which occurred during 2002-2004 across the nations of China, Singapore, Taiwan, and Canada. Although most travelers were at low risk for contracting SARS, people were advised not to travel to countries where SARS was prevalent.

*Safety Procedures*

Since the terrorist attacks on the United States on September 11, 2001, the U.S. government has attempted to increase security in airports, subways, and train stations. Although the government has established many precautions in order to protect Americans while traveling, U.S. citizens must be aware of continuing threats to security before traveling overseas. The events of September 11 have not only effected the way Americans feel about traveling but has also brought an awareness of the growing tensions between the U.S. and other countries. Thus, business travelers must be aware of the possible dangers they could face while in other countries.

Although terrorist attacks can take place in any nation, U.S. nationals should take extra precautions to remain safe in certain areas of the world. Before leaving for a business trip, one should obtain a Consular Information Sheet, issued by the Department of State, to learn valuable information about the country to be visited. The information sheets are available for every country in the world and give important information such as entry requirements, currency regulations, unusual health conditions, the crime and security situation, political disturbances, areas of instability, and special information about driving and road conditions. The sheets also provide the telephone numbers and addresses for U.S. embassies and consulates. One should take into consideration all of the information given on the Consular Information Sheet before making the decision to make a business trip overseas.[23] Additionally, Public Announcements are regularly published regarding possible international security issues. These announcements are made when the U.S. perceives a threat, even if it does not involve U.S. citizens as a particular target-group. Announcements have been issued in the past dealing with pre-election disturbances, violence by terrorists, as well as anniversary dates of specific terrorist events.

Business travelers can take specific actions to reduce the risk of being a victim while overseas. When planning for a trip, one should carefully consider what is to be packed in luggage. A businessperson needs to be aware of the culture that he or she will be entering and pack accordingly. U.S. culture can be quite different from that of the foreign nation. An American can easily be spotted by the clothes worn, so one key to not being a target overseas is to dressing conservatively. Do not dress in a way that draws attention to oneself, especially with expensive jewelry and clothes. Blending in with the culture is better than looking like a tourist. One should pack as light as possible and leave all valuable things behind.

*Safety on the Street*

In the end, remaining safe in a foreign nation requires, in most cases, the use of common sense. Always be aware of the local surroundings and do not get into situations that pose a potential risk. If safety might be jeopardized, one would wisely postpone overseas business travel until the risk of being harmed is not an issue. Travelers should use the same common sense overseas that would normally be used in the United States. One should avoid crowded places—such as subways, train stations, and elevators—because of the increased risk of being a victim of pickpockets. Foreigners should not travel alone at night. If necessary, one should avoid short cuts and poorly-lighted streets. The key to not being a victim is to act like a native, not a tourist. Travelers should walk around with confidence, not confusion. If a situation arises where police or help is needed, a few phrases should be learned in the foreign language so help can be sent.[24]

### Safety in the Hotel

As a rule of thumb, hotel doors should remain locked and meetings with business associates should take place in the lobby instead of the room. Due to the possibility of items in a hotel room being stolen, valuables or money should never be visible in the room. A hotel business card may be useful in the event of an emergency or if one gets lost. As with safety on the street, the best form of self-defense is to use common sense.[25]

### Safety on Public Transportation

Public transportation in other nations can be dangerous for the uninitiated business traveler. Criminal activity may be systematic and well organized on or near public transportation. Some tips for safe use of public transportation include the following:

- Never sit or stand too close to strangers.
- Do not accept food or drink from strangers. Criminals have been known to drug food and drinks in order to rob.
- Hide valuables in a safe place, if possible, and never expose large amounts of cash in a public place.
- One should not to fall asleep in places that are unfamiliar.
- Be careful to drive and walk in safe, well lit areas.
- If traveling by way of taxi, be sure the taxi is clearly identified with official markings.
- Always trust common instincts and avoid buses and city trains, if possible.[26]

### Travel and Medical Insurance

Travel protection consists of insurance coverage and assistance services that will safeguard a traveler before, during, and after the trip. Numerous benefits accrue to those obtaining travel insurance prior to overseas travel, such as protection of cost incurred due to a cancelled trip, twenty-four hour emergency medical referral and assistance during travel, reimbursement of unexpected travel expenses incurred during an emergency, and coverage during a medical emergency. Additionally, the astute traveler ensures that his or her health care insurance covers emergencies abroad. Some medical insurance policies do not cover medical emergencies outside of the United States. In cases where medical coverage is valid, a policy may not cover personal evacuation from a remote area or part of the country where medical facilities are inadequate. One should consider purchasing a short-term health and emergency policy that is designed specifically for travelers, especially the option that covers personal evacuation in the event of a serious illness or emergency.

NOTES

## Currency Guidelines

International currency exchange has been a major issue for business travelers. This problem has been effectively solved in Europe, with the development of a common currency—the Euro—among European Union members. However, when traveling to other areas of the world, currency exchange can be problematic. Currencies in the regions of Asia, Africa, or South America are not unified and can cause problems with exchange. Many airports have exchange locations in them, but the more remote the location the fewer exchange stands will be available.

While some U.S. international travelers may understand that different currencies hold different values, they may not be able to mentally convert the value from the U.S. dollar. Therefore, Americans end up paying too much for something, as foreign vendors often take advantage of the situation. Normally this is seen with tourists, but it can happen very easily with a businessperson. Another problem is the ability to freely convert one currency from another. This can be problematic in nations where the currency is not very valuable and the exchange rate is unfavorable.

The astute business traveler carries minimal cash, as credit and debit cards have become increasingly popular across borders. The issuing companies will convert the purchases at the most favorable rate available on the day of transaction. One can purchase traveler's checks locally and then cash them at virtually any bank in the world. This is a common way of avoiding the currency problems that exist. However, many people do not want to take the time or do not have the time before leaving the United States to visit a bank to obtain traveler's checks. Therefore, they are forced to rely on the exchange of currency in the country where they are going. Currency exchange can be a problem for the traveler who does not take the time to become educated on exchange rates. The business traveler must research exchange conversion rates prior to embarking on business travel overseas.

## Check List for Business Meetings and Travel Abroad

One should ensure—prior to departure—that trip essentials are handled, such as travel itinerary to medical information, as well as being educated on the country where the meetings will take place. The traveler should consider an additional list for the business meeting, which is the purpose for the whole trip in the first place. The wise traveler develops a list of important things to remember before leaving for a business trip:

- A successful business meeting starts before leaving the country. The meeting needs to be set up before leaving the United States, and the business needs to determine whether or not an interpreter will be needed before arriving in the country for the meeting. Those in the meeting should convey the correct message, because poor communication can have a devastating effect on the outcome of the meeting.
- Business cards are always something a businessperson makes sure they have on them; but when traveling overseas for a business trip, one should have business cards not only in English but also the language of the country in which the meeting will be held. Individuals also must familiarize themselves with the culture in which they will be entering. One needs to learn the basic cultural traits, such as hand signals, road signs, and common courtesy traits such as tipping.
- If a person uses electrical appliances during the presentation, he or she should make sure to bring a transformer and/or plug adapter. Many outlets used in other countries are different than those used in the United States.[27]

## Cross-Cultural Communications

The ability to communicate successfully with other cultures is imperative when conducting a business meeting oversees. "The advent of the global economy is changing the fundamental nature of our governments, businesses, organizations and populations. No longer are people constrained by state boundaries but have all become part of an interdependent international network."[28] If one intends on conducting business in an international territory, communication is a part of life. Cross-cultural communication is a crucially important matter that should not be overlooked. Parents fail to communicate with their children; bosses often do not communicate well with their staff; men and women often have trouble communicating to one another.

Communication failure tends to be a universal problem that people experience within their own culture and language. The lack of communication often leads to unnecessary problems. Therefore, communication is an important aspect of business in the United States, as well as when conducting business abroad. When one chooses to engage in business internationally, he or she must consider many aspects of cross-cultural communication. Language barriers, foreign holidays, the time-zone changes, the usage of global telephones, and global internet access can sometimes be overlooked when preparing for a business trip. Furthermore, knowledge of acceptable forms of body language and gestures will be a great asset when communicating properly in different cultures. The astute business traveler can prepare for proper communication techniques via formal and informal training programs aimed at helping improve cross cultural communication. Typical cross-cultural communication areas for consideration include language barriers, foreign holidays, time-zone changes, acceptable forms of business communications, and gestures.

### Language Barriers

"It is now recognized that linguistic and cultural knowledge are the two most vital areas of knowledge that organizations must come to acquire if they are to integrate, progress and succeed in the marketplace."[29] Inexperienced U.S. business travelers incorrectly assume that all of their international colleagues speak and understand the English language. English is frequently the language used in global business, even though it is not the language spoken by the majority of people in the world. English is taught in many other schools overseas, where it is a second language in many other countries. However, the method of instruction emphasizes reading and grammar to the point that foreigners often can read English fluently but are unable to understand it. The following suggestions are offered to English speaking travelers when dealing with non-English speaking persons:

- Slow down and be patient. Avoid the attempt to raise your voice louder.
- Remember others are trying something new and different to them; speak clearly.
- Keep sentences short.
- Avoid asking "either/or" questions and negative questions and contractions.
- Avoid idioms, colloquialisms, slang, and jargon
- Use visuals if ever possible, such as graphs, charts, or models.[30]

Finally, the business traveler should not go to the other extreme and assume business associates are not fluent in English, as this could lead to embarrassing or negative situations.

### Foreign Holidays

Travelers must consider foreign holidays before making international business travel arrangements. Foreign nations may not recognize the holidays that Americans typically observe. For example, German culture celebrates Vincent's Day, Assumption Day, and Reformation Day. Germany does not observe U.S. holidays, such as Good Friday, Easter, and Labor Day. Some cultures may have more religious holidays than others. Other nations may celebrate the birthdays of ancient emperors, as well as the dates of events not recognized in the United States. Holidays may be observed in a combined week, so one should not attempt to conduct a business trip during a holiday week. Therefore, a businessperson should be aware of the holiday schedule before scheduling the trip abroad and scheduling meetings with customers or associates.

### Time-Zone Changes

Just as in considering the holiday schedule before traveling, one should also be aware of the different time zones. This is an easy but important consideration when making travel arrangements, as the date may change depending on the direction of global travel. For example, two calendar days are lost, depending on the time of departure, when traveling from the eastern U.S. to China. Conversely, one only loses a couple of hours–despite all day travel–when returning from Europe to the U.S. The traveler should also realize that many other countries do not observe daylight savings time.

### Acceptable Forms of Business Communications

When traveling abroad, one needs to consider how to maintain communication between foreign associates, the home base office, family, and friends. The use of international prepaid phone cards is acceptable across the globe. Prepaid international phone cards are available for purchase at most retail stores. If using a reusable card, one should make sure that it has enough minutes "loaded" for all communication needs. However, some of these cards are only useful calling internationally from the United States. One should make sure that the phone card works from inside another country. Additionally, cell phone companies have added international service as an option to global travelers. Individuals should pay bills on time and have a prepaid phone card as a back-up. International travelers often have no way to recharge their cell phone batteries, because other countries sometimes have different electrical outlets and voltage settings that do not fit the standard battery chargers for U.S. cell phones.

Travelers should observe the same precautions whenever accessing the Internet and checking email. With prepaid phone cards, global roaming Internet access service is available. The technology provides worldwide access from anywhere to anywhere through a local number. Prior to departure, one must be sure that the account is paid in advance to assure access for the length of the entire trip. Global phone access and global internet access are two important items that business travelers need when traveling abroad. These items should be taken care of before departing on the trip.

### Acceptable Forms of Body Gestures

Body language is an important form of communication across cultures and sometimes differs greatly from the body gestures that are used in the United States. For example, a "thumbs up" in America is a positive gesture; however, it is an offensive gesture in certain other cultures. A "wink" to someone in America is also a positive gesture, but it often carries a different meaning in other cultures. This is an area in which one should be educated when traveling to a foreign country for business. To the inexperienced traveler, gestures that seem harmless and acceptable in American culture can be quite offensive to those in the foreign culture. Therefore, one should observe appropriate gestures while doing business in a foreign country.

### Other Cultural Factors

Culture is a set of behavior patterns that are learned and shared through common experience. Culture is learned—it impacts everyone and serves as the means of processing and interpreting information. Every land has its own culture, and every culture is different from one to another. Cultural factors are important areas that business travelers need to study prior to traveling abroad. "The single greatest barrier to business success is the one created by culture."[31] Other important areas that could become potential barriers include religious factors, history, local laws, and the relationship between customs and foreign goods.

### Religious Factors

Religious factors are a very serious situation in certain regions of the world. In the United States, people often take for granted the freedom to observe religious practices in any manner. A religious ruling class controls some nations where freedom of religion does not exist. Bibles and other religious paraphernalia can be very offensive to foreign cultures. Possession of such may involve negative legal repercussions. The religious beliefs of some cultures strongly affect all aspects of personal and business life.

### History

Just as respecting the religious beliefs of other nations is important, one also needs to respect the history of the culture. Business associates in other cultures may be sensitive to attitudes concerning their nation's history and culture. An example would be the Chinese civilization, which has flourished for over 3500 years. When visiting historical sites, care should be taken to show respect for the historical significance of that location. Such respect communicates to foreign associates a heightened level of appreciation for the culture, which may lead to more favorable business relationships.[32]

### Local Laws

The experienced business traveler understands and observes the laws of "the land" when traveling overseas. If one violates the rules and regulations of another nation, the United States Embassy can do little besides provide a list of local attorneys. If one violates a local law while in a foreign nation, the offender should ask the arresting authority to notify a consular officer at the nearest Embassy. Individuals should inquire about the local laws before arriving in a new culture and obey them while in that nation.

NOTES

*Customs and Foreign Goods*

Custom regulations obviously vary from country to country and are constantly under revisio Concerning the import and export of goods across borders, the experienced business traveler aware of contraband items. Many fruits and specific food products are banned from transpo across borders. One tip is to not attempt to convey contraband through the customs process of t foreign nation. Similar limitations may be placed on items upon return to the U.S. Current U. Customs law allows only four hundred dollars' worth of merchandise to be brought in the count before levying a tax against it. One should keep receipts of all purchases. A foreigner should nev carry a package for someone else when entering a new country.

*Transportation Modalities*

As in travel across the U.S., airlines, rails and ferries, taxis, and buses provide publ transportation services overseas. Traveling by rail is a more popular method of transportation other countries, especially in tourist areas. The experienced business traveler researches the vario modes of transportation available in the foreign nation and is aware of the procedures for securi such services. Trains and buses may require exact change, so one needs to be aware of the co and plan appropriately. One should always possess a passport and valid photo ID–in addition possessing a planned itinerary of the trip.

If choosing air travel, businesses have two options: commercial or charter flights. Chart flights, more convenient than commercial travel, are typically reserved for larger corporate use. the business decides to travel by charter, one should secure the service from a reputable compan Smaller "fly-by-night" airlines have been known to "go out of business" in the middle of the trav dates, abandoning business travelers.

Rails and ferries are available for cross-border travel. Train travel may be more cost effecti than air travel. For example, Europe and Asia boast rail systems that travel at high speeds and can as quick as air travel. International rail systems are rated high in safety performance and passeng safety. Ferries are also a common way to travel in certain areas, as they provide safe and reliab service as well. Many consider rail and ferry travel a safe and reliable method of travel overseas.

Car rentals offer another option for business travel. One should do business with a know company or one that has well identified markings. To avoid being a target, foreigners should n rent luxurious or flashy cars Since most U.S. auto insurances do not cover overseas rentals, t traveler should purchase the insurance offered by the rental company. Some companies only ha cars with the steering wheel on the opposite side of the car. Many accidents have resulted due the unfamiliarity of the vehicle. If at all possible, one should not rent a car while overseas—to sa much stress and money.

If one must rent a car while oversees, the embassy or consulate of the country teaches abo specific vehicle operator requirements. Many countries do not recognize a U.S. driver's licens However, most countries accept an international driver's license. An international driver's licen can be obtained prior to departure at the local American Automobile Association. Certain natio require a permit instead of tolls on certain roads. The absence of this permit may result in a seve financial fine. The traveler is responsible to observe all laws and road signs, even if they are n in English. Be aware of odd traffic patterns and the fact that many countries, compared to wh Americans are used to, drive on the opposite sides of the road.*

---

*Some of the information in this supplement was compiled from readily available public domain documents such as those provided by the United States government. Citations are included to reference all other aspects of this supplement not considered public domain.

# ENDNOTES

## CHAPTER ONE

1   The World Bank. (2006). Globalization. Retrieved February 03, 2013 from http://web.worldbank.org/WBSITE/EXTERNAL/EXT ABOUTUS/0,,contentMDK:23272496~pagePK:51123644~piPK:329829~theSitePK:29708,00.html

2   The World Bank. (2006). Assessing Globalization. Retrieved October 12, 2006 from http://www1.worldbank.org/economicpolicy/globalization/documents/AssessingGlobalizationP1.pdf p. 1

3   Ibid. p. 2

4   Legrain, P. (2003). Cultural Globalization Is Not Americanization. The Chronicle of Higher Education. May 9, 2003. Retrieved October16, 2006 from http://chronicle.com/free/v49/i35/35b00701.htm. Para. 5

5   Castles, S. (2002). Migration and Community Formation under Conditions of Globalization. International Migration Review, 36(4), 1143-1169.

6   WTO. (2006). What is the WTO? Retrieved September 11, 2006 from http://www.wto.int/english/thewto_e/whatis_e/whatis_e.htm.

7   NACLA. (2004). NAFTA Turns Ten 1994-2004. NACLA Report on the Americas, 37, 6-8.

8   Bureau of Economic Analysis. (2014). NIPA Tables v1.1.1 – Percent Change from Preceding Period in Real Gross Domestic Product – Period 1992-A & Q to 2012-A & Q. Retrieved January 1, 2013 from http://www.bea.gov/iTable/index_nipa.cfm Table 1.1.1 Percent change from preceding period real Gross Domestic Product.

9   McIntyre, D. (2013). Forecast: 10 most profitable U.S. companies in 2013. Retrieved on July 30 from http://www.usatoday.com/story/money/business/2013/01/20/10-profitable-companies-2013/1848581/

10. IMF (2013) World Economic Outlook Database 2013 GDP Percent Change Retrieved on January 4 2014 from http://www.imf.org/external/pubs/ft/weo/2013/02/weodata/weorept.aspx?pr.x=48&pr.y=9&sy=2011&ey=2018&scsm=1&ssd=1&sort=country&ds=.&br=1&c=924%2C456%2C578%2C534%2C443%2C582&s=NGDP_RPCH&grp=0&a=

11  CIA. (2009). The World Factbook – GDP (Purchasing Power Parity) retrieved January 10, 2014 from https://www.cia.gov/library/publications/the-world-factbook/rankorder/2001rank.html?countryName=Wallis%20and%20Futuna&countryCode=wf&regionCode=aus&rank=224

12  CIA. (2009). The World Factbook – United States. Retrieved January 5, 2014 https://www.cia.gov/library/publications/the-world-factbook/fields/print_2050.html and https://www.cia.gov/library/publications/the-world-factbook/fields/print_2061.html and http://www.census.gov/foreign-trade/statistics/highlights/toppartners.html

13. Sinnett, W. (2006). Global Sourcing for Global Markets. Financial Executive, 22, 46-48.

14  International Trade Administration. (2006). U.S. Export/Import Statistics - Coal (not anthracite). Retrieved February 3, 2013 from http://www.eia.gov/coal/production/quarterly/

15  Schlumberger. (2012). About Schlumberger. Retrieved February 3, 2013 from http://www.slb.com/about.aspx /

16  Scott, L., & Otnes, C. (1996). Something Old, Something New: Exploring the Interaction Between Ritual and Advertising. Journal of Advertising, 25, 33-39, § Conclusion, ¶ 1.

17  Moore, K. J., & Lewis, D. C. (2000). Multinational Enterprise in Ancient Phonicia. Business History, 42, 17.

18  Holy Bible (KJV). 1 Kings 5:1-18.

19  Pax Romana, Retrieved October 16, 2006 from http://www.unrv.com/early-empire/pax-romana.php

20  Woods, R. O. (2003). Harnessing the Void: How the Industrial Revolution Began in a Vacuum. Mechanical Engineering-CIME, 125, 38-41.

21  EIA. (2002). Acquisitions of U.S. Energy Assets by Foreign Investors in 2002 Remain High. Retrieved September 27, 2006 from http://tonto.eia.doe.gov/FTPROOT/financial/fdiad2002.pdf.

22  OECD. (2006). About OECD. Retrieved September 28, 2006 from http://www.oecd.org/about/

23  Computer Dealer News. (2001). Integrated LAN, Video in POS System. Computer Dealer News, August 31, 2001, 17-17, 40.

24  M. Salisbury. (2006). Containerized Ocean Trade. The Journal of Commerce, 7-29, 49.

25  ISO in Brief. ISO. Retrieved January 4, 2014 from http://www.iso.org/iso/standardsandconsumer.pdf

26  Forbes Inc. (20139). The Forbes Global 2000. Retrieved December 15 http://www.forbes.com/global2000/

27  Retrieved December 2013 from http://www.globaltrends.com/knowledge-center/features/shapers-and-influencers/190-corporate-clout-2013-time-for-responsible-capitalism

28  Corruption Perceptions Index 2013: Retrieved December 2013 from http://cpi.transparency.org/cpi2013/results/

29  UNICEF State of the World's Children 2011: Retrieved July 2013 from http://www.unicef.org/sowc2011/pdfs/SOWC-2011-Main-Report_EN_02092011.pdf

30  Global post. (2011). Top 5 worst natural disasters of 2011. Retrieved on July 30 from http://www.globalpost.com/dispatch/news/regions/asia-pacific/japan/111229/worst-natural-disasters-2011

31  H. Levins. (2004). Demand for Arabic Linguists Far Outweighs Supply. St. Louis Post-Dispatch, December 13, 2004.

## CHAPTER TWO

1   Merriam-Webster Online Dictionary, Retrieved September 2, 2006 from http://www.m-w.com/dictionary/culture

2   Answers.com, Retrieved October 15, 2006 from http://www.answers.com/topic/ethnocentrism

3   Harris, P. (2006). European Leadership in Globalization, Retrieved October 15, 2006 from http://www.emeraldinsight.com/Insight/ViewContentServlet?Filename=Published/EmeraldFullTextArticle/Articles/0540960205.html

4   Answers.com, Retrieved October 15, 2006 from http://www.answers.com/topic/polycentrism

5    Harris, P. (2006). European Leadership in Globalization, Retrieved October 15, 2006 from http://www.emeraldinsight.com/Insight/ViewContentServlet?Filename=Published/EmeraldFullTextArticle/Articles/0540960205.html

6    Ibid.

7    Penrose, John M., Rasberry, Robert W. and Myers, Robert J. (2004). Business Communication for Managers: An Advanced Approach. Mason, Ohio: Thomson: South-Western p. 19.

8    Almaney, Adnan. (1974). Intercultural Communication and the MNC Executive. Columbia Journal of World Business. p. 23. Retrieved July 13, 2006 from: Business Source Premier Database.

9    Ibid. p. 25.

10   Penrose, John M., Rasberry, Robert W. and Myers, Robert J. (2004). Business Communication for Managers: An Advanced Approach. Mason, Ohio: Thomson: South-Western p.21.

11   Ibid.

12   Robbins, Stephen P. (2005). Organizational Behavior: Eleventh Edition. New Jersey: Pearson: Prentice- Hall p. 323.

13   Ibid.

14   The Apostles Creed. Retrieved October 15, 2006 from http://www.achristiansway.20fr.com/CHRISTIANITY.html

15   Articles of Jewish Faith. Retrieved October 15, 2006 from http://www.noahide.org.uk

16   Islam Articles of Faith. Retrieved October 15, 2006 from http://www.islam.com/artialsfaith.htm

17   Ibid.

18   The Hindu Universe. Retrieved October 15, 2006 from http://www.hindunet.org/

19   Buddhism. Budda Dharma Education Association. Retrieved October 15, 2006 from http://www.buddhanet.net/

20   Our Beliefs. Western Reform Taoism. Retrieved October 15, 2006 from http://www.westernreformtaoism.org/ para. 3

21   About Confucianism. (2006). Retrieved October 15, 2006 from http://www.religion-cults.com/Eastern/Confucianism/confuci.htm

22   Confucius. The Great Learning. Retrieved October 15, 2006 from http://etext.library.adelaidecedu.au/mirror/classics.mit.edu/Confucius/learning.htmc

23   Shintoism. Shinto Online learning Association. Retrieved October 15, 2006 from http://www.jinja.or.jp/english/s-0.html

24   Argandona, A., (2001). Corruption: the corporate perspective. Business Ethics: A European Review, 2, pp.163-175, (p.163).

25   USINFO Trade and Economics. Report Underpins View of Corruption as Obstacle to Development (2006), Retrieved October 15, 2006 from http://usinfo.state.gov/xarchives/display.html?p=washfile-english&y=2006&m=November&x=20061107120940SAikceinawz0.6615412. (para.2)

26   Ibid.

27   Transparency International USA (2006), Retrieved October 15, 2006 from http://www.transparency-usa.org/

28   Transparency International USA Toolkit (2006), Retrieved October 15, 2006 from http://www.transparency-usa.org/toolkit.html

29   U.S. department of Justice. Foreign Corrupt Practices Act Anti-bribery Provisions (2006), Retrieved October 15, 2006 from http://www.usdoj.gov/criminal/fraud/fcpa/dojdocb.htm

30   Attitude. (2006). Retrieved July 24, 2006 from http://dictionary.reference.com/browse/attitude.

31   Merriam-Webster Online Dictionary, Retrieved September 15, 2006 from http://www.m-w.com/dictionary/attitudes

32   Doing Business. (2006). Retrieved July 23, 2006 from http://www.frommers.com/destinations/southamerica/1010027590.html.

33   France. (2003). Retrieved July 29, 2006 from http://www.cyborlink.com/besite/france.htm.

34   United Arab Emirates. (2003). Retrieved July 29, 2006 from http://www.cyborlink.com/besite/uae.htm.

35   Italy. (2003). Retrieved July 29, 2006 from http://www.cyborlink.com/besite/italy.htm.

36   Mexico. (2003). Retrieved July 29, 2006 from http://www.cyborlink.com/besite/mexico.htm.

37   Women in Society. Retrieved July 29, 2006 from http://countrystudies.us/germany/91.htm.

38   Role of Women. Retrieved July 29, 2006 from http://countrystudies.us/iran/53.htm.

39   Role of Women. Retrieved July 29, 2006 from http://countrystudies.us/mexico/60.htm.

40   Social Class. Retrieved July 29, 2006 from http://countrystudies.us/iran/48.htm.

41   Mooney, L. A., Knox, D., & Schacht, C. (2000). Understanding social problems (2nd ed.). Cincinnati, OH: Wadsworth.. pp. 5-9.

42   McCrae, Robert R. (2004) Personality and Culture Revisited: Linking Traits and Dimensions of Culture Retrieved August 18, 2006 from http://ccr.sagepub.com/cgi/content/abstract/38/1/52

43   McCrae, Robert R. (2004) Personality and Culture Revisited: Linking Traits and Dimensions of Culture Retrieved August 18, 2006 from http://ccr.sagepub.com/cgi/content/abstract/38/1/52

44   Minkov, Michael, Hofstede, Geert, (2011) "The evolution of Hofstede's doctrine", Cross Cultural Management: An International Journal, Vol. 18 Iss: 1, pp.10 - 20

45   Hofstede, Geert (1980). Culture's Consequences: International Differences in Work-Related Values. Beverly Hills CA: Sage Publications

46   Minkov, Michael, Hofstede, Geert, (2011) "The evolution of Hofstede's doctrine", Cross Cultural Management: An International Journal, Vol. 18 Iss: 1, pp.10 - 20

47.  Hofstede, Geert, Gert Jan Hofstede and Michael Minkov. Cultures and Organizations: Software of the Mind, 3rd ed. New York: McGraw-Hill.

48.  Minkov (2009). Predictors of differences in subjective well-being across 97 nations. Cross-Cultural Research, 43, 152-179

49.  Geert Hofstede (1998). Masculinity and Femininity: The Taboo Dimension of National Cultures. Thousand Oaks CA: Sage Publications.

50.  Hofstede, G. (1983). The Cultural Relativity of Organizational Practices and Theories, Journal of International Business Studies, 14 (2), 75-89

51.  Minkov, Michael, Hofstede, Geert, (2011) "The evolution of Hofstede's doctrine", Cross Cultural Management: An International Journal, Vol. 18 Iss: 1, pp.10 - 20

52   Hofstede, G. (1993) "Cultural Constraints in Management Theories", The Executive, Vol. VII No. 1, 1993, 81-94

53. Hofstede, G. (2001). Culture's consequences: Comparing values, behaviors, institutions, and organizations across nations (2nd ed.). Thousand Oaks, California: Sage Publications, Inc.

54. McCaskill, A, & Roussas, S. (2012). BSC versus a Traditional Measurement System: Collecting empirical data

55. Trompenaars, F. and C. Hampden-Turner (1993). Seven Cultures of Capitalism. Doubleday Press.

56. Ibid.

57. House, R. J., Hanges, P. J., Javidan, M., Dorfman, P. W., & Gupta, V. (Eds.) (2004) Culture, Leadership, and Organizations: The GLOBE study of 62 societies. Thousand Oaks, CA. SAGE Publications Inc

58. Chhokar, J. S., Brodbeck, F. C., & House, R. J. (Eds.) (2007), Culture and leadership across the world: The GLOBE book of in-depth studies of 25 societies. New York, NY. Lawrence Erlbaum Associates/Taylor & Francis Group, LLC.

## CHAPTER THREE

1. Brandly, M. (2002) A Primer on Trade. Retrieved on July 24, 2006 from http://www.mises.org/story/1084

2. U.S. Department of Commerce International Trade Administration (2006, July) Promoting Trade and Investment. Retrieved on July 19, 2006 from http://www.trade.gov/promotingtrade/index.asp

3. National Center for Policy Analysis (2003) Benefits of Subsidies to New Businesses. Retrieved on July 24, 2006 from http://www.ncpa.org/sub/dpd/?page=article&Article_ID=41834   Retrieved April 3, 2014 from http://trade.gov/media/publications/pdf/trade_finance_guide2007.pdf

5. Retrieved April 3, 2014 from http://issuu.com/aidfortrade/docs/exportfinance

6. Foreign Trade Zone Resource Center (2006) A Brief History of the U.S. Foreign-Trade Zones Program. Retrieved on July 20, 2006 from http://foreign-trade-zone.com/history.htm

7. Ibid, para. 2

8. Retrieved April 3, 2014 from http://trade.gov/media/publications/pdf/trade_finance_guide2007.pdf.

9. Moffat, M. (2006) Why are Tariffs Preferable to Quotas? Retrieved on July 22, 2006 from http://economics.about.com/cs/taxpolicy/a/tariffs_quotas.htm

10. http://www.sef.hku.hk/~larryqiu/Papers/LCR.pdf

11. Regibeau, P., Rockett, K. (2003, June) Administrative Delays as Barriers to Trade. Retrieved on July 23, 2006 from http://www.essex.ac.uk/economics/discussion-papers/papers-text/dp557.pdf

12. Court and its Procedure (2007). Retrieved on August 20, 2007 from http://www.judiciary.gov.bt/html/court/trial.php

13. United Nations Conference on Trade and Devlpoment (2000). The Standardization of Law and Its Effect on Developing Economies. Retrieved on August 20, 2007 from  http://www.unctad.org/en/docs/pogdsmdpbg24d4.en.pdf

14. WTO (2006) Intellectual Property: Protection and Enforcement, para. 6. Retrieved on July 25, 2006 from http://www.wto.org/english/thewto_e/whatis_e/tif_e/agrm7_e.htm

15. WTO (2006) What are Intellectual Property Rights? para. 1. Retrieved on July 25, 2006 from http://www.wto.org/english/tratop_e/trips_e/intel1_e.htm, para. 1

16. Ibid., para. 3

17. WIPO (2006) Summary of the Berne Convention for the Protection of Literary and Artistic Works, para. 6. Retrieved on July 25, 2006 from   http://www.wipo.int/treaties/en/ip/berne/summary_berne.html, para. 3

18. Ibid, para. 4

19. Frey, Donald E. (1998). Individualist Economic Values and Self-Interest: The Problem in the Puritan Ethic. Journal of Business Ethics. Oct 1998 Part 2, Vol. 17 Issue 14, p1573-1580, 8p. Retrieved July 6, 2006 from: http://www.springerlink.com/(xy1bh5y5qrv4xt551uzham45)/app/home/contributionasp?referrer=parent&backto=issue,6,11;journal,181,342;linkingpublicationresults,1:100281,1

20. http://www.sagepub.com/upm-data/42958_2_The_Cultural_Context.pdf

21. Morris, Michael H.; Davis Duane L.; Allene, Jeffrey W. (1994). Fostering Corporate Entrepreneurship: Cross-cultural Comparisons of the Importance of Individualism versus Collectivism (paragraph 6). Journal of International Business Studies, 1994, Vol. 25 Issue 1, p65-89, 25p, 6 charts, 1 graph. Retrieved July 6, 2006 from: http://www.palgrave-journals.com/jibs/journal/v25/n1/abs/8490849a.html

22. Ibid, (paragraph 7)

23. Ibid, (Table 1)

24. Ibid, (Table 2)

25. http://www.ascecuba.org/publications/proceedings/volume19/pdfs/mesolago.pdf

26. Ibid

27. The economy: Economic policy. Country Profile. Cuba. 2004. The Economist Intelligence Unit Limited 2004 p24-25, 3p.

28. The New Dictionary of Cultural Literacy, Third Edition, 2002. http://www.bartleby.com/59/18/marketeconom.html

29. The economy: Economic policy. Country Profile. Russia, 2005. The Economist Intelligence Unit Limited 2005 p34-36, 3p.

30. CIA World Fact Book. (2013). Retrieved on July 30 from https://www.cia.gov/library/publications/the-world-factbook/geos/rs.html

31. International Human Development Indicators. (2013). Human development index (HDI) value. Retrieved on January 2014 from table 1 http://hdr.undp.org/en/data

32. Yamada, Bundo. (Oct. 20, 1990). DEV Centre WP 28: Internationalization Strategies of Japanese electronics Companies:Implications for Asian Newly Industrializing Economies (NIEs). Retrieved July 18, 2006 from: http://ideas.repec.org/p/oec/devaaa/28-en.html

33. Fraser, Simon; Wresch, William. (2005). National Competitive Advantage in E-Commerce Efforts: A Report from Five Caribbean Nations. Perspectives on Global Development & Technology. Vol. 4 Issue 1, p27-44, 18p. Retrieved July 18, 2006 from: http://www.uwosh.edu/faculty_staff/wresch/Portercarib.htm

34. UNDP (2006). Human Development Report 2006: Power, poverty and the global water crisis. http://hdr.undp.org/hdr2006/

35. Stephenson, K. Arinaitwe. (March, 2006). Factors Constraining the Growth and Survival of Small Scale Businesses. A Developing Countries Analysis. Journal of American Academy of Business, Cambridge. Vol. 8 Issue 2, p167-178, 12p.

36    Ibid., p. 168

37    Ibid.

38    Craig, Ben. (4/1/2005). The Growing Significance of Purchasing Power Parity. Economic Commentary. P1-4, 4p, 2 graphs. Retrieved July 18, 2006 from: http://ideas.repec.org/a/fip/fedcec/y2005iapr1. html

39    Ibid.

40    UNDP (2006). Beyond Scarcity: Power, poverty and the global water crisis. http://hdr.undp.org/en/reports/global/hdr2006/

41    Barth, Steve. (Jul98). Risky business. World Trade. Vol. 11 Issue 7, p38, 6p, 1 chart, 5c.

42    Miceli, T.J., Sirmans, C.F. & Turnbull, G. K. (Feb2003). Land Ownership Risk and Urban Development. Journal of Regional Science. Vol. 43 Issue 1, p73-94, 22p. Retrieved July 21, 2006 from: http://papers.ssrn.com/sol3/papers.cfm?abstract_id=388549

43    Matz, Leonard. (Feb/Mar 2005). Measuring Operations Risk: Are We Taxiing Down the Wrong Runways? Bank Accounting & Finance. Vol. 18 Issue 2, p3-47, 5p. (page 3) Retrieved July 21,2006    fromhttp://business.highbeam.com/434984/article-1G1-129549344/measuring-operations-risk-we-taxiing-down-wrong-runways

44    A Merton approach to transfer risk. Risk.Sep 2005, Vol. 18 Issue 9, p110-114, 5p. (abstract). Retrieved July 21, 2006 from: http://www.risk.net/risk-magazine/technical-paper/1500234/a-merton-approach-transfer-risk

45    Court and its Procedure (2007). Retrieved on August 20, 2007 from http://www.judiciary.gov.bt/html/court/trial.php

46    Leiken, Robert S. (Winter96/97). Controlling the global corruption epidemic. Foreign Policy. Issue 105, p55, 19p, 1bw. (paragraph 1)

47    Strodes, James. (Dec97). ...Begins at home. World Trade. Vol. 10 Issue 12, p24, 2p, 1 cartoon, 1c.

48    Leiken, Robert S. (Winter96/97). Controlling the global corruption epidemic. Foreign Policy. Issue 105, p55, 19p, 1bw.

49    Hamra, Wayne. (Oct2000). Bribery in International Business Transactions and the OECD Convention: Benefits and Limitations. Business Economics. Vol. 35 Issue 4, p33, 14p, 1 diagram. (paragraph 6). Retrieved July 22,2006 fromhttp://connection.ebscohost.com/c/articles/3765386/bribery-international-business-transactions-oecd-convention-benefits-limitations

50    Ibid.

51    Hoxter, Curtis J. (7/20/2000). Military in some Latin American countries is upsetting the democratic process. Caribbean business. Vol. 28 Issue 28, p12, 1/2p.

52    Ibid.

53    Praying to make their kingdom nicer. Economist. 1/11/2003. Vol. 366 Issue 8306, p37-38, 2p, 1c. Retrieved July 22, 2006 from: http://www.economist.com/world/africa/displayStory.cfm?story_id=1525180

54    Ibid.

55    Bosnia Peace Operation: Pace of Implementing Dayton Accelerated as International Involvement Increased. GAO Reports. 6/5/1998. p1, 206p. Retrieved July 22, 2006 from: http://www.gao.gov/archive/1998/ns98138.pdf

56    Ibid.

57    Ibid.

58    Lenain, Patrick; Bonturi, Marcos; Koen, Vincent. (May2002). The fallout from terrorism. OECD Observer. Issue 231/232, p9, 2p, 1c. Retrieved July 22, 2006 from: http://www.findarticles.com/p/articles/mi_qa3648/is_200205/ai_n9059363

59    Robin, Raizel. (3/17/2003). Worst-case Scenario. Canadian Business. Vol. 76 Issue 5, p29, 1p, 1 diagram.

60    Ibid, p. 30.

61    Dunning, John H. (Jul98). An overview of relations with national governments. New Political Economy. Vol. 3 issue 2, p280, 5p. Retrieved July 24, 2006 from: http://www.tandfonline.com/doi/abs/10.1080/13563469808406355

62    Ibid.

## CHAPTER FOUR

1    Promoting Trade and Investment. U.S. Department of Commerce International Trade Administration. (¶ 2) Retrieved July 8, 2006 from: http://trade.gov/promotingtrade/index.asp

2    Drucker, Peter F. (2005). Trading places. The National Interest, p101(7). Retrieved July 29, from: 2006, http://nationalinterest.org/article/trading-places-430?page=3

3    U.S. Congress. (1776). Declaration of Independence. Retrieved July 16, 2006, from National Archives Web Site: http://www.loc.gov/rr/program/bib/ourdocs/DeclarInd.html

4    Smith, Adam. (1776). An Inquiry into the Nature and Causes of the Wealth of Nations. Library of Economics and Liberty, Book 4, (Chap. 2, ¶ 12.) Retrieved July 17, 2006 from the World Wide Web: http://www.econlib.org/library/Smith/smWN12.html

5    Ricardo, David (1821). On the Principles of Political Economy and Taxation. London: John Murray. Third edition.

6    Olin, Bertil. (1933). Interregional and International Trade. Cambridge: Harvard University Press.

7    Reeve, T., (2002). Factor Endowments and Industrial Structure. Publication number 731. (p. 5). Retrieved July 22 from Federal Reserve Web Site: http://www.federalreserve.gov/pubs/ifdp/2002/731/ifdp731.pdf

8    Vernon, R. (1966). "International Investment and International Trade in the Product Life Cycle," Quarterly Journal of Economics, 80:190-207.

9    World Trade Organization. (2006) World Trade Report 2006. (p. 60). Retrieved July 17, 2006 from World Trade Organization Web Site: http://www.wto.org/english/res_e/booksp_e/anrep_e/wtr06-2c_e.pdf

10    Porter, Michael. (1990). The competitive advantage of nations. New York: Basic Books.

11    Ibid.

12    Principles of the Trading System. (n.d). (Principles Section ¶ 1.) Retrieved July 25, 2006 from http://www.wto.org/english/thewto_e/whatis_e/tif_e/fact2_e.htm

13    Merriam-Webster Online. (2005). Retrieved July 25, 2006 from http://www.merriam-webster.com/dictionary/system

14    The GATT Years: from Havana to Marrakesh. (n.d.) (GATT: 'provisional' for almost half a century Section, ¶ 4.) Retrieved July 17, 2006 from World Trade Organization Web Site: http://www.wto.org/english/thewto_e/whatis_e/tif_e/fact4_e.htm

15    What is the World Trade Organization? (n.d.) (Did GATT succeed? Section, ¶ 5) Retrieved July 17, 2006 from World Trade Organization Web Site: http://www.wto.org/english/thewto_e/whatis_e/tif_e/fact1_e.htm

16    What is the World Trade Organization? (n.d.) (Above all, it's a negotiating forum, Section ¶ 2.) Retrieved July 17, 2006 from World Trade Organization Web Site: http://www.wto.org/english/thewto_e/whatis_e/tif_e/fact1_e.htm

17    Principles of the Trading System. (n.d) (Principles Sections ¶ 1-8.) Retrieved July 25, 2006 from http://www.wto.org/english/thewto_e/whatis_e/tif_e/fact2_e.htm

18    Principles of the Trading System. (n.d.) (Principles Sections ¶ 9-18.) Retrieved July 25, 2006 from http://www.wto.org/english/thewto_e/whatis_e/tif_e/fact2_e.htm

19    Reason, T. America for Sale. CFO Magazine Copyright 2006 economist.com. February 2006. (¶ 3) Retrieved July 29, 2006 from the world-wide web: http://www.cfo.com/article.cfm/5435380/c_5461573?f=insidecfo

20    Winning Investments. Foreign Direct Investment Magazine. Published June 5, 2006. Retrieved August 19, 2006 from: http://www.fdimagazine.com/news/fullstory.php/aid/1646/Winning__Investments.html

21    Irwin, D. A., & American Enterprise Institute for Public Policy Research. (1996). Three Simple Principles of Trade Policy. Washington, DC: American Enterprise Institute. Retrieved October 4, 2006, from Questia database: http://www.questia.com/PM.qst?a=o&d=97673215

22    Balance of trade. (2006, September 30). In Wikipedia, The Free Encyclopedia. Retrieved 07:12, October 3, 2006 from http://en.wikipedia.org/w/index.php?title=Balance_of_trade&oldid=78697689

23    Foreign Direct Investment. (n.d.) (Foreign Direct Investment Section, ¶ 1) Retrieved July 17, 2006 from World Bank Web Site: http://data.worldbank.org/indicator/BX.KLT.DINV.CD.WD

24    Trade and Foreign Direct Investment. (1996) (FDI and employment in the host country Section, ¶ 12) Retrieved July 17, 2006 from World Trade Organization Web Site: http://www.wto.org/English/news_e/pres96_e/pr057_e.htm

25    Leong, K., (1998). Managing global operations: focus on expatriates-Mary Blonigen, the Scots company. Production operations management. The Ohio State University Fisher College of Business. Retrieved October 4, 2006, from http://www.decisionsciences.org/decisionline/Vol29/29_4/pom_29_4.pdf#search=%22expatriates%22

26    China set to restrict foreign property investment. China Daily Retrieved July 29, 2006 from: http://www.chinadaily.com.cn/china/2006-07/17/content_642827.htm

27.   Fung, E & Shaw, J. (2011). China limits property purchases by foreigners. Wall Street Journal. Retrieved on July 30 from http://online.wsj.com/article/SB10001424052748704584504575615942546998222.html

28    Foreign Direct Investment (FDI). (n.d.) (¶ 2) Retrieved July 17, 2006 from United Nations Conference on Trade and Development Web Site: http://www.unctad.org/Templates/Page.asp?intItemID=3146&lang=1

29    Foreign Ownership of Property in Mexico. Blue Road Runner.com (¶ 1) Retrieved August 19, 2006 from: http://www.blueroadrunner.com/ownprop.htm

30    Brown Field Investments (2006). The free dictionary from Farlex. Investopedia.com. Retrieved October 6, 2006, from http://financial-dictionary.thefreedictionary.com/Green+Field+Investment

31    Trade and Foreign Direct Investment. (1996) (FDI and employment in the host country Section, (¶ 4) Retrieved July 17, 2006 from World Trade Organization Web Site: http://www.wto.org/English/news_e/pres96_e/pr057_e.htm

32    Labyrinth of Incentives. Foreign Direct Investment Magazine. Published December 2, 2002. (¶ 7) Retrieved August 19, 2006 from the World Wide Web: http://www.fdimagazine.com/news/fullstory.php/aid/187/Labyrinth_of_incentivesUnited_States.html

33    Story, L. (2012). As companies seek tax deals, governments pay high price. New York Times. Retrieved on July 30 from http://www.nytimes.com/2012/12/02/us/how-local-taxpayers-bankroll-corporations.html?pagewanted=all&_r=0

## CHAPTER FIVE

1    Boyes, William and Melvin, Michael. (1991). Markets, Demand and Supply, and the Price System. Economics. (p. 56) Boston, MA: Houghton.

2    Ibid., p. 165

3    Schwartz, A. J., (1993). Money Supply. Retrieved July 9, 2006 from http://www.econlib.org/library/Enc/MoneySupply.html

4    Ruffin, R. J. and Gregory. (1988). Productivity and Cost. In Ruffin, R. J. and Gregory, P. R. (4th Ed.), Principles of Economics. (p. 265). Glenview, IL: Scott, Foresman.

5    Ruffin, R. J. and Gregory. (1988). Demand and Supply. InRuffin, R. J. and Gregory, P. R. (4th Ed.), Principles of Economics. (p. 124-25). Glenview, IL: Scott, Foresman.

6    Kapoor, J. R…et al. (1994). Banking Services. Kapoor, J. R…et al. (3rd Ed.), Personal Finance. (p. 189). Boston, MA: Irwin.

7    Samuelson, P. A. and Nordhaus, W. D. (1998) Uncertainty and Game Theory. In Samuelson, P. A. and Nordhaus, W. D. (16th Ed.), Economics. (p. 204). New York: Irwin/McGraw-Hill.

8    Bank for International Settlements. (2008). Retrieved December 7, 2008, from www.fxcm.com/forex-vs-futures.jsp?&keyword=futures%20options&jc=14155470&s=14213061&lx=14144173&m=14023381&tra=3148430

9    Bank for International Settlements. (2013). Triennial Central Bank Survey 2013 of Foreign Exchange Turnovers. Retrieved December 31, 2013 from https://www.bis.org/publ/rpfx13fx.pdf

10   Ibid.

11   Cross, S.Y. (1998). The Foreign Exchange Market in the United States. Federal Reserve Bank of New York: NY FRBNY p. 41.

12   UBS Investment Bank (2004). Foreign Exchange and Money Market Transactions. Zurich: UBS AG.

13   Big Mac Index. (2012). The Economist. Retrieved from http://www.scribd.com/doc/102253973/Big-Mac-Index-July-2012

14   Fast food and strong currencies. The Economist, June 9 2005. Page 1. Retrieved July 26, 2006 from http://www.economist.com/markets/bigmac/displayStory.cfm?story_id=5389856

15    The Foreign Exchange Interbank Market Retrieved January 2014 from http://www.investopedia.com/articles/forex/06/interbank.asp

16    Jost, K. (1997). The stock market. Retrieved August 13, 2006, from http://library.cqpress.com/cqresearcher/cqresrre1997050200.

17    NYSE Euronext. (2012). New York Stock Exchange Ends Member Seat Sales. Retrieved on July 30 from http://www.nyse.com/press/1135856420824.html

18    (2006). The Investor's Advocate: How the SEC Protects Investors, Maintains Market Integrity, and Facilitates Capital Formation. Para. 1 Retrieved August 13, 2006, from http://www.sec.gov/about/whatwedo.shtml

19    Report Persuant to Section 21(a) of the Securities Exchange Act of 1934 Regarding the NASD and the NASDAQ Market. Retrieved August 13, 2006, from http://www.sec.gov/litigation/investreport/nd21a-report.txt

20    (2006). Currency Devaluation and Revaluation. Para. 1. Retrieved August 13, 2006, from http://www.newyorkfed.org/aboutthefed/fedpoint/fed38.html

21    Borlan, Bruce. (1994). The Great Depression and the New Deal. In Nash, G. B…et al. (3rd Ed.), The American People. (p. 824). New York: HarperCollins.

22    Roberts, J.M. (1995). The Shaping of a New World. In Roberts, J.M. (3rd Ed.), History of the World. (p. 936). London: Penguin

23    Perry, Marvin…et al. (1989). International Relations in an Age of Superpowers. Perry, Marvin…et al. (3rd Ed.), Western Civilization. (p. 826-27). Boston: Houghton

24    Bordo, M. D. (1993). Gold Standard. Retrieved July 9, 2006, from http://www.econlib.org/library/Enc/GoldStandard.html

25    U.S. Department of State. Smoot-Hawley Tariff. Para. 1 Retrieved October 15, 2006, from http://www.state.gov/r/pa/ho/time/id/17606.htm

26    Idid, Para. 2

27    Roberts, J.M. (1995). The Shaping of a New World. In Roberts, J.M. (3rd Ed.), History of the World. (p. 878-80). London: Penguin

28    Boyes, William and Melvin, Michael. (1991). Markets, Demand and Supply, and the Price System. Economics. (p. 1005) Boston, MA: Houghton.

29    De George, R. T. (1995). Famine, Natural Resources, and International Obligations. In De George, R. T. (4th Ed.), Business Ethics. (p. 550). Englewood Cliffs, NJ: Prentice Hall.

30.   IMF Quotes. Retrieved 2014 from https://www.imf.org/external/np/exr/facts/quotas.htm

31    Boyes, William and Melvin, Michael. (1991). Markets, Demand and Supply, and the Price System. Economics. (p. 1015) Boston, MA: Houghton.

32    Heakal, R., (2003). Floating and Fixed Exchange Rates. Retrieved July 18, 2006, from http://www.investopedia.com/articles/03/020603.asp

33    Heakal, R., (2003). What is a Currency Board? Retrieved August 12, 2006, from http://www.investopedia.com/articles/03/020603.asp

34    Eichengreen, B. (1992). European Economic Community. Retrieved July 10, 2006, from http://www.econlib.org/library/Enc/EuropeanEconomicCommunity.html

35.   European Commission. Economic and Financial Affiars: What is ERM II?. Retrieved January 2014 from http://ec.europa.eu/economy_finance/euro/adoption/erm2/index_en.htm

36    Wegs, J.R. and Ladrech, R. (1996). European Unity. In Wegs, J.R. and Ladrech, R. (4th Ed.), Europe Sine 1945. (p. 154-156). Boston: Bedford/St. Martin's

37    European Commission. Economic and Financial Affiars: Who can join and when. Retrieved January 2014 from http://ec.europa.eu/economy_finance/euro/adoption/who_can_join/index_en.htm

38    Wegs, J.R. and Ladrech, R. (1996). European Unity. In Wegs, J.R. and Ladrech, R. (4th Ed.), Europe Sine 1945. (p. 154). Boston: Bedford/St. Martin's

39    Europa. Retrieved on March 18, 2013, from http://europa.eu/about-eu/countries/index_en.htm

## CHAPTER SIX

1     Hufbauer, G. C., Schott, J. J. (1994). Western Hemisphere Economic Integration. Washington DC. Institue for International Economics.

2     Shaffer, Ellen R., Waitzkin, Howard, Brenner, Joseph, Jasso-Aguilar, Rebeca,(2005). Global Trade and Public Health. American Journal of Public Health, 00900036, Vol. 95, Issue 1 (§ Trade Rules ¶ 1 p.23-24)

3     Mwase, Ngila (1995). Economic integration for development in eastern and southern Africa. Round Table Vol. 36, Issue 1 (§Economic integration: theoretical overview ¶2)

4     Regional Economic Integration, (n.d.). Retrieved July 7, 2006, from http://www.accd.edu/sac/mgt/ibus/1305090/Chapter%208%Lecture.htm

5     Haftel, Yoram Z. (2004). From the Outside Looking in: The effect of Trading Blocs on Trade Disputes in GATT/WTO. International Studies Quarterly, Vol. 48 Issue 1 (¶ 2 p.121) and WTO Building Blocks or Trading BLocks retrieved 2014 from http://www.wto.org/english/thewto_e/minist_e/min05_e/brief_e/brief09_e.htm

6     UC Atlas of Global Inequality (2006). Regional Trade Blocs: The role and function of regional trade blocs. (§ General Debates on Trade Blocs ¶4) Retrieved September 1, 2006 from http://ucatlas.ucsc.edu/trade/subtheme_trade_blocs.php

7     Ibid. § General Debates on Trade Blocs ¶5

8     Kirkham, Richard, Cardwell, Paul James (2006). The European Union: A Role Model for Regional Governance. European Public Law. Vol 12 Issue 3 (§The Case for Regional Governance ¶ 1,2 p.405)

9     Yap, J. (2005). Economic integration and regional cooperation in East Asia. Retrieved on July 8, 2006, from http://www.eaber.org/intranet/documents/22/711/PIDS_Yap_05.pdf

10    Stages of Economic Integration: From Autarky to Economic Union (2006) Government of Canada. Retrieved on July 8, 2006, from http://dsp-psd.communication.gc.ca/Collection-R/LoPBdP/inbrief/prb0249-e.htm

11    Mahant, E. (2000) Regional Economic Integration -Bringing Values Back In. Retrieved on September 1, 2006 from http://www.apfpress.com/book2/pdf_files/3.pdf

12    Arnold, Dennis (2006). Free Trade Agreements and Southeast Asia. Journal of Contemporary Asia. Vol. 36, Issue 2 (p. 195 ¶ 2)

13    Mwase, Ngila (1995). Economic integration for development in eastern and southern Africa. Round Table Vol. 36, Issue 1 (§Regional integration benefits ¶2)

14    Seligson, Mitchell A. (1999). Popular Support for regional economic integration in Latin America. Journal of Latin American Studies Vol. 31 Issue 1 (p. 130 ¶1)

15    Goss, Brian Michael (2001). All of our Kids Get Better Jobs Tomorrow: The North American Free Trade Agreement in the New York Times. Journalism and Communication Monographs. Vol. 3 Issue 1 (p.4 ¶1)

16    Hufbauer, Gary C., Wong, Yee (2003). Security and the Economy in the North American Context: The Road Ahead for NAFTA. Canada – United States Law Journal Vol. 29(¶1 p. 53)

17    U.S. Customs and Border Protection (2006). North American Trade Agreement (NAFTA). (§NAFTA ¶ 1) Retrieved on September 1, 2006 from http://www.cbp.gov/xp/cgov/import/international_ agreements/free_trade/nafta/

18    USTR. 2006. NAFTA: A Strong Record of Success. Retrieved 7/18/06 from http://www.ustr.gov/assets/Document_Library/Fact_ Sheets/2006/asset_upload_file242_9156.pdf

19    Ibid.

20    USTA. (2012). Making NAFTA Work for U.S. Small- and Medium-Sized Business. Retrieved on April 23 from http://www.ustr.gov/ about-us/press-office/fact-sheets/2011/making-nafta-work-us-small-and-medium-sized-business and http://www.rosalienebacchus.com/ articles/RegionalTradeBlocks.html

21    USTA. (2012). Americas. Retrieved on April 23 from http://www. ustr.gov/countries-regions/americas

22    Ratner, D., Scott R. E. (2005). NAFTA's Cautionary Tale: Recent History Suggests CAFTA could lead to further U.S. job displacement. (¶ 10). Retrieved from http://www.epi.org/content.cfm/ib214

23    Mercosur Economic Research Network Website. Retrieved on July 6th, 2006 from http://www.redmercosur.org.uy/Index03/ objectives03.htm and http://www.rosalienebacchus.com/articles/ RegionalTradeBlocks.html

24    Profile: Mercosur-Common Market of the South (2007). Retrieved on APRIL 22, 2013 from http://news.bbc.co.uk/1/hi/world/ americas/5195834.stm and http://www.mercosur.int/innovaportal/ file/4657/1/folleto_marzo_2014_es.pdf

25    International Organizations. (2004). Andean. Retrieved on April 23, 2013 from http://www.worldstatesmen.org/International_ Organizations.html#Andean

26    Venezuela announces exit from Andean trade blocPeople's Daily Online. Retrieved on July 6th, 2006 from http://english.peopledaily. com.cn/200604/24/eng20060424_260673.html. Para. 4

27    Baumann. R (2008). Integration in Latin America trends and challenges. Retrieved on April 20, 2013 from http://www.eclac.org/ publicaciones/xml/2/32312LCBRSR190RenatoBaumannIntegrati on.pdf

28    (2006). Pisco sour. Economist, 00130613, Vol. 380, Issue 8492 ¶5

29    Ibid. ¶6

30    CARICOM. Retrieved on April 4, 2013 from http://www.caricom. org/jsp/community/member_states.jsp?menu=community

31    Glossary – Venezuela. Library of Congress. Retrieved September 30, 2006 from: http://lcweb2.loc.gov/frd/cs/venezuela/ve_glos.html

32    El Salvador Soccer War. Global Security. Retrieved September 30, 2006 from: http://www.globalsecurity.org/military/world/war/ elsalvador.htm

33    Caribbean Community and Common Market. The Columbia Electronic Encyclopedia, 6th ed. Columbia University Press. Retrieved from Infoplease: http://www.infoplease.com/ce6/history/ A0810434.html

34    Stout, James V, Ugaz-Pereda, Julieta (1996). Western Hemisphere Trading Blocs and Tariff Barriers for U.S. Agricultural Exports. Economic Research Service/USDA.p.138 § CACM ¶ 1. Retrieved September 30, 2006 from http://www.ers.usda.gov/publications/ aer771/aer771q.pdf

35    Ibid. p.139 § CACM ¶ 3,4.

36    (2006).The Central American Free Trade Agreement (CAFTA). World Almanac & Book of Facts, 00841382, 2006 § Trade and Transportation

37    European Union. On the road to EU membership. Retrieved on April 24, 2013 from http://europa.eu/about-eu/countries/on-the-road-to-eu-membership/index_en.htm

38    EUPOPA – The EU at a Glance. § Euro-jargon. Retrieved from http://europa.eu/abc/eurojargon/index_en.htm

39    Geographica – The Complete Illustrated Atlas of the World, 2005 Edition, p.145. Milsons Point, Australia: Random House

40.   (2010). Four Asian Tigers. Retrieved on April 27, 2013 from http://en.wikipedia.org/wiki/Four_Asian_Tigers#cite_note-Anonymous_2009_75-77-13

41    Association of South East Nations. Retrieved September 30, 2006 from http://www.aseansec.org/64.htm

42    Asia-Pacific Economic Cooperation. Retrieved September 30, 2006 from http://www.apec.org/

43    SARRC. (2013). Retrieved on April 12, 2013 from http://www. saarc-sec.org/

44    South Asian Association for Regional Cooperation. Retrieved September 30, 2006 from http://www.saarc-sec.org/main.php

45    (2006). Organization of Arab Petroleum Exporting Countries. §OAPEC Establishment ¶1Retrieved September 30, 2006 from http://www.oapecorg.org/About.htm

46    Ibid. §OAPEC Monthly Bulletin

47    Geographica – The Complete Illustrated Atlas of the World, 2005 Edition, p.313. Milsons Point, Australia: Random House

48    West Africa. (2005, February). New African. i437 p24 (1)

49    (2004). Department of Foreign Affairs – Republic of South Africa. §History ¶3

50    Langton, Danielle (2005). CRS Report for Congress. United States-Southern African Customs Union (SACU) Free Trade Agreement Negotiations: Background and Potential Issues Retrieved October 6, 2006 from http://www.nationalaglawcenter.org/assets/crs/ RS21387.pdf#search=%22Southern%20African%20Customs%20 Union%E2%80%94SACU.%20%22. p. 2, para. 2.

51    Ibid.

52    U.S. Energy Information Administration. International Energy Statics. Retrieved 2014 from http://www.eia.gov/cfapps/ipdbproject/ IEDIndex3.cfm?tid=50&pid=53&aid=1

53    OECD. (2012). Retrieved on April 27th from http://www.oecd.org/ about/membersandpartners/

54    Organization for Economic Co-Operation and Development. Retrieved October 6, 2006 from http://www.oecd.org/about/0,2337 ,en_2649_201185_1_1_1_1_1,00.html

55    Reviews (2003). New OEDC report offers insights into adolescents' reading performance. Reading Today Vol. 20 Issue 4 ¶3

CHAPTER SEVEN

1     Henricks, M. (1997). From a distance. Entrepreneur magazine (§ Beyond Bicultural, ¶ 3). Retrieved July 22, 2006 from http://www.entrepreneur.com/article/0,4621,227655-7,00.html

2     Koch, A.J. (2001). Selecting overseas markets and entry modes: Two decision processes or one? Marketing Intelligence and Planning, 19, p. 6.

3     Heriot, K.C., Poff, J.K. (n.d.). Costs of developing a foreign market for a small business: The market & non-market barriers to exporting by small firms, pp. 2-3. Retrieved July 22, 2006 from http://www.sbaer.uca.edu/research/icsb/2005/092.pdf

4     Palmetto Consulting. (2004). Costs of developing a foreign market for a small business: The market and nonmarket barriers to exporting by small firms (p. 8). Retrieved August 11, 2006 from http://www.sba.gov/advo/research/rs241tot.pdf

5     United Nations Industrial Development Organization. (2006). Alliances and Joint Ventures: Patterns of internationalization for developing country enterprises (pg. 19). Retrieved August 11, 2006 from http://www.unido.org/file-storage/download/?file_id=53677

6     United Nations Industrial Development Organization. (2006). Alliances and Joint Ventures: Patterns of internationalization for developing country enterprises (pg. 19). Retrieved August 11, 2006 from http://www.unido.org/file-storage/download/?file_id=53677

7     Ibid. p. 19

8     Entrepreneur magazine. (2005). How to take your company global (§ Going Global, ¶ 1). Retrieved July 23, 2006 from http://www.entrepreneur.com/article/0,4621,312297-2,00.html

9     Delaney, L. (2004). 20 factors to consider before going global. Entrepreneur magazine Retrieved August 11, 2006 from http://www.entrepreneur.com/article/0,4621,319156,00.html

10    Kurlantzick, J. (2003). Stay Home? Entrepreneur magazine (§ New Strategies, ¶ 1). Retrieved July 24, 2006 from http://www.entrepreneur.com/article/0,4621,305948-3,00.html

11    Anderson, E., and Gatignon, H. (1986). Modes of Foreign Entry: A Transaction Cost Analysis and Propositions. Journal of International Business Studies, pgs. 1-26

12    Levitt, T. (1983). The globalization of markets. Harvard Business Review.

13    Hult, G. T. M., & Ketchen, D. J. (2001). Does market orientation matter? A test of the relationship between positional advantage and performance. Strategic Management Journal.

14    Huber, G. P. (1991). Organizational learning: The contributing processes and the literature. Organization Science.

15    Drew, S. A. W. (1997). From knowledge to action: The impact of benchmarking on organizational performance. Long Range Planning.

16    Javorski, B. J., & Kohli, A. K. (1993). Market orientation: Antecedents and   consequences. Journal of Marketing.

17    Pan, Y. & Tse, D. (2000). The Hierarchical Model of Market Entry Modes. Journal of International Business Studies.

18    Zacharakis, A. (1997). Entrepreneurial Entry into Foreign Markets: A Transaction Cost Perspective. Entrepreneurship Theory & Practice.

19    Osland, G. E., C. R. Taylor and Zou Shao Ming (2001), "Selecting International Modes of Entry and Expansion", Marketing Intelligence and Planning.

20    Keillor, B., Davila, V., Hult, G. T., (2001). Market entry strategies and influence factors:A Multiindustry/Multiproduct investigation, Marketing Management Journal.

21    Eriksson, K., Johansson, J., Majkgard, A., & Sharma, D. D. (1997). Experiential knowledge and the cost in the internationalization process. Journal of International Business Studies.

22    Hitt, M. A., Hoskisson, R. E., & Kim, H. (1997). International diversification: Effects on innovation and firm performance in product-diversified firms. Academy of Management Journal.

23    Czinkota, M. (1982). Export development strategies: US promotion policies. New York: Praeger.

24    Peng, M. W., Hill, C. W. L., Wang, D. Y. L., (2000). Schumpeterian dynamics versus Williamsonian considerations: A test of export intermediary performance, Journal of Management Studies.

25    Luostarinen, R., Welch, L., (1990). International Business Operations, Kyriiri Oy, Helsinki.

26    Pearce II, John A., Robinson Jr., Richard B. (2003). Strategic Management: Formulation, Implementation, and Control.. 8th ed. pg. 57. New York: McGraw-Hill/Irwin.

27    Ibid. pp. 58-60.

28    Narver, J. C., & Slater, S. F. (1990). The effect of a marketing orientation on business profitability. Journal of Marketing.

29    Erramilli, M.K., Agarwal, S., and S-S. Kim "Are Firm-Specific Advantages Location-Specific Too?" Journal of International Business Studies.

30    Zou, S., & Cavusgil, S. T. (2002). The GMS: A broad conceptualization of global marketing strategy and its effects on firm performance. Journal of Marketing.

31    Arnold, David. (2003). Strategies for Entering and Developing International Markets.   Financial Times (Oct 2003), Chapter 2, ¶ 1. Retrieved from http://www.phptr.com/articles/article.asp?p=101588&rl=1

32     Slaughter, M. (2010). How U.S. multinational companies strengthen the U.S. economy. Retrieved on May 16, 2013 from http://www.uscib.org/docs/foundation_multinationals_update.pdf.

33    Hester, S. (1985) Export trading companies: A marketing vehicle for small textile and apparel firms, Journal of small business management, Vol. 23.

34    Joyner, Nelson T. (N.d.). How to Find and Use an Export Management Company. ¶1. Retrieved from http://www.fita.org/aotm/0499.html.

35    USA Trade (2005) Developing an export strategy, (Electronic Version) Retrieved July 13, 2006 from www.usatrade.com. Chapter 4, .p.4.

36    Power Home Biz (2006), Export definitions. (Electronic Version) Retrieved July 13, 2006 from www.powerhomebiz.com/vol7/export.htm, p.1.

37    Bascal, Robert. (1997). The Role of the Facilitator: Understanding What Facilitators Really DO! ¶ 3. Retrieved from http://www.iaf-world.org/i4a/pages/Index.cfm?pageid=3291.

38    USA Trade (2005) Developing an export strategy, (Electronic Version) Retrieved July 13, 2006 from Developing an Export Strategy, USA Trade.gov, 2005, Chapter 6, p.3.

39    Slow, Steady Growth To Continue for Franchise Businesses in 2013. Retrieved 2014 from http://www.franchise.org/Franchise-News-Detail.aspx?id=58916.

40    Prusaitus, S (2005). International marketing theory and practices: An investigation of marketing communications in the film industry in latin america. , Florida State University, p. 25.

41    UNIDO (2004) Alliances and joint ventures: Patterns of internationalization for developing country enterprises, Unido Series, p. 13.

42    Ibid. p. 14.

43    Kock, S (2003) Project business as a distinct entry mode: A conceptual discussion, IMP Conference, Logano, Switzerland, p11.

44    Kemp, R.G.M. (2004) Managing interdependence for joint venture success: An empirical study of dutch international joint ventures. Gronigen Press, p.216.

45    USA Trade (2005) Developing an export strategy, (Electronic Version) Retrieved July 13, 2006 from Developing an Export Strategy, USA Trade.gov, 2005, Chapter 6, p.4.

46    Gulati, R (1998) Alliances and networks. Strategic management journals, v. 19, p. 293-317.

47    Ibid.

48    UNIDO (2004) Alliances and joint ventures: Patterns of internationalization for developing country enterprises, Unido Series p. 18, 2004

CHAPTER EIGHT

1    Jones, G. & George, J. (2003). Contemporary Management (3rd ed.). New York: McGraw-Hill Companies. p.615.

2    Bruner, R., et. al. (1998). The Portable MBA (4th ed.). New Jersey: John Wiley & Sons, Inc. p.128.

3    Bartlett, C. & Ghoshal, S. (1989). Managing Across Borders: The Transnational Solution. Massachusetts: Harvard Business School Press. p.32

4    Blocher, E., Chen, K., Cokins, G., & Lin, T. (2005). Cost Management. New York: McGraw-Hill. p.387.

5    Alexander, K. (2002). Business the Ultimate Resource. Massachusetts: Perseus Publishing. p.179.

6    Caslione, J. & Thomas, A. (2002). Global Manifest Destiny. Illinois: Dearborn Trade Publishing. p.155.

7    Ibid., p.157.

8    Ibid., p.158.

9    Grayson, D. & Hodges, A. (2002). Everybody's Business. New York: DK Publishing, Inc. p.39

10   Eccles, R. & Nohria, N. (1992). Beyond the Hype – Rediscovering the Essence of Management. Boston: Harvard Business School Press. p. 117.

11   Heizer, J. , & Render, B. (1999). Operations management (5th ed., p. 209). New Jersey: Prentice-Hall.

12   Inman, R. A. (2006) Business Reference. Encyclopedia of Management - Comp-De. (§ Inventory Types, ¶ 21). Retrieved July 15, 2006 from: http://www.referenceforbusiness.com/management/Int-Loc/Inventory-Types.html

13   Fitzpatrick, W. M. , & Burke, D. R. (2000). Virtual partnering for transactional and relational competitive advantage (¶ 3). Global Competitiveness. Retrieved July 23, 2006, from http://www.allbusiness.com/periodicals/article/719310-1.html

14   Fitzpatrick, W. M. , & Burke, D. R. (2000). Virtual partnering for transactional and relational competitive advantage (¶ 14). Global Competitiveness. Retrieved July 23, 2006, from http://www.allbusiness.com/periodicals/article/719310-1.html

15   Ibid., (¶ 15).

16   Ibid., (¶ 16).

17   Fixed Assets. (n.d.). Bitpipe. Retrieved August 16, 2006 from: http://www.bitpipe.com/tlist/Fixed-Assets.html

18   Daniels, J. D. , & Radebaugh, L. H. (1998). International business: Environments and operations (8th ed., pp. 352-353). United States: Addison Wesley Longman.

19   Gorg, H. (n.d.). Analyzing foreign market entry: The choice between Greenfield investment and acquisitions (p. 4). Retrieved July 23, 2006, from http://www.tcd.ie/Economics/TEP/1998/981.pdf#search='Greenfield%20investment'

20   Inman, R. A. (2006) Business Reference. Encyclopedia of Management - Comp-De. (§ Continuous Improvement). Retrieved July 20, 2006 from: http://www.referenceforbusiness.com/management/Comp-De/Continuous-Improvement.html

21   Evans, J. R., & Lindsay, W. M. (1999). The management and control of quality (4th ed., p. 118). Cincinnati: South-Western College Publishing.

22   Kline, J.J. (1992). Total quality management in local government. Government Finance Review (¶ 5). Retrieved June 16, 2006 from http://www.allbusiness.com/periodicals/article/337928-1.html

23   Frednell, L.D., & Robbins, T.L. (1995). Modeling the role of total quality management in the customer focused organization (¶ 3). Journal of Managerial Issues. Retrieved June 16, 2006 from http://www.allbusiness.com/periodicals/article/534858-1.html

24   Briggs, S., & Keogh, W. (1999). Integrating human resource strategy and strategic planning to achieve business excellence (¶ 18). Total Quality Management, pS447. Retrieved June 16, 2006 from Infotrac database.

25   International Organization for Standardization. Overview of the ISO System. (§ How ISO Standards Benefit Society, ¶ 1-4). Retrieved July 19, 2006 from http://www.iso.ch/iso/en/aboutiso/introduction/index.html

26   Blocher, E.J., Chen, K. H., Cokins, G., Lin, T. W. (2005). Cost Management: A Strategic Emphasis (3rd ed., p 14). NY: McGraw Hill/Irwin.

27   Thompson, A. A., Strickland III, A. J., and Gamble, J. E., ((2006) Crafting & Executing Strategy. (15th ed. p 139). NY: McGraw Hill/Irwin

28   Beasley, J. E. (n.d.). Just in Time (JIT). Retrieved July 5, 2006 from: http://people.brunel.ac.uk/~mastjjb/jeb/or/jit.html

29   Ibid.

30   BBC. (2001, September 25). Just-in-Time Manufacturing. Retrieved July 5, 2006 from: http://www.bbc.co.uk/dna/h2g2/A593769

31   Ibid.

32   Norman, J. (1998). Entrepreneur.com. Business Start-ups. How to Manage Inventory. Retrieved July 24, 2006 from: http://www.entrpreneur.com/article/0,4621,229017-1,00.html

33    Donovan, R., M. & Co. (n.d.) Inventory Control: Improving the Bottom Line. Retrieved July 15, 2006 from: http://www.rmdonovan.com/inventory_control.htm

34    McLeavey, D. W. & Narasimhan S. L. (1985). Production Planning And Inventory Control. Massachusetts: Allyn and Bacon, Inc.

35    Moyer, McGuigan & Kretlow. (2006). Contemporary Financial Management. (10th ed.). Thomson, South-Western; Ohio.

36    Craig, T. (1996, June). Global Logistics. Information is a Key Ingredient. Retrieved July 13, 2006 from: http://www.ltdmgmt.com/mag/art3.htm

37    Langevin, A. & Riopel, D. (2005). Logistics Systems: Design and Optimization. New York; Springer Science & Business Media.

38    Ibid.

39    Buelow, D. M. (2001, November). Eight Symptoms of Poorly Optimized Distribution Networks. Retrieved July 10, 2006 from: http://www.supplychainbrain.com/archives/11.01.opinion.htm?adcode=30

40    Langevin, A. & Riopel, D. (2005). Logistics Systems: Design and Optimization. York; Springer Science & Business Media.

41    Ruch, W. A., Harold, E.F., Wieters, C. D. (1992). Fundamentals of Production/Operations Management. (5th edition). St. Paul, MN: West Publishing Company.

42    Buelow, D. M. (2001, November). Eight Symptoms of Poorly Optimized Distribution Networks. (§5-High levels of invetory). Retrieved July 10, 2006 from: http://www.supplychainbrain.com/archives/11.01.opinion.htm?adcode=30

43    Ruch, W. A., Harold, E.F., Wieters, C. D. (1992). Fundamentals of Production/Operations Management. (5th edition). St. Paul, MN: West Publishing Company.

44    Sanderson, T. (2001, December). Developing an Internet Transportation Management Strategy. Retrieved July 10, 2006 from: http://www.supplychainbrain.com/archives/12.01.opinion.htm?adcode=30

45    Meachum, M. (1997, April). Returnable Packaging: Logistics Providers Hel Make It a Green-Green Solution. Retrieved July 10, 2006 from: http://www.supplychainbrain.com/archives/4.97.logistics.htm?adcode=90

46    Buelow, D. M. (2001, November). Eight Symptoms of Poorly Optimized Distribution Networks. Retrieved July 10, 2006 from: http://www.supplychainbrain.com/archives/11.01.opinion.htm?adcode=30

47    Kelton, K. (1998, Fall). A Business Case for Enhancing Supply Chain in the Metals Industry Information Systems Management, Vol. 15 (4): 72-76. Retrieved July 7, 2006 from: http://www.ism-journal.com/Contents1998.html

48    Rogers, S. (2004, April). Supply Management: Six Elements of Superior Design. Supply Chain Management Review. (¶ 4). Retrieved July 5, 2006 from: http://www.manufacturing.net/scm/index.asp?layout=articlePrint&articleID=CA412838

49    Kelton, K. (1998, Fall). A Business Case for Enhancing Supply Chain in the Metals Industry Information Systems Management, Vol. 15 (4): 72-76. Retrieved July 7, 2006 from: http://www.ism-journal.com/Contents1998.html

50    Ibid. ¶pg. 15

51    Ibid

52    Rogers, S. (2004, April). Supply Management: Six Elements of Superior Design. Supply Chain Management Review. Retrieved July 5, 2006 from: http://www.manufacturing.net/scm/index.asp?layout=articlePrint&articleID=CA412838

## SUPPLEMENTAL MATERIAL

1.    Compensation review: Retrieved from: http://blog.iese.edu/expatriatus/2011/11/05/expatriate-compensation-a-review/

2.    Ibid.

3.    Capell, P. (2004). Employers Seek to Trim Pay for U.S. Expatriates. Retrieved November 16, 2005 from http://www.careerjournal.com/myc/workabroad/20040412-capell-expat.html

4.    Haldemann, P. (1999). Building the Bridge for a Successful Expatriation Process. Retrieved November 15, 2005, from http://www.relojournal.com/sept2000/business_report.htm

5.    Swaak, R. (2002). Managing the Expatriation Process Is One of the Thorniest Issues for Global Managers. Retrieved November 15, 2005, from http://www.frankallen.com/Executive_Reports/HR_and_The_Global_Marketplace/Repatriation/repatriation.html_

6.    Australian Centre for International Business. (2001). Expatriate Management: A Business Model for Diversity Management. Retrieved November 13, 2005, from http://www.diversityaustralia.gov.au/_inc/doc_pdf/exp_manage_model.pdf

7.    Treven, S. (2001). Human Resource Management in International Organizations. Retrieved November 13, 2005, from http://www.efst.hr/management/Vol6No1-2-2001/11-Treven.doc

8.    Elenius, J., Garvik, L., & Nilsson, F. (2003). An Evaluation of the Repatriation Process at Company X. Retrieved November 14, 2005, from http://www.handels.gu.se/epc/Archive/00003646/01/inlaga%5F2003%5F16.pdf

9.    Swaak, R. (2002). Managing the Expatriation Process Is One of the Thorniest Issues for Global Managers. Retrieved November 15, 2005, from http://www.frankallen.com/Executive_Reports/HR_and_The_Global_Marketplace/Repatriation/repatriation.html_

10.   Australian Centre for International Business. (2001). Expatriate Management: A Business Model for Diversity Management. Retrieved November 13, 2005, from http://www.diversityaustralia.gov.au/_inc/doc_pdf/exp_manage_model.pdf

11.   Sims, R. & Schraeder, M. (2005). An Examination of Salient Factors Affecting Expatriate Culture Shock The Journal of Business and Management, Vol. 10 Issue No. 1. pp. 73-88.

12.   Salacuse J. (2005). Ivey Business Journal. Negotiating: The Top Ten Ways that Culture Can Affect Your Negotiation. Retrieved November 18, 2005 from http://www.iveybusinessjopurnal.com/ibjmarchapril/2005.htm

13.   Chew, J. (2004). Managing MNC expatriates through Crises: A Challenge for International Human Resource Management. Retrieved on August 8th 2013 from http://rphrm.curtin.edu.au/2004/issue2/expats.html

14.   Government Printing Office. (July, 1996). Service member's personal protection guide: A self-help handbook to combating terrorism. Retrieved 10 November, 2005 from http://www.dtic.mil/doctrine/jel/cjcsd/cjcsi/gude5260.pdf

15. Kwintessential. (2004). Retrieved on Augusts 7th, 2013 from http://www.kwintessential.co.uk/resources/country-profiles.html

16. Mashable. (2013). 10 apps for international travel. Retrieved on September 2nd 2013, from http://mashable.com/2013/04/29/international-travel-apps/

17. United States Department of State. Passports. (2006). Retrieved October 15, 2006 from http://travel.state.gov/passport/passport_1738.html

18. United States Department of State. Visas. (2006). Retrieved October 15, 2006 from http://travel.state.gov/visa/visa_1750.html

19. United States Council for International Business. ATA Cartnet Export Service (2006). Retrieved November 1, 2006 from http://www.uscib.org/index.asp?documentID=718

20. United States Department of State. U.S. Embassies, Consulates, and Diplomatic Missions (2006). Retrieved October 15, 2006 from http://usembassy.state.gov/

21. United States Department of Commerce International Trade Administration. Export Assistance Center (2006). Retrieved November 1, 2006 from http://www.export.gov/eac/index.asp

22. United States Department of State. Medical Information for Americans Traveling Abroad. Retrieved November 1, 2006 from http://travel.state.gov/travel/tips/health/health_1185.html

23. United States Department of State. Consular Information Sheets. Retrieved November 1, 2006 from http://travel.state.gov/travel/cis_pa_tw/cis/cis_1765.html

24. A Safe Trip Abroad. (2006). Retrieved November 1, 2006 from http://www.friendlytravels.com/asafetripabroad.htm

25. Ibid.

26. Ibid.

27. Small Business Notes. (2006). Retrieved November 5, 2006 from http://www.smallbusinessnotes.com/international/exporting/businesstravel.html

28. Ibid.

29. Proozm. Voice Between Network Announces New Foreign Language Translation Website. (2006). Retrieved November 15, 2006 from http://www.przoom.com/news/1359/, ¶ 3.

30. Ibid, ¶ 4.

31. Cultural Savvy. (2006). Retrieved November 15, 2006 from http://www.culturalsavvy.com/

32. Martin, B. & Larsen, G. (1999). Taming the tiger: key success factors for trade with China. Marketing Intelligence & Planning. Volume 17 Number 4 1999 pp. 202-208

# INDEX